V ELEETINGS FROM WHITLEY BAY.

LORD
MANDE IN BUSH -
didn't know fat
was over

Spoilt
Bastard
Robot
Wars

Nellie
show axed

YOU'VE GOT
A BLOODY CHEEK

AIRPLANE.
PLOT
LIFT.

LAWYERS
WATCH.
Advert.

INTERNET
Q+A.

MAN HAS
① HAIR
PLANT

② GETS BILL

③ HAIR CAME
OUT

25
YEARS OF
VIZ
SILVER PLATED JUBILEE

William Cook

BOXTREE

First published 2004 by Boxtree
an imprint of Pan Macmillan Ltd
Pan Macmillan, 20 New Wharf Road, London N1 9RR
Basingstoke and Oxford
Associated companies throughout the world
www.panmacmillan.com

ISBN 0 7522 2525 1

9 8 7 6 5 4 3 2

A CIP catalogue record for this book is available from the British Library.

Design by Perfect Bound Ltd and Fulchester Industries
Colour reproduction by Aylesbury Studios (Bromley) Ltd
Printed and bound in Great Britain by Butler & Tanner

CONTENTS

VIZ
STARTS TODAY £5 SNAP!
NEW PRICE SENSATION
IT'S 20p!
FRU 'T' NIGHT FEVER!
START YOUR NUTS! NUDE MOTORCYC
All your favourites plus BILLY THE FISH
A CHAMPAGNE TRIP TO FRANCE ON CONCORDE FOR EVERY READER RETURNING ON THE QE2 ONLY TOP!
HOW TO WIN THE LOTTERY EVERY WEEK!
FREE MONEY AND SEX!
ROGER MELLIE THE FAT SLAGS
We've got pictures of the Queen's ARSE
BANDITS and how to beat them!
LET'S TALK TURKEY
QUEEN'S 'I'M A BED' NAKED SEX ROMPS!
FREE World Cup 98 CYBERMOT Worthless football gimmick
FREE SUBBUTEO TABLE
SEX, MURDER & LAVATORIES EVERYTHING YOU WANT FROM A GOOD MAGAZINE
"I've seen the STARS' COCKS and they're nothing special!" says BBC toilet attendant
DINOSAUR BANDWAGON SPECIAL
FREE TAKE THAT! BICYCLE SEAT COVER INSIDE
Girls! It's your big chance to sit on our faces!
TITS OFF FOR THE LADS
PISS OFF
LINDA BARKER
Fat Slags Sid the Sexist Mr Logic
Jonathon Ringpiece Roger Mellie Bottom Inspectors
Big Vern Biffa Bacon
Finbarr Saunders
Roger Mellie
Fellas! Meet our CELEBRITY WHORES Top stars go on the game!
With Fat Slags Sid the Sexist
Roger Mellie Tommy Salter
Capt. Morgan & more! etc.
BRITAIN'S STOOLS ARE GETTING FIRMER
The magazine everyone was talking about
HAPPY 50th
IN THE CHURCH Sacked Reverend reveals all!
BANGA! BANGA! BANGA! BANGA!
ROGER MELLIE THE FAT SLAGS
SPOILT BASTARD SID THE SEXIST
LUVVIE DARLING WANKER WATSON
FELIX & HIS AMAZING UNDERPANTS
SAVE £16 with our FREE SPICE GIRLS EYE TEST
SUMMER FETE
TOMBOLA
TOMBOLA
TOFFEE TENT
BEER TENT
WOBBLY CASTLE
TEARS OF THE CLOWNS! Exposed!
POP IN THE YEAR 2000
NOT PARTICULARLY CHRISTMAS ISSUE
FREE INSIDE
THE BEATLES, CONCORDE & LINFORD CHRISTIE'S GENITALS
BRITISH
EURO 2004
COME ON TIM!
POSTMAN PLOD FAT SLAGS 8 ACE
RAFFLES FARMER PALMER
SASHA SLAPPA DRUNKEN BAKERS

PART ONE **THE STORY**

In November 1979, in Newcastle upon Tyne, a nineteen-year-old DHSS clerk called Chris Donald, his old schoolfriend Jim Brownlow and his fifteen-year-old brother Simon published 150 copies of a new comic called *Viz*. Priced 20p – or 30p to students – the 'Bumper Monster Christmas Special' (actually just twelve pages) went on sale in a suburban pub where local punk bands hung out. Within a few hours, they'd sold every copy.

A decade later, *Viz* was selling over a million copies per issue, outselling every other magazine in Britain apart from the *Radio Times*, *TV Times* and the *Reader's Digest*. And twenty-five years since it started, it's still going strong. Its characters have become comic icons, it's read by everyone from the softest student to the hardest squaddie, and its famous fans range from Stephen Fry to Steve Coogan, from Jonathan Ross to John Peel, from Vic & Bob to Ant & Dec. This book is a celebration of those first twenty-five years.

Mainly, of course, it's simply a book of comic art – and, like anything remotely comical, it requires absolutely no explanation. However the story of how that artwork came about is actually pretty interesting, and often quite amusing. It's the tale of a handful of unknown Geordies (plus a few foreign interlopers from as far afield as Pontefract and Anglesey) who transformed a tiny fanzine into Britain's biggest humorous magazine. Along the way, they provoked the ire of gypsies, scousers, monarchists, the highly reputable manufacturer of an internationally renowned and respected brand of sports and leisurewear, and DC Thomson, publishers of the *Beano* and the *Dandy*. They unwittingly inspired an irritating media trend known as laddism. They even helped revive the showbiz career of Keith Chegwin. Oh, and quite by chance, they also completely reinvented the Great British sense of humour. What follows, more or less, is a rough summary of how they did it.

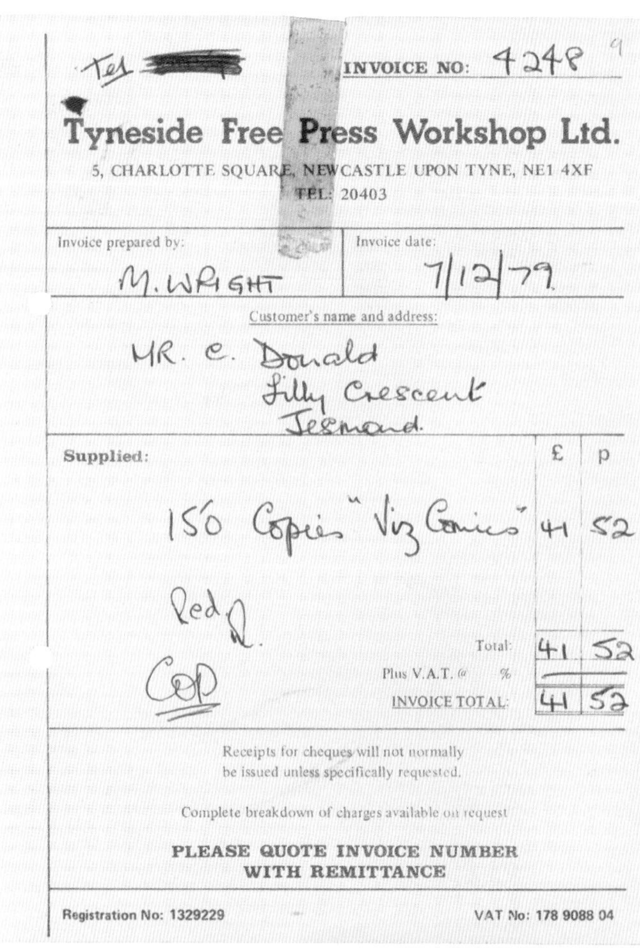

Tel INVOICE NO: 4248

Tyneside Free Press Workshop Ltd.

5, CHARLOTTE SQUARE, NEWCASTLE UPON TYNE, NE1 4XF
TEL: 20403

Invoice prepared by:	Invoice date:
M. WRIGHT	7/12/79

Customer's name and address:

MR. C. Donald
Lilly Crescent
Jesmond.

Supplied:	£	p
150 Copies "Viz Comics"	41	52
Recd R.		
COD		
Total:	41	52
Plus V.A.T. @ %		
INVOICE TOTAL:	41	52

Receipts for cheques will not normally be issued unless specifically requested.

Complete breakdown of charges available on request

PLEASE QUOTE INVOICE NUMBER WITH REMITTANCE

Registration No: 1329229 VAT No: 178 9088 04

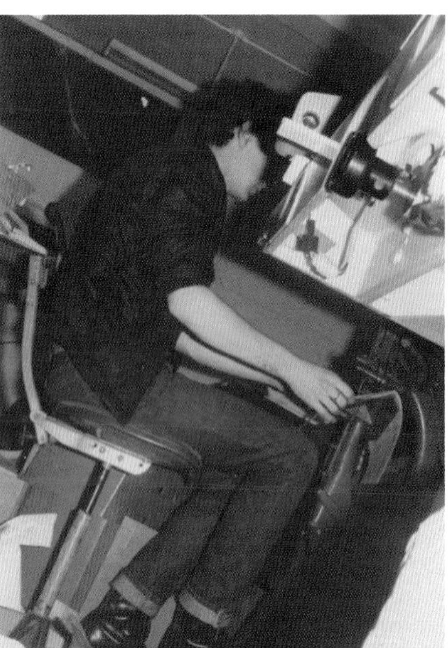

This page and opposite: Issue one - 150 copies were printed at the Tyneside Free Press at a cost of £41.52.

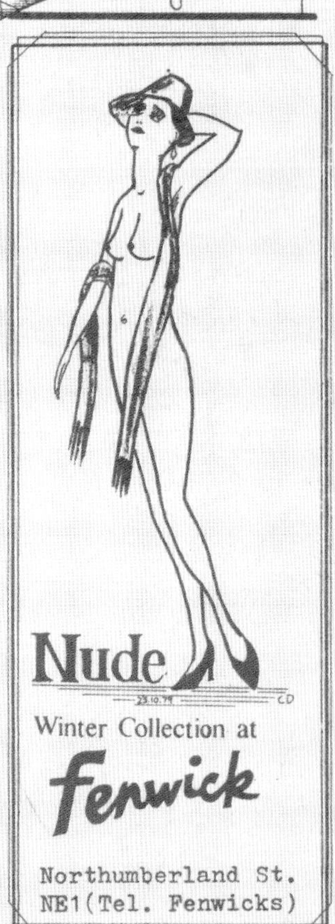

Poland 7c., Lesotho 15c., Cuba 8c., Sharjah 78c., Qatar 9c., Western Samoa 5c., Students 30p, Sierra Leone 6c., Ethiopia 50c., Iran 4 dollaratollahs, Ghana 6c.

1

Viz 12/79

The Lily Crescent Locomotive Club.

1ST EVER EDITION. Official monthly paper.

L O C O M O T I V E   T I M E S

NOVEMBER 1975 ISSUE ONE PRICE 15p

EDITOR: Christopher Donald
REPORTERS: C.Donald,James Brownlow.

....

THE LILY CRESCENT LOCOMOTIVE CLUB,
LILY CRESCENT,
JESMOND,
NEWCASTLE UPON TYNE 2.

CHAIRMAN: C.Donald, Lily Crescent.

- -

CONTENTS

The Lily Crescent Locomotive Times, *Chris Donald's first homemade periodical, and a forerunner of far bigger things to come. Intrepid reporter Jim Brownlow would become one of the founding editors of* Viz.

CLUB NEWS:

At the time of writing our magazine is in only its first week,so any readers wishing to obtain a copy each month may do so by joining the l.c.l.c.,for only 10p each month. This money covers the cost of your paper, wich would otherwise be 15p per month.

On Friday I was handed the firt column obtained from our 1st writer,JAMES BROWNLOW, WHOM I am sure most readers know well. He will be keeping us up to date with goings on at HEATON C.S., a very important part of our rly. scene.We can never get to the carriage sidings on our outings, so I am sure Jims column will make interesting reading.

Recently discusions were held concerning possible visits to GLASGOW and LONDON. The Glasgow trip would be a L.C.L.C.

Funnily enough, Chris Donald never really read that many comics as a kid. 'Me dad wouldn't let us watch ITV and he wouldn't let us read kids' comics because he was a big one for improving ourselves,' he says. 'He wouldn't let us get the *Beano* and he wouldn't let us get the *Dandy* because they were rubbish.' In fact, the only comics Chris really read regularly were *Valiant* and his brother's *Look & Learn*. This was Steve, who inspired cartoon pedant Mr Logic, created by their younger brother, Simon.

Unlike Chris, Simon read comics avidly, especially the American superhero kind. 'I used to try and copy all of the Marvel artists,' he says. 'I used to study the way they drew.' His ambition was to work for Marvel. He even wrote to them, asking how to go about it. When he won the school woodwork prize, he bought a book called *How to Draw Comics the Marvel Way*. Yet his idea of fun was resolutely British. When he won another school prize, he bought a book of Two Ronnies sketches. Marvel Meets The Two Ronnies – it's not a bad shorthand for the bizarre hybrid that became *Viz*.

Chris quite liked reading periodicals, but he was always far more interested in making them. He even made newspapers for his teddy bear to sell in his own toy paper shop. But then Chris discovered trainspotting, which inspired his first man-sized paper, the *Locomotive Times*. This was the official publication of the Lily Crescent Locomotive Club, named after the street where he lived. He still has the launch issue. Highlights included a guided tour of the local sidings for an additional 20p.

'I used to go trainspotting every weekend, more or less,' says Chris. 'We used to go to Chesterfield and Crewe and York, and mystery tours that invariably went to Whitby, which was unfortunate because there's not much that happens there for trainspotters.' Chris once carried a chair from his house to a nearby railway bridge to photograph a particular train, which was due to pass by underneath, and when a passing woman muttered something disparaging, he followed her home and demanded to know what she'd said.

'How dare you,' he protested. 'I'm a perfectly well-behaved person taking a photograph of a train from a chair on a bridge.' This steely determination was central to the subsequent success of *Viz*. The *Locomotive Times* folded after just one issue, but from then on, if Chris was keen on something, he tended to make a magazine about it. 'We had a football team in the street and I did the programme,' he recalls. 'I managed the team as well, but I think the whole object of the exercise was to do the programme.'

'How dare you! I'm a perfectly well-behaved person taking a photograph of a train from a chair on a bridge.'

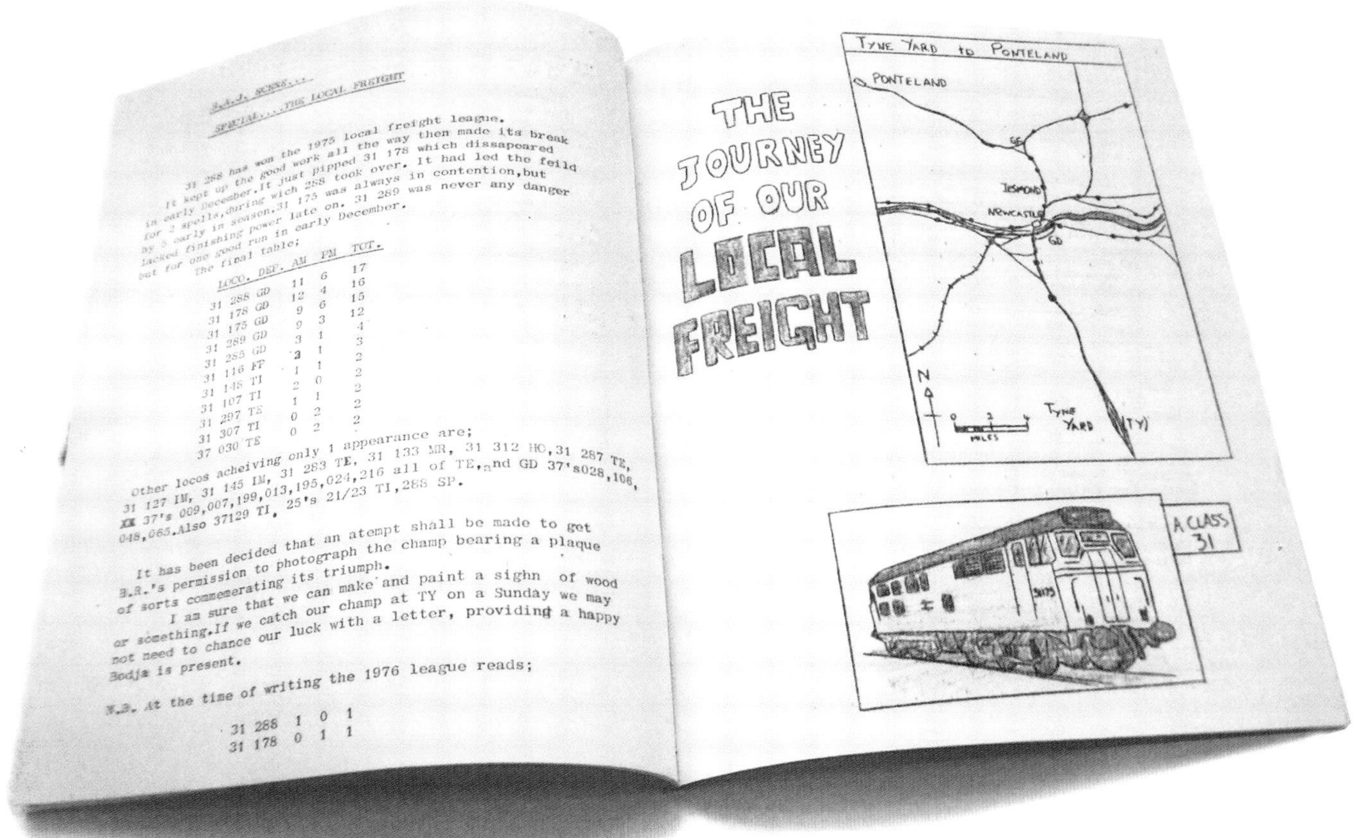

SPECIAL....THE LOCAL FREIGHT

31 288 has won the 1975 local freight league. It kept up the good work all the way then made its break in early December. It just pipped 31 178 which dissapoared for 2 spells, during wich 288 took over. It had led the feild by 5 early in season. 31 175 was always in contention, but lacked finishing power late on. 31 289 was never any danger but for one good run in early December.

The final table;

LOCO.	DEP.	AM	PM	TOT.
31 288	GD	11	6	17
31 178	GD	12	4	16
31 175	GD	9	6	15
31 289	GD	9	3	12
31 285	GD	3	1	4
31 116	FP	2	1	3
31 148	TI	1	1	2
31 107	TI	2	0	2
31 297	TE	1	1	2
31 307	TI	0	2	2
37 030	TE	0	2	2

Other locos acheiving only 1 appearance are; 31 127 IM, 31 145 IM, 31 283 TE, 31 133 MR, 31 312 HO, 31 287 TE, 37's 009,007,199,013,195,024,216 all of TE, and GD 37's 028,106, 048,065. Also 37129 TI, 25's 21/23 TI, 288 SP.

It has been decided that an atempt shall be made to get B.R.'s permission to photograph the champ bearing a plaque of sorts commemerating its triumph.

I am sure that we can make and paint a sighn of wood or something. If we catch our champ at TY on a Sunday we may not need to chance our luck with a letter, providing a happy Bodja is present.

At the time of writing the 1976 league reads;

31 288	1	0	1
31 178	0	1	1

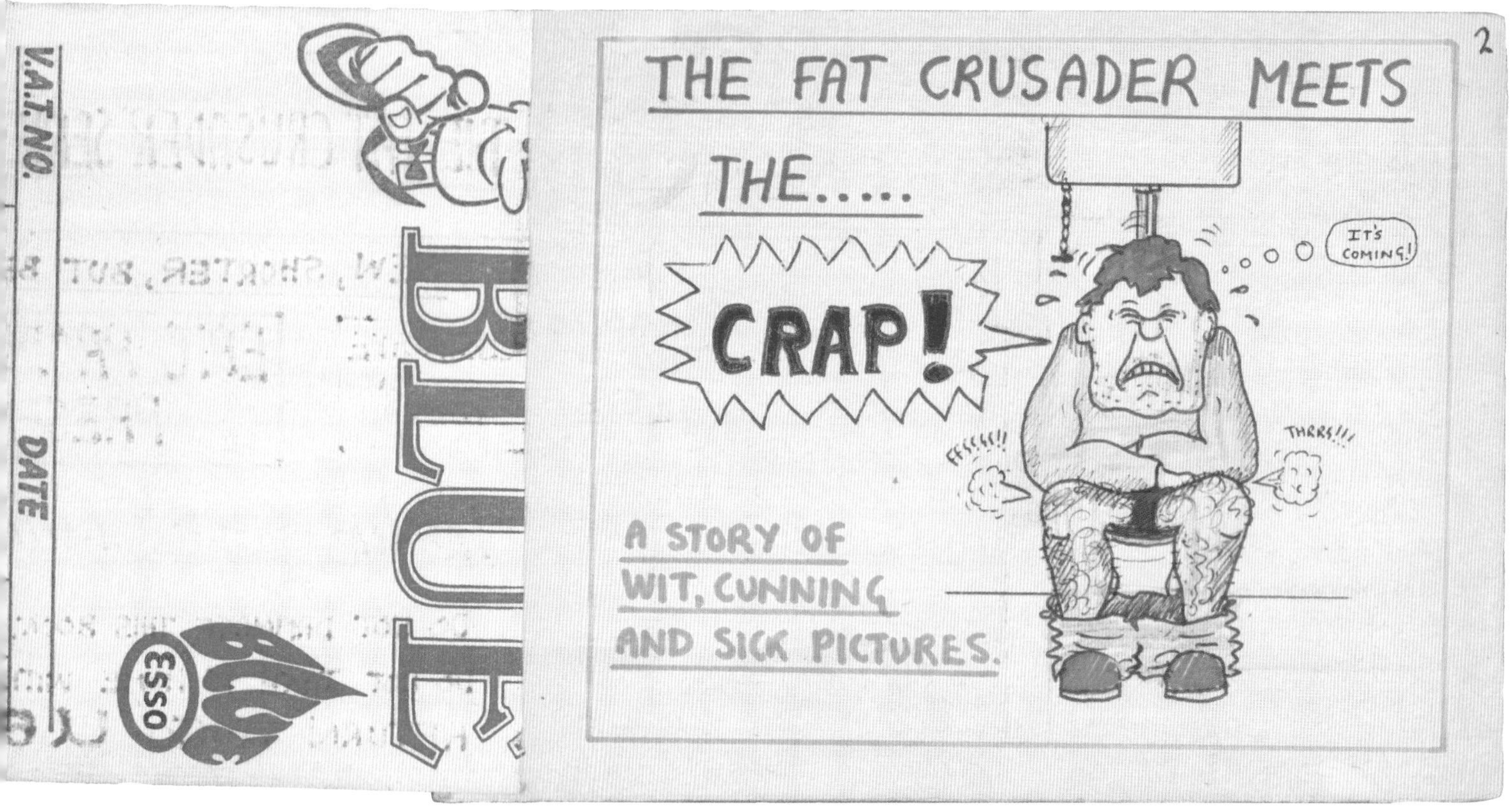

Above: The Fat Crusader, *Chris Donald's first comic, which became a big hit at school. The paper was supplied by his dad, who sold Blue Esso paraffin.*

Chris's dad wasn't that keen on comics, but he had a keen sense of fun. He bought Steve, Chris and Simon funny books and played them Goons LPs. He saved up his Green Shield stamps to get them tape recorders, which they used to record their own comic sketches and spoof radio shows. If you think this sounds escapist you're absolutely right. Creating a secret world of your own can be a great escape from real life, and the Donald brothers had quite a lot of reality to escape from. 'We were all into escapism in a lot of ways,' confirms Simon. 'Our mother was ill. She was disabled from when I was born, although she'd actually had MS probably since Steve was born, and it obviously caused a lot of problems. There was a lot of dysfunction in the family so I think escapism was quite natural for all of us, and I think there was a lot of having to be funny in order to cope with situations.'

One situation they all had to cope with was the dramatic divide between home and school. 'Suddenly, for the first time, you met all these hooligans,' says Simon. 'It was quite a big problem for all three of us in that we'd come from this cosy neighbourhood, Jesmond, which is pretty posh, and we ended up in school in Heaton. I'm not saying Heaton's rough, but it's certainly a lot more working class than Jesmond.' And the school took pupils from tougher districts like Walker and Byker. 'We had a riot that made it onto the front page of the national press,' says Simon. 'One of the big cartoonists actually did a cartoon about our riot.' It was like a scene straight out of *Viz*.

'It's the outside view that's necessary for the comedian,' says Steve. 'You can't make comedy out of something that you completely identify with, because you can't separate yourself from it.' With one foot in middle-class Jesmond and the other in working-class Heaton, Steve, Chris and Simon were all outsiders of a sort.

It wasn't just the difference between home and school that made the Donald brothers a bit different – it was the difference between their parents. Their mother grew up in middle-class Jesmond. Their father grew up in working-class Shieldfield. Their mother had been a window dresser at Fenwicks, the local department store. Their dad had been a milkman, delivering milk to the street where she lived. 'He never drank, never smoked and saved every penny, in the hope that he would one day be able to buy a house in Jesmond,' says Simon. And after years of hard graft, he did.

Their dad eventually bought a house in the same street where their mother was raised, yet like many industrious working men who've pulled themselves up by their own bootstraps, he remained one step removed from his new neighbours. 'My parents' friends were teachers with beards, and dad was constantly laughing at how lefties couldn't keep their houses clean,'[1] says Chris. Yet these bearded teachers were now his social circle. 'He worked hard all his life and achieved what he set out to do, which was to bring himself up to the standard of living that he aspired to, and that his chosen wife had been brought up to expect,' explains Steve. 'As an aspiring person, working his way up, he'd be trying to get rid of his accent, whereas we, when we went to Heaton, had to acquire a Geordie accent in order to get some protective camouflage.' But the best camouflage of all was *Viz*.

At school, Chris became close friends with a boy from Blackburn called Jim Brownlow. 'We didn't fit in with any of the little cliques,' says Chris. 'We ended up wandering around on our own all the time. We would occasionally get called homs and poofs because we were two blokes who were hanging around together.' And one of the things they did together was draw cartoons. 'I found out how you can draw people being sliced up like a bacon slicer – a bit like Tom & Jerry,' says Chris. 'We were ashamed to show them to anyone because we knew people would say that we were mad and sick. I kept them in a drawer in my bedroom.'

Fortunately, Chris's next creation was a lot more accessible. *The Fat Crusader* was a superhero, inspired by a quiet classmate called Scotty Dixon. The strip also depicted other pupils, and some teachers, and soon these meticulous little booklets were being passed around the entire school. A few issues found their way into the staff room, where they got a similarly good reception. Some people even asked Chris to feature them in future editions. Chris still had no idea he could ever make a living out of drawing daft cartoons, but *The Fat Crusader's* popularity was a sign of things to come.

When Chris left school, he wanted to train as a geography teacher (he liked maps) but he didn't get the grades, so he went to work at the DHSS instead. He thought he'd go to college a year later, but his dad said it was a job for life. 'I was administering voluntary National Insurance contributions for people who were living abroad in non-EEC non-reciprocal countries,' he recites, robotically. 'If your National Insurance number ended in 42, 43 or 44 A or B, you wrote to me.' It sounds soul-destroying, but it was actually a useful apprenticeship for *Viz*. There's nothing quite like the petty rigmarole of office life for developing your sense of the ridiculous, and quite a lot of this civil service bureaucracy subsequently found its way into *Viz*. 'There were a lot of things about the DHSS that Chris thoroughly enjoyed, because he's very anal and he likes forms,' says Simon. 'He brought so much of that into the *Viz* office and it used to drive everyone else mad.' But it was a methodical sort of madness that would stand Chris, and *Viz*, in good stead.

To relieve the tedium, Chris started writing unofficial match reports for the staff five-a-side team. His write-ups were just as popular around the office as *The Fat Crusader* had been at school. They were also just as impertinent. 'They had some fairly choice language,' says Chris. 'One old lady took offence at something I'd written and complained to the Higher Executive Officer.' But the

'There was a lot of things about the DHSS that Chris thoroughly enjoyed, because he's very anal and he likes forms.'

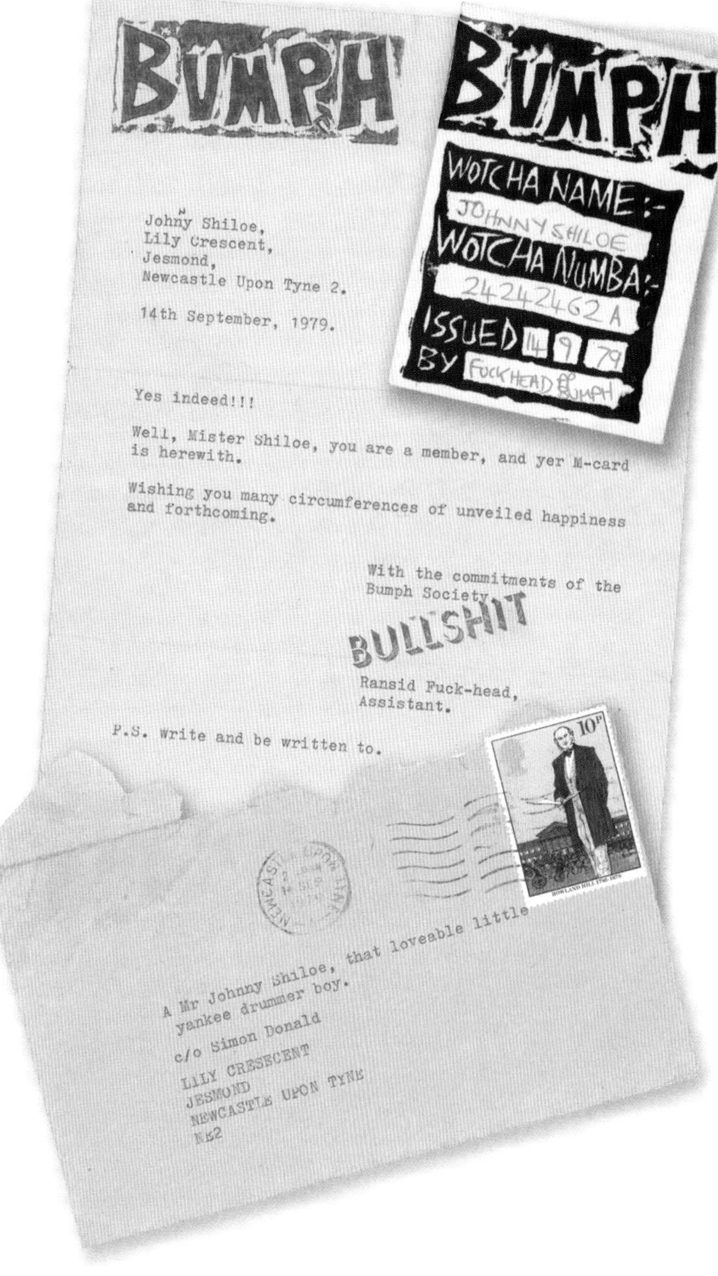
BUMPH

BUMPH
WOTCHA NAME:- JOHNNY SHILOE
WOTCHA NUMBA:- 24242462 A
ISSUED 14 9 79
BY FUCKHEAD BUMPH

Johnny Shiloe,
Lily Crescent,
Jesmond,
Newcastle Upon Tyne 2.

14th September, 1979.

Yes indeed!!!

Well, Mister Shiloe, you are a member, and yer M-card is herewith.

Wishing you many circumferences of unveiled happiness and forthcoming.

With the commitments of the Bumph Society,

BULLSHIT

Ransid Fuck-head,
Assistant.

P.S. Write and be written to.

A Mr Johnny Shiloe, that loveable little yankee drummer boy.
c/o Simon Donald
LILY CRESCENT
JESMOND
NEWCASTLE UPON TYNE
NE2

The Bumph Club was another of the Donald brothers' early form-filling exercises.

ARNOLD THE MAGAZINE

AUGUST 1978 : EPIC PRODUCTIONS (UK) LTD : CHRIS DONALD / JIM BIZZ GROOVER : PRICE 2p

LATEST

TONY BLACKBURN, RADIO ONE D.J., HAS ENTERED HOSPITAL FOR A HEAD TRANSPLANT. THE DONOR IS BELIEVED TO BE A SCOTS PINE.

POLICE TODAY TOOK INTO CUSTODY A MAN IN CONNECTION WITH A ROBBERY. THEY SAID "COME ON, YOU", AND HE SAID, "OH GOD."

FOR SALE

OLD CLOTHING

POPE'S HAT, SHOES ROBES ETC.
(CAN DELIVER)
THE VATICAN, ROME.

SICK AND TIRED OF BABIES?

WE CAN HELP!

OUR PATENTED, MEDICALLY APPROVED DEVICES COULD STOP YOUR PROBLEMS.

SEND A S.A.E. + £10 to

JOE'S RUBBER JOHNIES LTD, BACK STREET, BLYTH.

26262 FOR TICKET DESIGN FOR DISCOS PARTYS ETC BY CHRIS DONALD FILTH CHEAP.

FROM A MERE RABBIT TO A REAL MAN

STARRING PHILIPS ATLAS.

A TRUE STORY. (NOT SO)

1. SITUATIONS VACANT

SALMON TASTER

NO EXPERIENCE OR QUALIFICATIONS NEEDED.

JOHN WEST LTD.

CATHOLIC CHURCH LTD. (ROME) INVITE APPLICATIONS FOR THE POST OF

POPE (MANAGING DIRECTOR)

GOOD PROSPECTS FOR RIGHT APPLICANT. COMPANY CAR & HOUSE, SERVANTS, VERY GOOD SALARY

APPLY THE VATICAN TEL. ROME 246 (OR ASK AT YOUR LOCAL BRANCH)

LOOKING FOR A JOB?

WE'RE DOING ONE ON TUESDAY.

MEET OUTSIDE BARCLAYS BANK, JESMOND, 10pm. (BRING YOUR OWN GEAR)

THE CONTINUING SAGA OF BIPO BARRINGTON OF THE SQUADRON

ONE DAY, IT WAS THE WAR. BIPO WAS CRUISING AT 1500 FEET ON THE LOOK OUT FOR THE BALLY HUN. WITH HIM WAS BOFFO HIGGINS, HIS ACE CHUM. READ ON...

THERE WAS NO SIGN OF GERRY, BUT....

SUDDENLY, THERE WERE '109'S AT 10 o'CLOCK.

AS THE KROUTS PASSED, THEY SHOT BIPO DOWN, AND SWORE AT HIM.

ENGLISH ARSEHOLE!

RAT-A-TAT-A-TAT

BIPO GROUNDED HIS CRATE IN A FIELD. (AND GOT OUT.)

HE SOON BEFRIENDED A BIG FRESIAN COW.

AND THEY HAD A LOVELY PICNIC.

THE END

OUR THANKS TO THE RAF FOR THEIR HELP.

2. SITUATIONS WANTED

YOUNG LADY, 21 yrs, SEEKS PART TIME EVENING EMPLOYMENT. GOOD LOOKING, EXPERIENCED, AND LOW PRICED. LEGS SPREAD LIKE MARGERINE. GOOD TITS. £25 A GO. CALL AT: 121 PINK LANE, N/CLE 1.

MALCOLM'S VAST WORLD OF KNOWLEDGE ABOUT BOKSES

LAST WEEK MALCOLM TOLD US HOW WE CAN PROTECT OUR GROINS FROM BALLS WITH A BOX. THIS WEEK WE LEARN...

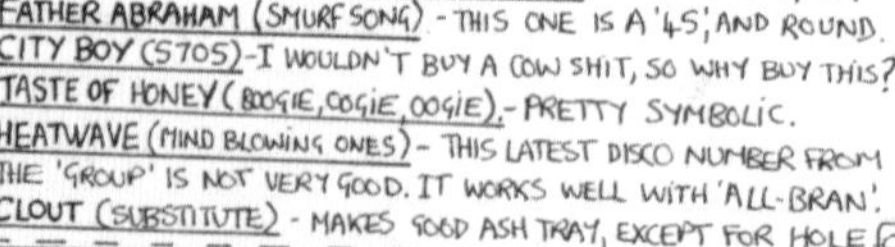

Singles

RAYDIO (LOVE THING) - PUTTING PRESSURE ON THE BEE GEES FOR TURDS OF THE YEAR.

BONEY M (BROWN GIRL IN THE RING) - BULL SHIT.

TRAVOLTA/NEWTON JOHN (THE ONE WHAT I WANT). - WHAT A BODY, EH?

FATHER ABRAHAM (SMURF SONG) - THIS ONE IS A '45', AND ROUND.

CITY BOY (5705) - I WOULDN'T BUY A COW SHIT, SO WHY BUY THIS?

TASTE OF HONEY (BOOGIE, OOGIE, OOGIE). - PRETTY SYMBOLIC.

HEATWAVE (MIND BLOWING ONES) - THIS LATEST DISCO NUMBER FROM THE 'GROUP' IS NOT VERY GOOD. IT WORKS WELL WITH 'ALL-BRAN'.

CLOUT (SUBSTITUTE) - MAKES GOOD ASH TRAY, EXCEPT FOR HOLE

AND...... THE GIANTS ON ALBUM

MOODY BLUES (OCTAVE) - I DON'T LIKE IT.

SATURDAY NIGHT FEVER SOUNDTRACK - IF YOU HAVE A COPY OF THIS DOUBLE ALBUM, TAKE IT TO THE NEAREST POLICE STATION, THEY ARE USED TO DEALING WITH SCUM. THE BEE GEES REALLY ARE TOO BAD.

STREET LEGAL by BOB DYLAN. EAT SOME NICE TINNED SALMON, BOB.

E.L.O. (OUT OF THE BLUE) A SPECTACULAR MULTI-MILLION £ LASER SHOW & A BIG SPACESHIP CAN'T HIDE THE FACT THAT E.L.O. STINK.

WAR of THE WORLDS (VARIOUS TWATS) JUSTIN HAYWARD SINGS. ENOUGH SAID.

BUZZCOCKS (ANOTHER MUSIC IN A DIFFERENT KITCHEN) TEN OUT OF TEN!

stranglers (BLACK & WHITE) THIS IS A NICE RECORD PLEASE BUY IT.

EDDIE & THE HOT RODS (LIFE ON THE LINE) BARRIE MASTERS & CO. ARE MORE PLASTIC THAN FRENCH BERTRAND (AND HE'S GOT A PLASTIC DICK). BAD.

BONEY M. (BONEY M'S NEW ALBUM) THIS RECORD COULD BE IMPROVED A LITTLE. THE METHOD I SUGGEST IS TO HURL IT FROM A WINDOW.

Radio Stars (SONGS FOR SWINGIN' LOVERS) BLOODY BLEEDING MARVELOUS.

FOR THE TIP TOP: JILTED JOHN (JILTED JOHN). & THE ONE THAT I ONE'T (TRAVOLTA/NEWTON-JOHN)

THE END. NEXT WEEK WE'LL HAVE GOLF TIPS FROM A NEW TOP PRO!

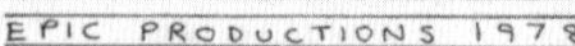
EPIC PRODUCTIONS 1978

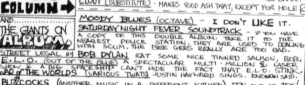

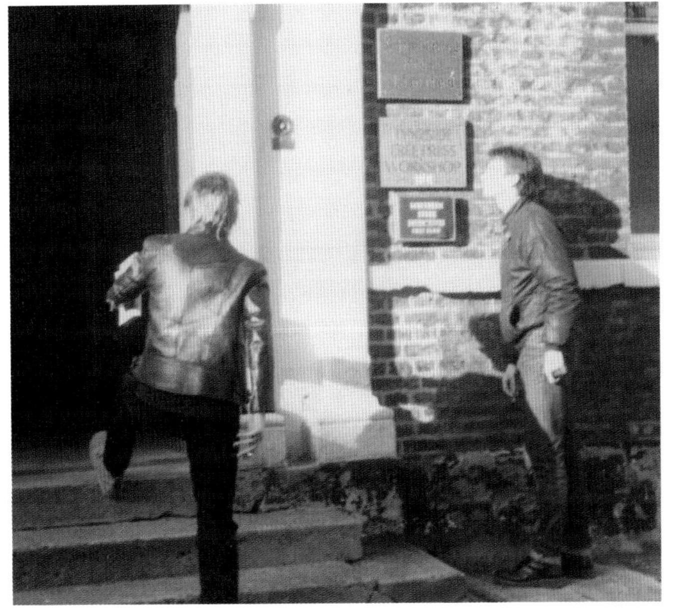

Left: Chris and Jim's Viz *prototype,* Arnold The Magazine. *Jim's Rude Kid would become an early* Viz *favourite.*

Above: Welcome to the glamorous world of magazine publishing – the Tyneside Free Press.

Below: Another Viz *prototype,* The Daily Pie.

Higher Executive Officer didn't discipline him. Instead, he suggested that Chris apply for a part-time job on the staff bulletin.

Chris got the job, but it didn't involve much writing. 'I was an errand boy for the editor,' he says. Yet Jim was still around, and in their spare time they created two one-off comics – *The Daily Pie* and *Arnold the Magazine*. Both publications consisted of a single sheet of A4, copied ten times at their local Prontaprint, and sold to their friends in local pubs for 10p – the price it cost to print it. Simon also sold some copies at his local youth club.

These comics went down just as well as *The Fat Crusader*, and since Chris was now earning a salary, and still living at home, he had a bit of cash to spare. He decided that for his next comic, he'd blow some of his hard-earned wages on a proper print run. It seems fitting that the most popular comic of the Thatcher years was bankrolled by the DHSS.

Chris contacted a couple of high street firms, but they wanted several hundred pounds to print a hundred copies, and his take-home pay was only £170 a month. Eventually, he found a 'hippy' printer called the Tyneside Free Press who would do him 150 copies for sixty quid, as long as he folded and stapled them himself. This was just about within his budget. Now all he needed was a new comic, and somewhere new to sell it.

THE DAILY PIE

THE TRAGIC NEW "MAGAZINE" FOR KIDS WHO CAN AFFORD IT

Written & Produced by Kwith Donood and Gym Braunloe.

EPIC PRODUCTIONS 1978 LTD, WILLY ENTERPRISES (UK) LTD, "YOU ARE A BASTARD" (UK) LTD, U.S.S. ENTERPRISE ENTERPRISES LTD.
(All rights reserved by the author/artist.)

NON PROFIT PRICE 90P

NOW INCORPORATING "MEAT"

TOMMY'S BIRTHDAY.
ONE DAY, IT WAS TOMMY'S BIRTHDAY...
HE WAS BLOWING OUT THE CANDLES ON HIS BIRTHDAY CAKE
HE BLEW,
PUFF!!
AND HE BLEW.
BUT HE COULD NOT BLOW THEM OUT.
OH! HIS HEAD HAS COME OFF.
THE END (C. Donald)

ADVERTISEMENT
BUY
THREE NUNS IN A SOAP DISH.
NEW MAGAZINE!!

COME TO THE SHOPS DEAR!
FUCK OFF!

YOUR STARS BY GYPSY
You (Jan 1st-Dec31st)
Today you made a bad decision and bought something crappy.

RAYMOND, THE LARGE CATERPILLAR
HE'S SO BIG, I CAN'T GET ANY WORDS IN!
THE END

EAT AT
JOURNEY
THEY SET OUT ON FOOT, OVER HILL AND DALE...

Right and opposite: Newcastle's nascent punk scene featured Arthur 2 Stroke and The Noise Toys. Below: Anti-Pop venue The Gosforth Hotel, where the first issue sold out in a night.

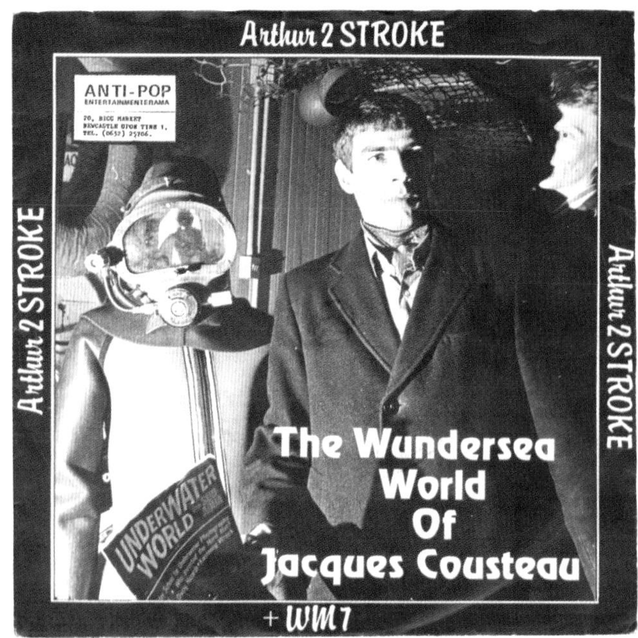

By the late Seventies, punk had finally reached Newcastle, and the focus of this fledgling scene was the Gosforth Hotel. Sting used to play there with a group called Last Exit, but by now the house band was a group called Arthur 2 Stroke And The Chart Commandos. Chris, Jim and Simon all used to go there to see them play. Named after a bloke called Arthur who'd had two strokes, this band was managed by a punk collective called Anti-Pop, which provided gigs, publicity and equipment for dozens of apprentice groups. 'We weren't into stitching people up or signing contracts,' says Andy Inman, who ran Anti-Pop with Arthur 2 Stroke front man Phil Branston. 'It was punk with an overdose of hippy.' A decade older than Chris, Phil was a bit of a guru figure for anyone who wanted to be a part of this new craze, especially in his onstage incarnation as Arthur 2 Stroke.

'All our friends were joining bands and getting in with all these trendy people,' says Chris. 'In order to be a groupie, I had to do something, so I thought, I'll do a fanzine and I'll be hip and trendy.'[2] Chris and Jim were hardly punks. Jim listened to The Stranglers and The Buzzcocks, but he didn't dress like them. Chris was still listening to his mum's Seekers

'It was very much part of that whole punk ethic that you didn't need corporations or big business to do your own thing.'

records. However Arthur 2 Stroke were hardly the Sex Pistols. Like a lot of new wave bands, they were funny rather than ferocious – a self-deprecating contrast to pompous prog rock. Simon was in a band that played the Gosforth. He was also a punk poet, a bit like John Cooper Clarke. Chris wrote some funny poems for Simon to perform, but he wasn't cut out to be a performer himself. Starting a punk fanzine was the best way to join in the fun.

Chris and Jim took some cartoons to the Anti-Pop office in the Bigg Market, the hub of Newcastle's raucous nightlife. Phil and Andy thought they were hilarious. 'Do another comic,' said Phil, 'and make it a fanzine for Anti-Pop.' With their DIY design and chaotic content, fanzines like *Sniffing Glue* had become a potent part of the punk scene. 'It was very much part of that whole punk ethic that you didn't need corporations or big business to do your own thing and sell your thing – you just did it yourself,' says Simon. 'It was a cottage industry and everybody helped everybody else out.'

Like all successful small businesses, these fanzines fed each other. Local Letraset press barons would trade fanzines with other editors, posting off bundles of bedsit publications and receiving bundles of unfamiliar fanzines in return. Far-flung editors distributed each other's journals around their own local outlets, and in this erratic fashion *Viz* eventually

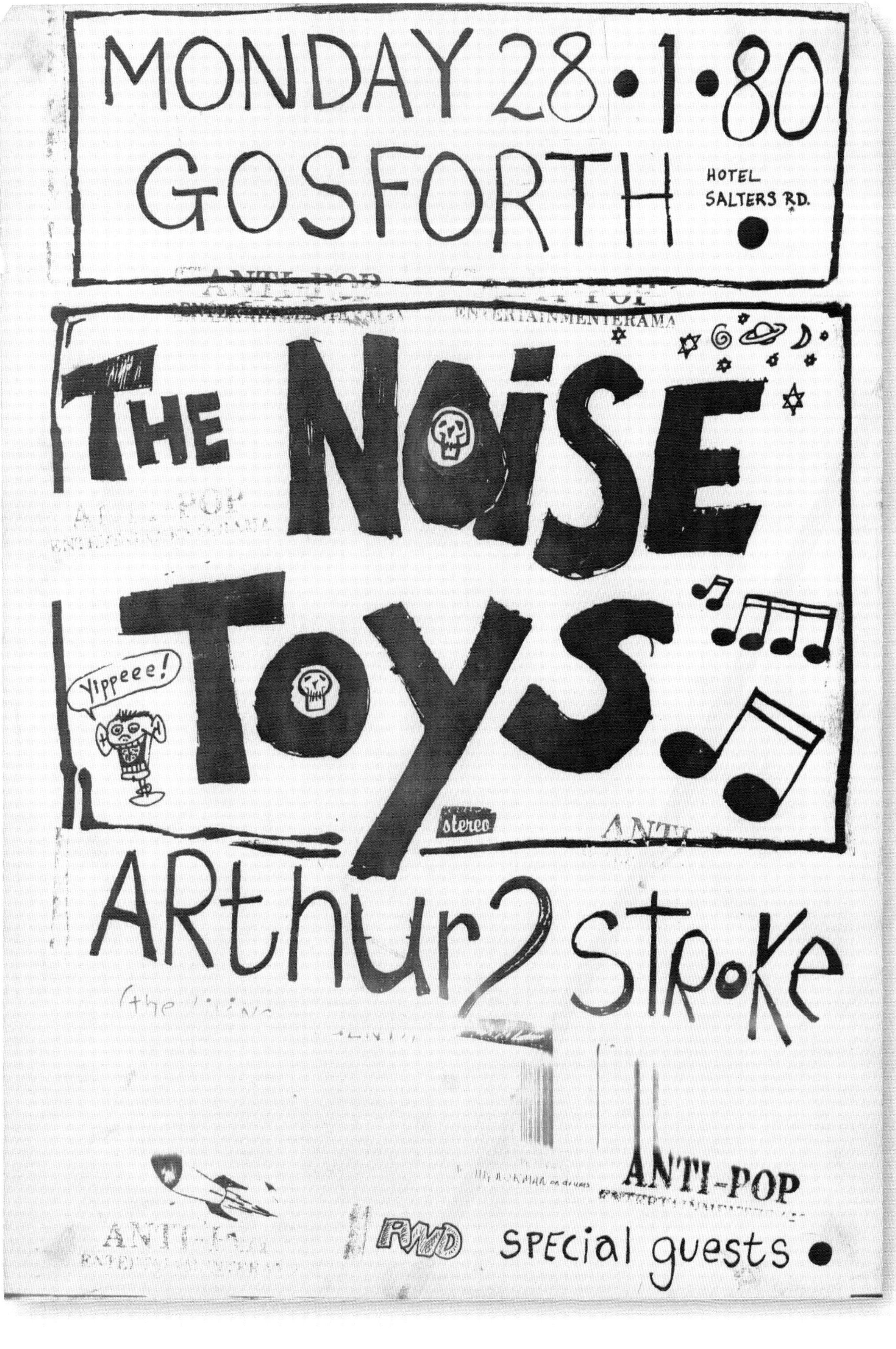

MONDAY 28•1•80
GOSFORTH
HOTEL
SALTERS RD.

ANTI-POP
ENTERTAINMENTERAMA

THE NOISE TOYS

Yippeee!

stereo

ARthur2 StRoKe

ANTI-POP

RMD SPECial guests •

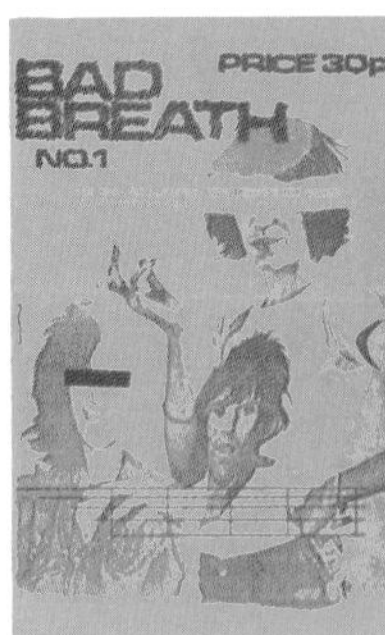

Chris's contribution to Bad Breath, *a local music fanzine.*

acquired a national profile – finding little clusters of avid readers across the country who far preferred rude cartoons to endless record and gig reviews.

'We had no idea what this thing was going to be called,' says Simon. 'It wasn't originally called *Viz*.' Viz Comics was supposed to be the brand name of the parent company, rather like Marvel Comics. The proper title was *The Bumper Monster Christmas Special*, but that was a bit of a mouthful, and since the word Viz was on the cover, and no better name emerged, it eventually became known as *Viz*, more or less by accident. Like a lot of great titles, it didn't really mean anything. It just sounded good – that's all. Chris made a lino cut of the *Viz* logo. Its main asset was that it was relatively easy to produce, comprising six straight lines and just three letters.

Chris had already done a cartoon for a local fanzine called *Bad Breath*, but that mag was all about music, and he found the whole thing pretentious. He was sure they could do a lot better. And they could. A quarter of a century later, that first issue still feels fresh and vital – and though the drawing was a bit wobbly, the attitude was all there. A curt introduction thanked 'all the artists we ripped off'. A teaser on the cover promised readers a free ice cream. 'If you don't complete and return this form, you will be shot,' warned a note inside. It was as iconoclastic as punk rock, but without any of the same self-importance. And reading it again today, it remains a cult classic.

As well as numerous strips by Chris and Jim, plus a couple from outside contributors (such as Martin Stevens from the Noise Toys, one of the punk bands who played the Gosforth) there was also a cartoon from Simon, who went on to draw quintessential *Viz* characters like Johnny Fartpants, Sid The Sexist, Mr Logic, Simon Lotion (Time And Motion Man), Aldridge Prior (He's A Hopeless Liar), Millie Tant (And Her Radical Conscience) and Auberon Waugh's own personal favourite, the Bottom Inspectors. In true *Viz* fashion, Simon's first ever strip was gloriously vulgar, advancing from fornication to vomiting in just three frames. As he says himself, 'the theme of my first three strips was people eating so much that they were sick'. Simon's *Viz* debut coincided with a shift in his comic tastes. 'Marvel comics suddenly seemed stupid,' he says. 'They took themselves far too seriously.' Unlike *Viz*. Simon now turned his attention to British children's strips, and although *Viz* still carried the odd superhero

'The theme of my first three strips was people eating so much that they were sick.'

pastiche, it was comics like the *Beano* and the *Dandy* rather than Marvel that became its benchmark.

The crisp, clear art of Herge's Tintin books was another inspiration. 'They were immaculate but they weren't too complicated,' says Chris. 'I always try to draw like that.' And he did. Yet like the issues that followed, the first *Viz* wasn't all cartoons. There was a rather sycophantic feature plugging their punk patrons, Anti-Pop, plus an article about Prince Charles's private life, written in sub-*Private Eye* style by one of Chris's penpals. 'Another *Viz* Exclusive Shock Horror Revelation Scoop From Our Surrey Correspondent' read the vaguely sarcastic headline. 'We've got nothing better to write about', added an apologetic note alongside. The article's speculative content was far tamer than many future *Viz* royal exclusives, but its knowing tone summed up everything that *Viz* subsequently set out to avoid.

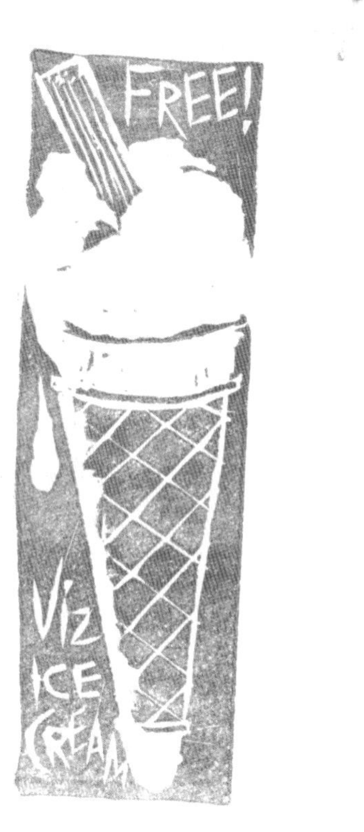

This page and overleaf: Some highlights from the first issue of Viz.

IT'S THE...
DISCO DANCING CHAMPION OF THE WORLD
BY CHRIS DONALD
JESUS! THIS GUY'S A TOTAL WOW!!
IT WAS JUST ANOTHER SATURDAY NIGHT AT THE 'ERUCTO DISCO' IN THE HEART OF THE BIG CITY.
Eructo Disco
TICKETS £5
NO SHITS
GENTS
NOTE COIN-OP CUBICLES 5p A TURD
PUSH
DOWN IN THE GENTS, WHILE ALL THE GUYS WERE TAKING A LEAK...
BIG BLOBS FOR BIG KNOBS
'STOP BABIES'
TURN KNOB (THIS KNOB)
THE DISCO DANCING CHAMPION OF THE WORLD WAS GETTING HIS FACE RIGHT.
PRESENTLY, OUR MISTER COOL WAS HOT TO TROT, AND HE MADE A 'B-LINE' FOR THE DISCO-FLOOR.
HYYACK!
LOOK AT THE GUY MOVE... HE'S ELECTRIC!
SWOOSH!
HEY! THIS GUY'S GOT DYNAMICS
BUT THEN.... THE CHAMP RUNS INTO A SPOT OF BOVVER!
THUG
I'M A THUG
SCREECH!!!
HIT
HOWK!
AND SO THE CHAMPION HAD HIS HEAD FLATTENED.
THE MORAL:- "DON'T GET YOUR HEAD FLATTENED"
THE END
Christopher Donald 3-5.10.79
VICTOR PRATT THE STUPID TWAT
DO YOU WANNA COME F'RA RIDE ON ME NEW BIKE VIC?
NAR MAN! CAN'T Y'SEE I'M ON THE PHONE.
13.10.79 C Donald
TOMMY'S BIRTHDAY.
ONE DAY, IT WAS TOMMY'S BIRTHDAY...
HE WAS BLOWING OUT THE CANDLES ON HIS BIRTHDAY CAKE.
HE BLEW,
PUFF!!
AND HE BLEW.
BUT HE COULD NOT BLOW THEM OUT.
OH! HIS HEAD HAS COME OFF.
THE END (C.Donald)
"TOMMY'S BIRTHDAY" © FIRST PUBLISHED JULY 1978 "THE DAILY PIE" ©1978
DOCTOR, PEOPLE TELL ME I LOOK LIKE A MELON!
PISS OFF! I'VE HEARD IT.
© CD 15.11.79
Pierre by B. Dylan.
SACRE BLEU
LE PETIT LAPIN FRANCAIS
VOICI UN ARBRE!
UN THISTLE
1. PIERRE ALLE AU CAMPAGNE POUR UN PETIT SPOT DE RECREATION.
VOICI! UN NOTICE!
DANGER ATOMIC RANGE
2. PIERRE LIT UN NOTICE. LE NOTICE DIT... "DANGER ATOMIC RANGE"
QU'EST-CE QUE C'EST ATOMIC?
3. ZUT ALORS!!! PIERRE TROUVE UN NUKE N'EST PAS?!
LE BOUME!
4 LE BOUME! PAUVRE PETIT BUNNY-LAPIN. C'EST LE PROGRES!!
CLUB CARTOONS ©
6

14 year old in sex romp scandal

by SUN REPORTERS

14 YEAR OLD ANN HIGGINS AT HOME YESTERDAY

A 51 YEAR OLD UNEMPLOYED BINGO CALLER ACCUSED HER FORMER HUSBAND OF RAPING THEIR 14 YEAR OLD DAUGHTER, AT DRATSAB MAGISTRATES COURT YESTERDAY. "IT ALL BEGAN WHEN HE STARTED FONDLING HER BREASTS," SHE CLAIMED.

FORMER HUSBAND, BILL, NOW UNEMPLOYED, OF SCROGG WAY, DRATSAB, AND LIVING WITH 13 YEAR OLD EX-NUN, MAGGIE SKUMM, DENIED THE CLAIM. "WE WERE VERY CLOSE, BUT NEVER HAD SEX," HE CLAIMED. HE ACCUSED FORMER HEAD MASTER AND TOWN MAGISTRATE NIGEL RAMSBOTTOM OF HAVING SEX WITH HIS DAUGHTER DURING LESSONS.

"HE LEAD HER ASTRAY," HE CLAIMS. "IT ALL BEGAN WITH HIM FONDLING HER BREASTS," HE ADDED.

FORMER HEAD MASTER AND MAGISTRATE RAMSBOTTOM, NOW LIVING WITH KINKY SOHO MASSEUSE JAYNE GROYNE, WOULD NOT MAKE ANY COMMENT.

"SHE CONSENTED TO SOME CASUAL SEX IN CLASS," HE SAID, "BUT SHE TOLD ME SHE WAS 23."

HIS MISTRESS, 42 YEAR OLD BUXOM PROSTITUTE, JAYNE GROYNE, OFFERED OUR REPORTER, "NUDE RELIEF," FOR £25. "I DON'T GO ALL THE WAY WITH STRANGERS," SHE ADDED, BUT SHE DID ADMIT TO A CASUAL RELATIONSHIP WITH FORMER MALE MODEL, 51 YEAR OLD ANDREW JONES. "IT ALL BEGAN WHEN HE STARTED TO FONDLE MY BREASTS," SHE SAID, BUT ADDED THAT HE WAS, "NO GOOD IN BED ANYWAY."

14 YEAR OLD ANN HIGGINS, CENTRE OF THE MASSIVE RAPE. RUMPUS IS NOW IN THE CARE OF 31 YEAR OLD SOCIAL WORKER MIKE JONES, FORMER HIPPY AND LECTURER, OF BINGE COURT, DRATSAB. HE DENIES THAT HE IS HAVING AN AFFAIR WITH THE SHAPELY 14 YEAR OLD, WHO IS EXPECTING A 'LOVE CHILD" IN 3 MONTHS. SHE DENIES THAT THE FATHER IS 41 YEAR OLD DIVORCED POOLS COLLECTOR ARTHUR SCROGG. SCROGG, A 41 YEAR OLD POOLS COLLECTOR, CLAIMS THAT 14 YEAR OLD ANN HAD OFFERED HIM CASUAL SEX WHEN THEY HAD MET AT SOHO SEX DEN, 'ENIDS'. HIS FORMER WIFE, NOW LIVING WITH 33 YEAR OLD FILM PRODUCER GAVIN PARTRIDGE, CLAIMS THAT SHE RETURNED HOME TO FIND THE COUPLE MAKING LOVE ON THE KITCHEN TABLE. "WE WERE GOOD FREINDS," SAID ANN. "IT ALL BEGAN WHEN HE STARTED FONDLING MY BREASTS," SHE ADDED. ANN, A PRETTY 14 YEAR OLD, ALSO DENIES THAT SHE AGREED TO '3 IN BED' SEX SESSIONS WITH SEX-CHANGE SOCIAL WORKER AND FORMER NUN, STEWART PRATT. THE CASE CONTINUES.

CD. © 21.10.79

7

Left and below: Newcastle poet Andrew Tait was a stalwart of the Viz *Top Ten Chart.*

This lack of journalistic cant was just one of the things that made *Viz* so different. Unlike *Private Eye*, it was never remotely political. It has never alienated its readers by aspiring to the same insider status. It has never become part of the media establishment, nor does it pretend to be. It's more like a gatecrasher at a posh celebrity party. When *Viz* was named Magazine of the Year in 1989, at a swanky VIP bash at London's Grosvenor House Hotel, its editorial team were ejected for foul and abusive language, after being plied with free drink by the staff of a midmarket national newspaper.

Unlike the Fleet Street press, *Viz* didn't talk down to its readers or claim it knew any more than they did. Its tabloid piss takes were written by and for people who knew the red tops were full of rubbish, but enjoyed reading them anyway. Consequently, its tabloidese rang truer than the more condescending parodies in *Private Eye*. And unlike so many alternative comedians, it never resorted to moaning about Margaret Thatcher. Anti-Thatcher rants by right-on stand-ups like Ben Elton merely bolstered her omnipotent public image. *Viz* was far more subversive – it totally ignored her. Although the comic started a few months after Mrs Thatcher became Prime Minister, if anything its main targets were actually woolly lefties. 'People assumed it was left wing – it wasn't,' says Chris. 'It was liberal but it wasn't left wing.'

Nevertheless, some people still seem to think that just because it's Northern, *Viz* must be Old Labour. 'How does it feel to be a socialist and a millionaire?' a butcher once asked Chris. 'How does it feel to be a vegetarian and a butcher?' asked Chris. 'But I'm not a vegetarian,' replied the butcher. 'And I'm not a socialist,' replied Chris. As his brother Steve says, 'That cynicism which makes us comedians also makes us less left wing.'

Plenty of publications try to prick other people's pomposity. *Viz* was the only one that actually dared to prick its own. Its Top Ten was calculated on the basis of how much groups paid *Viz* to appear on its pop page, rather than how many records they sold. 'If you haven't got any money then don't bother sending us your records,' read a typical disclaimer. 'We don't want to know.' The first three figure bribe wasn't even from a bona fide band at all, but a local music teacher, struggling poet and telephone prankster called Andrew Tait, whose subsequent publicity stunts included demonstrating outside 10 Downing Street, going on hunger strike, threatening to swallow a packet of woodlice killer and sending an electric toaster to Bob Dylan.

Viz never patronized its readership, or tried to cuddle up to them. 'The page you write and it's always shite', read the frank slogan on the Letters Page. 'It can be a soul-

• The Viz Top Ten •

RECORD BREAKER!

Two-ton Tait tops Top Ten tree!

Tyneside tunesmith **ANDREW TAIT** has carved a niche for himself in the anals of pop history — along with such great names as Jimi Hendrix, John Lennon and Elvis Presley. For Andrew has become the first ever popstar to buy his way into the Viz Top Ten with a three figure bribe, and he did it in true style — handing over a massive **£200.01** to secure himself a place in pop history — and the prized number one position in this issue's chart.

Andrew Tait hands over the magnificent cheque for £200.01 to the reigning Miss Viz Top Ten, Cindy Smallpiece (36-24-36).

1	**ANDREW TAIT** *Songs From The Heart Of The Primal Goat*	£200.01
2	**DOGS D'AMOUR**	£50.01

destroying task reading through the letters,' admits Chris. 'A percentage of them are really, really thick and they say some absolutely disgusting, appalling things. You have to put it to the back of your mind that those people read it.'[3] The staff usually wrote the best ones themselves, although part of their appeal was that it was impossible to tell which was which. 'A lot of the letters on the letters page are sort of sneaky digs at the type of readers they have and the type of people they are,' says Steve. And *Viz* was just as prickly when readers tried to cuddle up to them. 'We did this thing in the comic taking the piss out of Michael Winner's restaurant column, and he wrote us this letter saying he thought it was really funny, so we put a picture of him in with the caption Fat Cunt,' reveals Chris.[4] Based in Newcastle rather than London, *Viz* has never hobnobbed with its targets. At their tenth birthday party, guests wore badges denoting their celebrity status – A, B or C. 'Do not stare at the celebrities', read a warning on the invitation. 'Pretend not to recognize them.'

Above and below: Arthur 2 Stroke and his Chart Commandos became Tony O'Diamond and Top Group Fantastic at the Viz 10th anniversary party.

In 1979, such innovations were still just a cheeky twinkle in Chris's mind's eye, but there was enough of that Fuck You brio in the first issue to make it utterly unlike anything anyone had ever come across before. This wasn't the genteel pranks and japes of the *Beano* or the *Dandy*. This was real schoolboy humour – the sort of jokes you heard behind every bike shed, from the roughest comprehensive to the poshest public school. You never laugh like you did at school, and reading *Viz* was like being back in the boys' bogs, sharing cigarettes and taking the piss out of the teachers. '*Viz* was into that humour that people only think they have with their mates,' says Andy. 'Lots of groups of mates have it all over the place, and if you could meet up with each other you'd probably have thousands of friends.'

Although everybody knew these jokes, nobody had ever thought of putting them down on paper, and by daring to do so, *Viz* located an underpopulated corner of the market. 'There were no magazines on the shelves at that time that had bad language in them apart from pornography,' explains Simon. '*Viz* had all this street language in it that had never been in print before.' And although everyone used this language, they certainly weren't used to reading it. In 1979, there were plenty of comics for kids, but hardly anything funny for anyone in their late teens or early twenties.

'*Viz* was into that humour that people only think they have with their mates,'

This page and opposite: Issue two of Viz with its free gift of a balloon stapled inside.

Even the newspapers were a lot more earnest and elderly than they try to be today. The tabloids were inane, the broadsheets were stuffy – and both formats were terribly old-fashioned. *Private Eye* was middle-aged and *Punch* was geriatric. If you were too old for *Whizzer and Chips* or *Shiver and Shake* and too young for *The Spectator* or *The New Statesman*, there was hardly anything amusing to read apart from the three main music papers – *Sounds*, *Melody Maker* and the *NME*. These rock and roll weeklies weren't entirely witless – they even had a few good cartoons – but unless you were mad about music, it was like buying a Big Mac for the sesame seeds on the bun. 'The only humour magazines that you could buy at all were *Punch* and *Private Eye*, both of which were heavily political, and *Punch* in particular was extremely stiff,' explains Simon. *Viz* was neither. Without really knowing how or why, *Viz* had found a niche.

'I really had no idea where I was supposed to be going in life and this was the first time I ever thought there was something that I was doing that people were interested in.'

Naturally, Chris & Co had no idea that they'd stumbled upon a publishing masterplan. 'The comic wasn't done with any intention of making money,' says Steve. Indeed, when Chris and Jim caught the 33 bus into town to collect the comic from the printers, the print run was so small that all the copies fitted into a single cardboard box. Yet compared to *The Daily Pie*, it still felt like the big time. 'It was a revelation to see our cartoons in jet black ink on creamy newsprint,' recalls Chris. 'The fact that the printers had bound four of the twelve pages the wrong way round didn't bother us in the slightest.' [5] It didn't bother Phil, either. 'This is just what we want,' he said.

Nevertheless, when Chris & Co set off to the Gosforth Hotel that winter evening, to try and flog the first issue, their expectations were so modest that they only took about half the comics with them. However *Viz* sold so well that Simon had to rush back home half way through the gig to collect the rest, and by the end of the evening, they'd sold every single copy. It was a pattern that would be repeated many times in years to come.

It felt great to see people actually reading *Viz* and – best of all – laughing at it. 'The feedback was incredibly good,' says Chris. It wouldn't pay its way for years. Total revenue from this first sell out was thirty quid – printing alone cost sixty. Yet although he was out of pocket, Chris was still encouraged. 'I couldn't see how it was going to be viable to do it on a commercial basis, but I still wanted to do another one,' he says. 'Going to the gigs and selling it was good fun – doing the cartoons was secondary.'

Conversely, drawing cartoons was the career Simon had always dreamed of. 'I couldn't believe that this could happen,' he says, still sounding a bit wistful as he looks back on it all today. He didn't care that the print run was tiny, or that the distribution was virtually non-existent. He'd always wanted to be a cartoonist and now, for a while at least, he was one. 'People were buying my cartoon strip,'

he says. 'It was terribly exciting. I had trouble at school, I didn't seem to fit into the whole education thing, I really had no idea where I was supposed to be going in life and this was the first time I ever thought there was something that I was doing that people were interested in.' Simon left school at sixteen. Unlike Chris, he didn't even stay on to do A Levels. And although it would be a long time before *Viz* gave him a decent living, it did give him an outlet he'd never really found at school. 'It was the one thing that I could focus on, in the hope that we could make something of it,' he says. 'Anything was better than sitting around watching the telly, or sitting in the pub all day trying to make one pint last for four hours.' He didn't worry whether it could ever become a proper business, or whether it would remain a hobby. All that really mattered was, it got him out and about.

In different circumstances, Chris and Simon could quite easily have gone on to university, but it was probably a good job they didn't. With no student distractions, *Viz* remained the main focus of their lives. Journalism has always been swamped with posh college kids with fake working-class accents – the sort of poseurs *Viz* lampoons in strips like Student Grant. Chris and Simon were both from the nicer side of Newcastle. Even if they'd kept *Viz* going while they were away at college, doing degrees would have cemented their middle-class credentials, and separated them from half their readers. The best comedy always bridges the class divide. By staying put, they kept their populist edge and maintained the comic's classless appeal.

Egged on by Phil and Andy (who bought the very first copy) they started work on a second issue, which finally appeared five months later, in April 1980. This time, they upped the print run to 500, but that issue sold out too. Highlights included another free gift – a balloon, stapled to the back page. 'It was a great joke,' says Simon. 'I kept trying to persuade the publishers to pay to do that joke again because only 500 people ever saw it.' However it wasn't long before they were printing a thousand at a time.

As well as hawking the comic in the Gosforth Hotel, Chris started flogging it from pub to pub. 'I used to hate walking into bars selling them, but something drove me to do it,' he says. 'I remember one drunken, bent-nosed farming student in the "agrics" bar at Newcastle University snorting at me, grabbing a dozen comics out of my hand and tearing them in half. You should have seen the look I gave him once I had got out of the building.' [6]

Thankfully, before too long, he found some more sympathetic outlets – an independent record shop called Listen Ear, a city centre pub called the Trent House and a community bookshop in Jesmond, which they mocked with gusto in the comic. 'They were the butt of a lot of the jokes, but because they were liberal and right on, they had to sell it because it was a homemade magazine,' says Chris. 'It was like goat's yoghurt. They had to sell it whether they liked it or not.' It even went on sale (unofficially) in the local HMV. 'The staff were ordered to hide the comics if anyone from head office entered the store.' [7] However, their most important patron was the Kard Bar, run by a printer turned shopkeeper called Brian Sandells.

Brian's shop sold posters which were popular with youngsters, and he was used to youngsters coming in and asking if he'd sell their fanzines too. He always said no. 'They were atrocious,' he says. 'They were toilet paper. They were awful. I couldn't see the humour.' But when Chris brought in *Viz*, for the first time Brian said yes. 'It was so anarchic,' he says. 'You could see it was going to hit people in the face and upset them.' There was the language it was written in, for one thing – a world away from the comics he'd grown up with. 'The F-word cropped up a lot,' he recalls. 'Nobody else would dare do that kind of thing.' But although the swearing caught the eye, Brian could see there was more to *Viz* than just a flurry of four-letter words. 'There was a lot of thought put into it,' he says. 'It was so well produced.'

Soon, Brian was stocking several hundred copies of every issue, and even then he had no trouble selling them. 'Heavens above,' he thought. 'This is exactly what the youngsters want.' Brian had an attic full of defunct pop pin ups – Donny Osmond, David Cassidy, that sort of thing. 'Why don't you give them away as free gifts?' he suggested. They were far too big, but that didn't deter Chris & Co. They simply cut them into four and gave away a quarter of a Bay City Rollers poster with every copy of the next issue.

Brian was so impressed, he even offered to take on their distribution – but like a lot of locals, he only ever saw *Viz* as a local joke. 'My idea of distribution was going to Durham and Berwick,' he says. 'No way did I think it could sell in London.' *Viz* spoke with a Geordie accent, and Brian didn't believe its Tyneside vowels would travel. 'Fifty miles south, no one will have a clue what it's all about,' he thought. Thankfully, *Viz* found another distributor and proved him wrong. 'Thank God they didn't come to me,' says Brian. 'They'd still be doing what they were doing years and years ago.' The comic's tone of voice was regional, but its appeal was universal.

Pretty soon, Brian started being approached by other people touting similar comics – but he hardly ever saw one he even felt like stocking, let alone one good enough to compete head to head with *Viz*. 'I'm sorry, it's not for me,' he'd say. 'It's not up to the same kind of standard.'

Opposite: Early posters advertising the comic. This page: Newcastle curry magnate, Lord Harpole outside the Rupali Restaurant.

Occasionally he'd take a few on sale or return, but invariably they just sat there on the counter. As its professional competitors would discover, the *Viz* blueprint may look simple but it's actually impossible to copy.

Brian began buying ad space in the comic. 'I always paid them upfront, mainly so they could get the damn thing printed.' And he always left the design to Chris. 'I don't want to do the adverts,' Brian told him. 'You must do them for me, because I want them in the style of *Viz*.' These advertisements, and others like them, were almost as entertaining as the cartoons – sending up the advertisers and giving their products a self-deprecating panache. Some of them were almost too successful. Local curry house proprietor Abdul Latif (aka Lord Harpole) became such a familiar face in *Viz* that visitors to Newcastle are often pleasantly surprised to find he's a real person, not a character in the comic. For Southern readers, it's almost surreal to eat a meal in his celebrated Rupali Restaurant. *Viz* was an audacious cut and shut of fact and fiction, and half the fun was trying to find the join.

The punters lapped it up, but output remained sporadic. There were three issues in 1980 and another three in 1981, but in 1982 there were only two issues and just one in 1983. 'Issue 10 came out on FA Cup Final day in '83,' recalls Simon. 'The next issue didn't come out until FA Cup Final day the following year.' Although the content was improving with every issue, *Viz* was grinding to a halt. With no second issue due that year, Brian persuaded Chris to do a greatest hits reprint in time for Christmas. Issue 10 was simply a compilation of Issues 1 to 4, with no new material, yet it still sold out straight away. 'For God's sake, get another issue out!' Brian used to scream at them, to absolutely no avail. 'People were coming in and pestering me,' he recalls. 'When's the next one coming in? When's the next one coming in?' Brian had to tell them that he simply didn't know.

The comic may have been in short supply, but there was no shortage of new readers. By now, Brian's shop alone was selling up to a thousand copies per issue – and the word was spreading, as students at Newcastle University and Polytechnic took the comic home in the holidays and showed it to their friends. 'The fact that it was Geordie was lost on many of its Southern readers at first,' says Steve. 'They just thought it was completely strange and weird and rude and new, and they loved it despite the fact that they didn't understand a lot of the dialect.' For outsiders, the Tyneside patois was all part of the appeal. 'Only ten or twenty per cent of it was written in the vernacular, but they obviously found that funny,' says Chris. Outlets now ranged from Norwich to Bournemouth, from wholefood stores to dirty bookshops. In an ad hoc way, *Viz* was gradually migrating nationwide.

By now, Chris had left the DHSS. 'My boss had been off for a week, so I'd taken the opportunity to do no work, lark about and generally misbehave. When she came back she told me off sternly. That was it. Half an hour later my resignation was on her desk, slipped under a bundle of other things.' [8] Chris had burnt his boats, but even his dad didn't blame him. 'I sometimes dream about going back, but the DHSS is a bit like nuclear science. It's a fast-moving world, and once you lose touch with modern developments in Social Security legislation affecting persons working overseas, there's no catching up again.' [9] The only thing he really missed was the tea trolley.

Around the same time that Chris left the DHSS, Simon left school with two O Levels (Art and English) and joined the new family business – signing on the dole. 'Steve had come back from college, Chris had given up the DHSS, I'd just left school and me dad had just been made redundant,' says Simon. 'We're all living at the same address, we've all got the same surname, so we're all signing at the same box on the same day at the same time. My mother was on benefits as well, but because she was disabled she didn't have to sign on. The family fucking outing, on the number 33 bus – every single fucking male member of the family went to sign on.'

Simon laughs about it now, but back then it wasn't quite so funny. Friends would see them on the bus, and ask where they were off to. 'It was a very depressing time,' he says. 'There wasn't even any dead end jobs that you could just pick up in order to turn over a bit of cash.'

There's never a good time or place to be out of work, but the North East in the early Eighties was particularly dismal. 'Newcastle was a very difficult place to be a success in at that time,' says Andy. 'Nobody had a job.'

But if Chris or Simon had found a job, *Viz* might well have fallen by the wayside. Like a lot of folk during the Thatcher years, with no easy way to make a living, they were thrown back on their own resources. It wasn't much fun at the time, but in the long run, unemployment saved them from the workaday drudgery that would have eclipsed their other interests. The benefit office became

'The DHSS is a bit like nuclear science. It's a fast-moving world, and once you lose touch with modern developments in Social Security legislation affecting persons working overseas, there's no catching up again.'

An early cartoon inspired by Chris's time at The Ministry.

Clockwise from above: Simon, Chris, Jim, Steve and Paul Whicker.

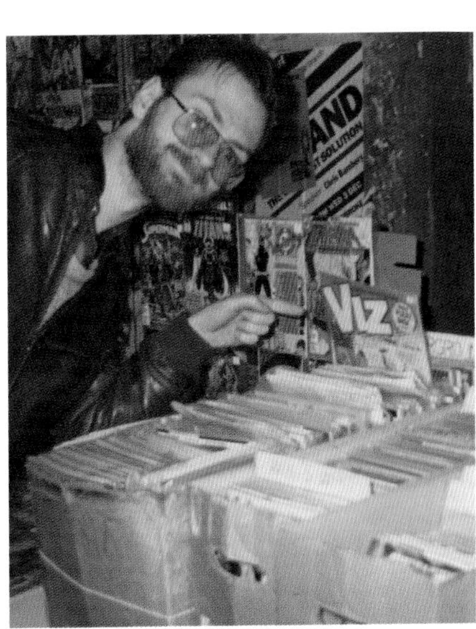

their Open University, giving them enough enforced free time to do the comic, depriving them of distractions, and even providing them with some unlikely inspiration. 'Me big brother got pulled in for going in to sign on wearing a yellow construction worker's hat,' recalls Chris. 'He'd got this Walkman thing and he attached the speakers to the hat.' The incident was pure Mr Logic.

Eventually, Steve became an author, illustrator and cartoonist (he also did special effects for movies like *Labyrinth* and *Little Shop of Horrors*) but, although he contributed to *Viz*, he was never as involved as Chris and Simon, or – initially, at least – Jim Brownlow. Jim's overall contribution may look relatively modest in pure percentage terms, but it's mighty hard to picture *Viz* developing the same way without his input. Diehard fans still adore his Paul Whicker The Tall Vicar – a drunken, randy, violent, foul-mouthed Church of England cleric whose height is by far his least unusual attribute. Likewise, his Rude Kid is the *Viz* signature in a single gag. Jim's fingerprints are all over the early issues, and inspired many more to come.

However as Jim's participation dwindled, the relationship between Chris and Simon became the main partnership in *Viz*. It's far too flip to label them as extrovert and introvert, but Simon is younger and more outgoing while Chris is older and more introspective, and this clash of personalities helped to give *Viz* its spark. 'There's always a little bit of friction between brothers,' says Anvil Springstien, who's known them for twenty years. 'They were always cursing at one another. Chris was always cursing at Simon, and Simon was always cursing at Chris.'

Even in public, this tension was sometimes palpable. One magazine came up with the bright idea of getting the main members of the editorial team to talk about each other behind each other's backs. Everyone was refreshingly rude, but Chris and Simon's remarks about each other were even feistier than the rest. 'He can't edit himself, either in

his work or when he's talking,' said Chris of Simon. 'He doesn't have the ability to be selective in what he says. He starts talking and then he'll just go on until you interrupt him – he just talks and talks and talks.'

'He's not a happy man,' said Simon of Chris.

'In what sense?' asked the man from the mag.

'In the sense that he's completely fucking miserable all the time,' said Simon.[10] But the pearl is the disease of the oyster, and if Chris and Simon hadn't been so dissimilar, maybe *Viz* wouldn't have been so full of fun.

It wasn't an equal partnership. Chris created *Viz*, and gave the comic its distinctive voice. Yet although Chris was always its driving force, Simon gave *Viz* something extra – that elusive factor X. His cartoons were often more basic (the Bottom Inspectors, Johnny Fartpants) but they were often the cartoons that people talked about the most (Sid the Sexist, Millie Tant). 'I don't think the friction between us is a benefit,' says Simon, 'but I think the fact that we're so different is.'

Compared to some brothers, they actually have quite a lot in common (they're both season ticket holders at Newcastle United, for a start – their seats are just a few feet apart) but they create two very different first impressions. Someone once described Simon as streetwise, and Chris as a bespectacled Oxford don. That was probably a bit over the top, but superficially there's some truth in it.

An early controversy boosted sales.

MP slams cash for North magazine

Four-letter comic on public cash

Chris Donald — working on Viz!

By SIMON WORTHINGTON

PUBLIC money has been pumped into a Tyneside-based comic which contains four-letter words.

The magazine Viz has mock advertisements with swear words.

It also contains a comic strip entitled Captain Incontinent and obscenities.

Artist Chris Donald, 24, launched Viz

ance grant from the Manpower Services Commission.

Yet MSC chiefs admit they never saw a draft of the comic nor have they seen a copy since.

But a North M.P. and Newcastle councillor have slammed the Government-formed body for putting cash into

Tynemouth Conservative M.P. Neville Trotter, said: "I do not think this is right.

Attention

"The MSC should have this magazine drawn to their attention. If they had seen a draft this might not have happened.

"It's quite unnecessary to publish four-letter words. It's a great pity the

One of Chris's adverts for a local pub.

After an obligatory spell on the other side of the benefits counter, signing on with Steve and Simon, Chris joined the Enterprise Allowance Scheme. This state sponsored ruse was a Thatcherite amnesty for moonlighters, paying unemployed people £40 a week to come off the dole and set up their own firms. 'It was a figure-manipulating thing to get the unemployment records down,' says Chris, 'but it was a good idea.' And without it, Viz might not have prospered. Officially, Chris was supposed to be building a career as a graphic designer, but he 'forgot' to mention Viz to the Enterprise Allowance people, and now his self-employed status allowed him to run the comic on the side. Eventually, the local paper found out and ran a story – 'Four Letter Comic On Public Cash' – but this minor scandal merely proved the age-old adage that no publicity is bad. The week after that parochial exposé, Chris sold an extra 500 copies. 'Sales just rocketed,' he says.

'Because I was cheap loads of people came to me and some nights I'd have six or seven posters to do for the next day.'

By now, *Viz* was selling so well that Chris was struggling to keep up. Jim had found a building job, and Chris was spending almost all his time on admin., and hardly any time putting the comic together. As well as selling *Viz* around town, Chris was trying to distribute it nationally, which involved painstaking chores like ploughing through all the regional *Yellow Pages* in Newcastle Central Library, so he could write to record shops around the country and ask them if they'd stock the comic.

As if this wasn't enough to be getting on with, Chris was also working for Anti-Pop promoter Andy Inman. 'He was paying me absolutely fuck all to do all these posters for him,' says Chris. 'Because I was cheap loads of people came to me and some nights I'd have six or seven posters to do for the next day.' He did all sorts of artwork for local bands, from posters to record sleeves, plus ads for an alternative clothing company. Yet it was all pretty badly paid and time consuming too. 'He'd stay up all night for a fiver,' says Andy. No wonder he found it hard to find time for *Viz*.

'I wasn't a terribly good graphic designer,' says Chris. 'I was a terrible plagiarist.' He can't have been that bad, what with all the work he was getting, but he thought he ought to get some training, so he did a foundation course at the local art college. Yet Chris was now twenty-one, and most of the other students had come straight from school. 'It was a nightmare,' he says. 'I just felt like I was about eighty.'

He quite liked the lecturers, but although these 'burnt out hippies' knew about *Viz*, they weren't particularly impressed. They suggested he become a greetings card designer. 'You must be kidding,' thought Chris.

Chris went back to freelance graphics, but though the work kept piling up, the money was still awful. 'I remember doing an advert for the *Yellow Pages* once, and the guy must have been paying a fortune to put it in, and I tried to charge him thirty-five quid.' He said he'd give Chris a fiver for cash. Another client was paying £750 a time for ad space in a national magazine, and giving Chris just £15 to design the advert that went in it.

The *Viz* side of things wasn't much better. 'We weren't even getting beer money out of it.' says Simon. Any money that came in went to pay for the next issue, but the main problem wasn't the cashflow but the workload. Chris would post off half a dozen comics at a time to some tiny independent outlet, and then have to chase them up a few months later, all for a few quid. His local postmistress complained that he was buying too many stamps. 'It was dying, basically, because I was getting bogged under with all the administration,' says Chris. 'The more it sold the harder it got.' Without a proper publisher, it was hard to see how *Viz* would survive.

Yet against all odds, *Viz* refused to lie down and die. Despite its increasing scarcity, sales kept on building. By 1983 it was selling 5,000 copies every issue – pretty good going for a comic that still wasn't on sale in normal newsagents. An unknown TV researcher called Jonathan Ross asked them to help him write a TV show he was planning. They said they'd think it over, but they never did anything about it. That show became The Last Resort. 'We've only ever done one thing, and that is retire to our bedrooms and draw cartoons and write little jokes,' says Chris. 'We've had offers to do all sorts of things, but we don't know how you do them.' [11] And so they turned down these offers and stuck to doing what they did best.

This page: Pics from Viz's first visit to London in 1981 - note Simon's 'Viz Comic Tour' T-shirt.

Nevertheless, *Viz* was featured on a couple of TV shows, and in 1984 *Viz* got a phone call from a man called Bob Paynter at IPC. IPC had seen *Viz* on TV and they wanted to see a copy. *Viz* sent IPC some back issues, and IPC sent *Viz* a cheque for three first-class train tickets to London. 'We'd never seen money,' says Simon. Dole money was all he'd ever had. They'd only been down to the Big Smoke a few times before.

IPC was (and is) a vast publishing empire, with dozens of mainstream titles, ranging from *Marie Claire* to the *NME*. 'There was a guy in a proper butler's outfit serving drinks out of a cabinet,' marvels Simon. 'We'd never seen anything like this in our lives.' Teaming up with IPC would have solved the comic's admin problems, but on the brink of his first big

IT'S BIG. IT'S GREEN. AND IT'S THROBBING.
'NEW IMPROVED'
WITH ADDED TOILET HUMOUR
VIZ
EVERY TWO MONTHLY August 1985
50p
Not for sale to minors
COMIC
MAKES OTHER MAGAZINES LOOK CRAP
ARE YOU SEXY?
Find out on page 5
BILLY BRAGG EXCLUSIVE
SPRINGSTEEN COLOUR POSTER
Win £1.00 in our terrific Vicar Joke Competition
FREE INSIDE
Super pair of DURAN DURAN PAPER UNDERPANTS
JOHNNY FARTPANTS
BIFF
PC VICTOR FOXTROTT
BILLY THE FISH
SGT. DEATH
and many more
ARE YOU CUMMIN' AT ME WITH THAT PARASOL?
PLUS Heart Wrenching Photo Romance
'Too Young To Love'
ON SALE HERE. 50p.

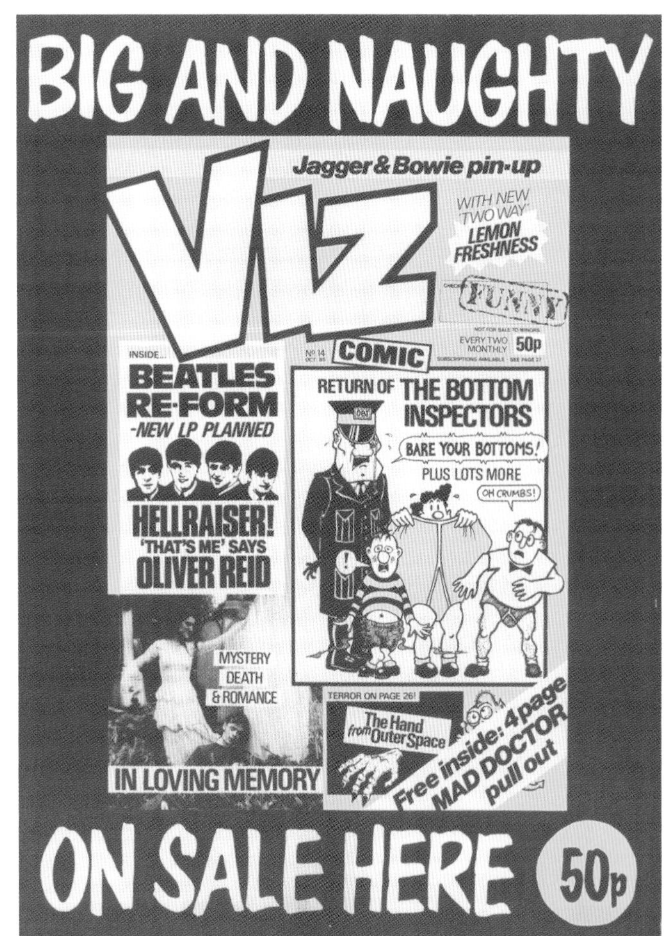
BIG AND NAUGHTY
Jagger & Bowie pin-up
VIZ
WITH NEW 'TWO WAY' LEMON FRESHNESS
FUNNY
EVERY TWO MONTHLY
50p
COMIC
INSIDE...
BEATLES RE-FORM
-NEW LP PLANNED
HELLRAISER!
'THAT'S ME' SAYS
OLIVER REID
RETURN OF THE BOTTOM INSPECTORS
BARE YOUR BOTTOMS!
PLUS LOTS MORE
OH CRUMBS!
MYSTERY DEATH & ROMANCE
IN LOVING MEMORY
TERROR ON PAGE 26!
The Hand from Outer Space
Free inside: 4 page MAD DOCTOR pull out
ON SALE HERE 50p

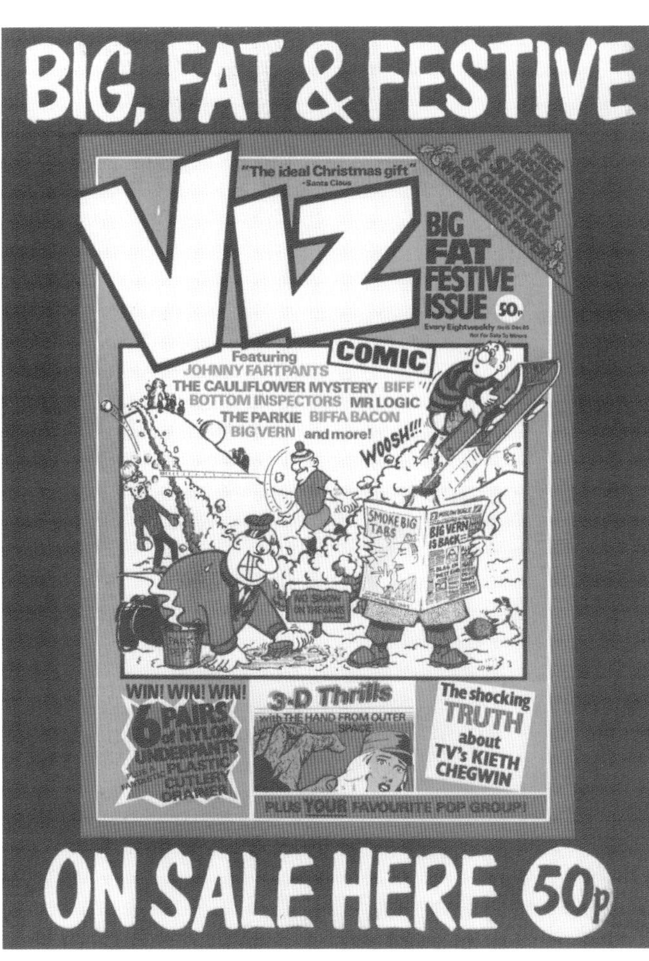
BIG, FAT & FESTIVE
"The ideal Christmas gift"
-Santa Claus
FREE INSIDE! 4 SHEETS OF CHRISTMAS WRAPPING PAPER
VIZ
BIG FAT FESTIVE ISSUE
50p
COMIC
Featuring
JOHNNY FARTPANTS
THE CAULIFLOWER MYSTERY
BIFF
BOTTOM INSPECTORS
MR LOGIC
THE PARKIE
BIFFA BACON
BIG VERN
and more!
WOOSH!!!
SMOKE BIG TABS
BIG VERN IS BACK
WIN! WIN! WIN!
6 PAIRS of NYLON UNDERPANTS
PLASTIC CUTLERY DRAINER
3-D Thrills
WITH THE HAND FROM OUTER SPACE
The shocking TRUTH about TV's KIETH CHEGWIN
PLUS YOUR FAVOURITE POP GROUP!
ON SALE HERE 50p

BIG, RED & GORY
NOW WITH GRAPHIC VIOLENCE
VIZ
BUCKETS OF BLOOD AND GUTS!
COMIC
50p
Better than all your other crappy magazines put together
NON STOP HORROR AND DEATH
DR. BOLUS AND THE REVENGE OF THE VOODOO SPIDERS
BILLY BANANAHEAD
S.W.A.N.T.
BIFF
NORMAN'S KNOB
GOOD JOB MY AMAZING UNDERPANTS ARE BULLET PROOF
The HAND from OUTER SPACE
TERROR OF THE EXPLODING SNOOKER STAR!
WIN 20p
PEANUTS
SHAKIN' STEVENS signs for FULCHESTER UNITED!
ON SALE HERE 50p

Johnny Fartpants
THERE'S ALWAYS A COMOTION GOING ON IN HIS TROUSERS!

HALLO READERS! MY NAME IS JOHNNY FARTPANTS!
RUMBLE!
QUAKE!
I'VE GOT A NOISY BOTTOM!

SOMETIMES I CAN'T HELP LETTING OFF...
DID YOU HAVE A NICE DAY IN SCHOOL, JOHNNY?
SCHOOL
QUACK!
Well... erm...

YOW! WHAT A STINK!
sorry mum.
YOU SEE A SMELLY GUFF CAN BE VERY EMBARASSING...

... LIKE THE OTHER DAY...
HELLO VICAR!
HULLO JOHNNY
PHOOT!
Oh...

JESUS, WHAT A WHIFF!
POH!, I'VE BLOWN A HOLE IN MY KNICKERS!
SEE WHAT I MEAN?

BUT BELIEVE ME FOLKS, A RUMBLING BOTTOM CAN BE VERY USEFUL...
YOU'RE FARTPANTS AREN'T YOU? I'M GOING TO GIVE YOU A GOOD BASHING!
!
OH NO! I'LL TAKE A PROPER KICKING FROM BASHER BLOGGS!

PARP!
YOINK! WHAT A HUMMER!

IN FACT I CAN USE MY STINKY BOTT FOR SOME NAUGHTY PRANKS...
OH NO! THERE'S ONLY ONE COPY OF 'JOKE FUNNIES' LEFT AND WE ALL WANT IT!
JOKE FUNNIES
PUMP POWER!

SEW A BUTTON ON THIS!
OH, CRIKEY HE'S GOING TO LETOFF!
BBBRRRRRRRRRRPHOOT!
READER'S VOICE
THAT SOUNDED LIKE A FRIDGE DOOR OPENING!

SHOP TOTALLY EMPTY
JOKE FUNNIES
A ZANY JAPE EH?...

... NOW I'LL GO HOME FOR TEA
A REAL FEAST OF BEANS, PICKLED EGGS, WITH CURRY AND LOTS OF CABBAGE WATER!

KEEPING TO A STRICT PUMP-DIET IS VERY IMPORTANT...
SO I CAN BREW ONE UP IF I SEE BASHER BLOGGS COMING!

INSIDE...
YOU'VE BEEN UP TO YOUR FARTING TRICKS AGAIN HAVEN'T YOU SON?!
NO, HONEST!

THEN WHAT DO YOU CALL THIS ?!
!
ULP!
YOU ARE IN FOR A SPANKING YOUNG MAN! GO TO YOUR ROOM!

IN HIS ROOM...
DON'T WORRY FOLKS, BY FIRMLY CLASPING THIS ORDINARY HOUSE-BRICK BETWEEN MY BUM CHEEKS, I'LL BE PERFECTLY SAFE!

BUT...
BEFORE I START, YOU CAN TAKE THAT BRICK OUT OF YOUR BOTTOM!
READER'S VOICE
OH NO! YOU'LL GET WHACKED!

AH, BUT LITTLE DOES DAD KNOW, THIS LONG, SLOW PUMP WILL FORM A PROTECTIVE CUSHION AROUND MY BUTTOCKS AND SAVE ME FROM A WHACKING!

—SD·CD·JB·AB—

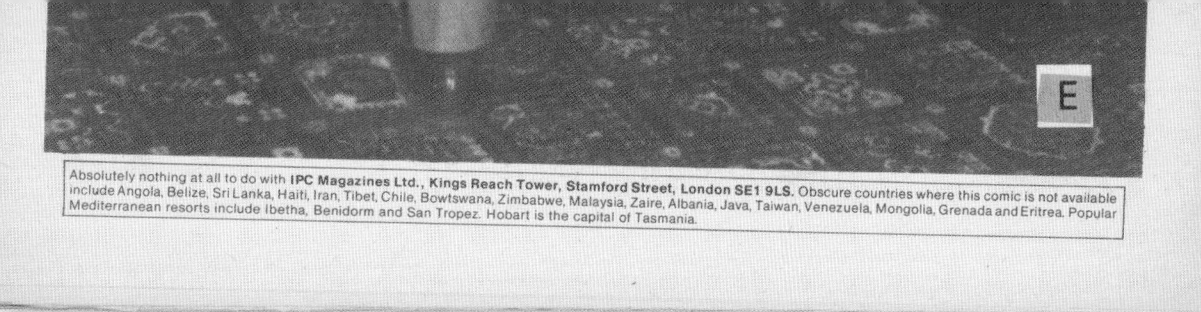

Opposite: Johnny Fartpants makes his first appearance in issue 12, November 1984.
Right: IPC's decision not to publish Viz *is reflected in the credit strip of issue 12.*

break, Chris found he had mixed feelings. 'I was in two minds,' he says. 'I couldn't keep on publishing it myself any more – it was getting too big to manage – but I had a bit of distrust for them as a big corporation.'

'We were selling a magazine to a group of people who didn't buy magazines, and that was a problem that they [IPC] had recognized and had been working on for ages and they couldn't seem to put it right,' says Simon. 'Men between 18 and 24, some of them bought *Sounds* and *NME* and *Melody Maker*, and that was pretty much it.' At that time, magazines like *Loaded*, *FHM* and *Maxim* didn't exist. 'They were looking for a magazine that would sell to these people, and they had noticed that was exactly what we were doing.'

IPC told them they'd been planning a magazine of their own. 'What they had in mind was a sort of *Private Eye* for students,' says Chris. 'It was a younger version of *Private Eye*.' But *Private Eye* was nothing like *Viz* and never would be. 'It's aimed at intellectuals, it's aimed at people who are interested in politics and it's also quite in-jokey,' argues Simon. And *Viz* was none of these things. There was also a practical problem. IPC wanted their new magazine to be fortnightly, like *Private Eye*, but Chris didn't think that would be possible. 'Fuck me,' he thought. 'At the minute, we're six monthly – 16 pages every six months. They want 24 pages every two weeks.' Yet despite their reservations, they agreed to do a dummy. IPC gave them £1,500 to do it, but they wanted the full 24 pages – and they wanted it in a month.

Initially, Simon didn't share his brother's qualms. 'I'd never felt so happy,' he says. 'It really looked like my hobby was going to become my work.' By now, he'd been on the dole for four years. Suddenly, here was the prospect of proper wages, maybe even a lifelong career. Even IPC's initial £1,500 felt like a lot of money. 'Somebody was offering us a job doing what we wanted to do. Obviously there was compromise but we didn't know there was another way.' He rang his girlfriend from a callbox to tell her the good news, and as soon as they got back to Newcastle, they set to work.

'I was in two minds. I couldn't keep on publishing it myself any more – it was getting too big – but I had a bit of distrust for them as a big corporation.'

The dummy consisted mainly of the best strips they'd done so far, plus a brand new character called Johnny Fartpants. 'There's Always A Commotion Going On In His Trousers', ran the strapline for the first strip. IPC also wanted a bit of politics (Johnny isn't renowned for his political satire) so Chris did a piece about the Greenham Common Women, who were camping outside an American Cruise missile base in Berkshire, to protest against warlike men in general and nuclear weapons in particular (it was telling that when he had to write about politics, Chris went against the grain by mocking the left rather than the right). Chris thought IPC would simply say yes or no, but unfortunately it wasn't so simple. 'They sent it back with all these changes and it was ridiculous,' he says. 'They'd missed the whole fucking point of it.' Even Johnny Fartpants was conspicuous by his absence.

A lot of young wannabes would have bitten their lips and doffed their caps, but *Viz* was made of sterner stuff. 'We went through the version they'd done and wrote a huge critique of it, defending the original and explaining in great detail why their jokes didn't work and why our jokes had worked,' says Chris. 'They were taking the comic to bits and ruining it.' It felt like the swagger that made *Viz* so special had been surgically removed.

'We were still hoping for the deal,' says Simon, but even Chris's audacious response didn't resolve matters either way, and eventually Chris sent IPC an ultimatum – did they want to publish *Viz* or not? In November 1984, five years after that first issue, he received a reply from John R. Sanders, Managing Director of IPC – Youth Group.

Sanders said he was very sad to inform them that, rather contrary to his own judgement, IPC had decided not to publish *Viz*. Apparently, IPC thought that after *Viz* had been toned down enough to satisfy them, the remaining material wouldn't make the sort of profit IPC required. IPC, explained Sanders, was in the mass circulation market, and they didn't regard *Viz* as sufficiently mass circulation.

Five years later, *Viz* was selling more than a million copies per issue, but it's very difficult to imagine a 'toned-down' version selling even a fraction of that amount.

'They didn't want anything rude,' says Chris. 'They didn't want any swearing.' Clearly, IPC's 'toning-down' would have eradicated the essence of the comic. 'Mr Logic said "penis",' recalls Chris. 'They wanted to change that to "donger". Mr Logic wouldn't say "donger",' protested Chris, perfectly logically at the time. 'He says "penis" because he's Mr Logic.' As Chris says today, 'you'd have been having that argument with them forever.'

Looking back, it was lucky IPC said no. 'That would have been us fucked,' says Chris. 'If I'd gone along with IPC then I should think I'd have fallen out with them within a year or two, and they'd have walked off with whatever remained of the comic and driven it into the ground.' Yet despite his trepidation about their plans, he doubts he would have been bold enough to turn them down. As Simon says, 'The fact that our talks with IPC ended in failure was the best thing that ever happened to *Viz*.'

Even at the time, without the benefit of hindsight, IPC's response wasn't all bad news. Sanders's letter also contained some kind words of encouragement that went well beyond the usual rejection slip platitudes. He told them he thought it had possibilities, that he hoped they'd make a go of it themselves and that it had great potential – that they shouldn't think the letter meant they should give up. Bob Paynter was even more encouraging. Paynter gave them another £500, and suggested they give Richard Branson's Virgin a try.

By now, *Viz* was on sale in the Newcastle branch of Virgin, and even though it was only appearing once or twice a year, this one record shop alone was selling at least a thousand copies of each issue. Since Richard Branson had dozens of record shops around the country, Chris sent him a copy of the comic, plus a letter pointing out how many they could sell if local sales were mirrored nationwide. At the time, Chris's dream was to sell 30,000 copies per issue. He ended up selling forty times that figure.

Chris's letter and the comic ended up on the desk of John Brown at Virgin Books. 'It was the funniest thing I'd ever seen in my life,' says John. 'From the moment I looked at it, I knew it would be a big success.' It took him all of thirty seconds to realize this could be huge. 'I really want to publish this,' John told his boss. 'It's brilliant.' 'Fine,' said his boss, so John phoned Chris and asked if he could come to Newcastle and meet him.

In stark contrast to the IPC trip, they conducted the meeting in a local café, and the homely location reflected the down-to-earth nature of the deal. 'He obviously liked the comic but all he talked about was the bloody business side of it,' says Chris. John wanted to know how much *Viz* cost to produce per issue, apart from printing. 'Forty quid,' said Chris. John couldn't believe it could be so cheap, but Chris had never paid any of his cartoonists. The only other expenses were paper and Letraset, and even that was just a few extra quid.

'His eyes were eventually lighting up when he realized that it was actually costing nothing to produce it,' says Chris. And best of all, unlike IPC, he didn't want any editorial input. 'You do the creating and we'll do everything else,' he told Chris.

John wasn't just being magnanimous. 'I couldn't have

'It was the funniest thing I'd ever seen in my life. From the moment I looked at it, I knew it would be a big success.'

Opposite: The Bottom Inspectors, and Viz publisher John Brown. Left: Chris in his office bedroom at Lily Crescent.

'I Tippexed out 27 words before I had the nerve to show it to her. She didn't seem too impressed with what remained.'

improved on it,' he says. Indeed, the only time he ever volunteered a criticism, it rebounded on him. 'I think this one's very bottomy,' said John, when he saw the first issue they'd done for him. 'There's a particularly large amount about bottoms.' In the next issue, out came the Bottom Inspectors. 'I've never opened my mouth since then.'

'He decided that for *Viz* to succeed, it had to remain entirely unchanged,' says Simon. 'It was the bravest move. Some people would say brave, some people would say foolish – but fuck me, he's a millionaire as a result of it.'

In fact, John was in a unique position. 'People joined Virgin to manage the shops and the next thing they knew, they were running an airline,' he says. 'It was very, very entrepreneurial and they just let me get on with it.' It's hard to imagine any other company giving him the same sort of leeway. 'If I was employed by a magazine publisher, it would have been very, very different,' he says. 'If I was employed by another book publisher, I wouldn't have been able to do it, because it was a magazine.' A magazine would have employed Chris & Co, giving them a steady wage, but no share of future profits. Instead, they signed a book contract, complete with royalties, which made a big difference when *Viz* reached the million mark. 'When it couldn't afford it, no-one was paid,' says John, 'and when it could, they were paid a lot.'

It didn't make their fortunes overnight. Chris was on £80 a week at first, and Simon was on £40. Simon was now living in a flat in Heaton, but Chris still lived at home, and for the next three years they carried on producing the comic from his bedroom. Their parents were none the wiser – Chris didn't think they'd approve. Their cover was finally blown when a TV crew turned up on the doorstep to film an item for a television show, and their mother asked to see the comic. 'I Tippexed out 27 words before I had the nerve to show it to her,' confesses Chris. 'She didn't seem too impressed with what remained.'[12] Even after Chris moved out, and into a flat with his fiancée, they still used his childhood bedroom as their office, commuting there every day from various flats in Newcastle. They didn't move into a proper office until 1988, the year sales reached half a million.

Signing a proper contract did herald a few modest changes. Chris finally felt flush enough to ditch his graphic design work, while Simon was able to buy a car to deliver the comic around town. If he took the passenger seat out of his Mini, he could carry 2,000 at a time. It was a step up from lugging bundles around Newcastle in his granny's old shopping trolley. And thanks to Virgin, they didn't have to staple them together any more.

The only problem was, John wanted a new 32-page comic every two months. The last three issues had only been 16 pages, and they'd been eight or nine months apart. It had taken them more than five years to put out just twelve issues – now Virgin wanted six a year. 'You can't do it,' said Brian Sandells. 'There'll be a clause that if you don't produce it'll cost you money. He'll bankrupt you in no time.'

Initially, at least, Chris shared some of Brian's concern. 'Fuck!' he thought. 'Where am I going to get the stuff from?' He was used to getting several pages from Simon plus a couple more from Jim and doing the rest himself, but now that was impossible. *Viz* badly needed some new blood. Chris put a small ad in *Private Eye* ('bum rates paid for top cartoonists') and got a reply from a bloke called Simon Thorp (aka Thorpy) who went on to create *Viz* evergreens like Farmer Palmer and Student Grant.

'He's the best drawer of us by miles,' said Chris. 'The first cartoon he sent in, we published it straight away.'[13] Even the letters he wrote were funny – Chris could tell they were on the same wavelength – but the first time they met, at a *Viz* party, it took a bit longer for things to click. 'He had a holdall and a tweedy jacket and a shirt and a tie,' recalls Chris. 'His mum had smartened him up.'[14]

'Can I take your bag?' asked Chris's wife, Dolores.

'Yes,' said Thorpy, 'but take care of it – it's got my kidney machine in it.'

'Fucking hell!' thought Chris. 'That's why he's so good at drawing. He's a reclusive. He's actually ill.' 'It turned out it was a joke, but we didn't find out until ages later,' says Chris. 'We've never got any of his jokes.'[15]

Thorpy always wanted to be a cartoonist, but he never thought it was feasible. 'At school they wouldn't countenance that suggestion,' he says. He was doing Art, Maths and Physics A Levels, so he told his teachers he wanted to be an architect, but in actual fact he wasn't interested in architecture at all. He liked the idea of doing

Dear Chris

Thanks for the Viz 23's and the cheque.

Please find enclosed "Nigel Smith Space Adventurer of the Future." I don't know how one might go about printing such a thing – whether it would be worth half-toning or just left as per normal. (It looks OK out of my megalithic Xerox). Ho hum.

Look out for more Wacky Lafs in the not-too-distant future.

Simon.

'Fucking hell! That's why he's so good at drawing. He's a reclusive. He's actually ill.'

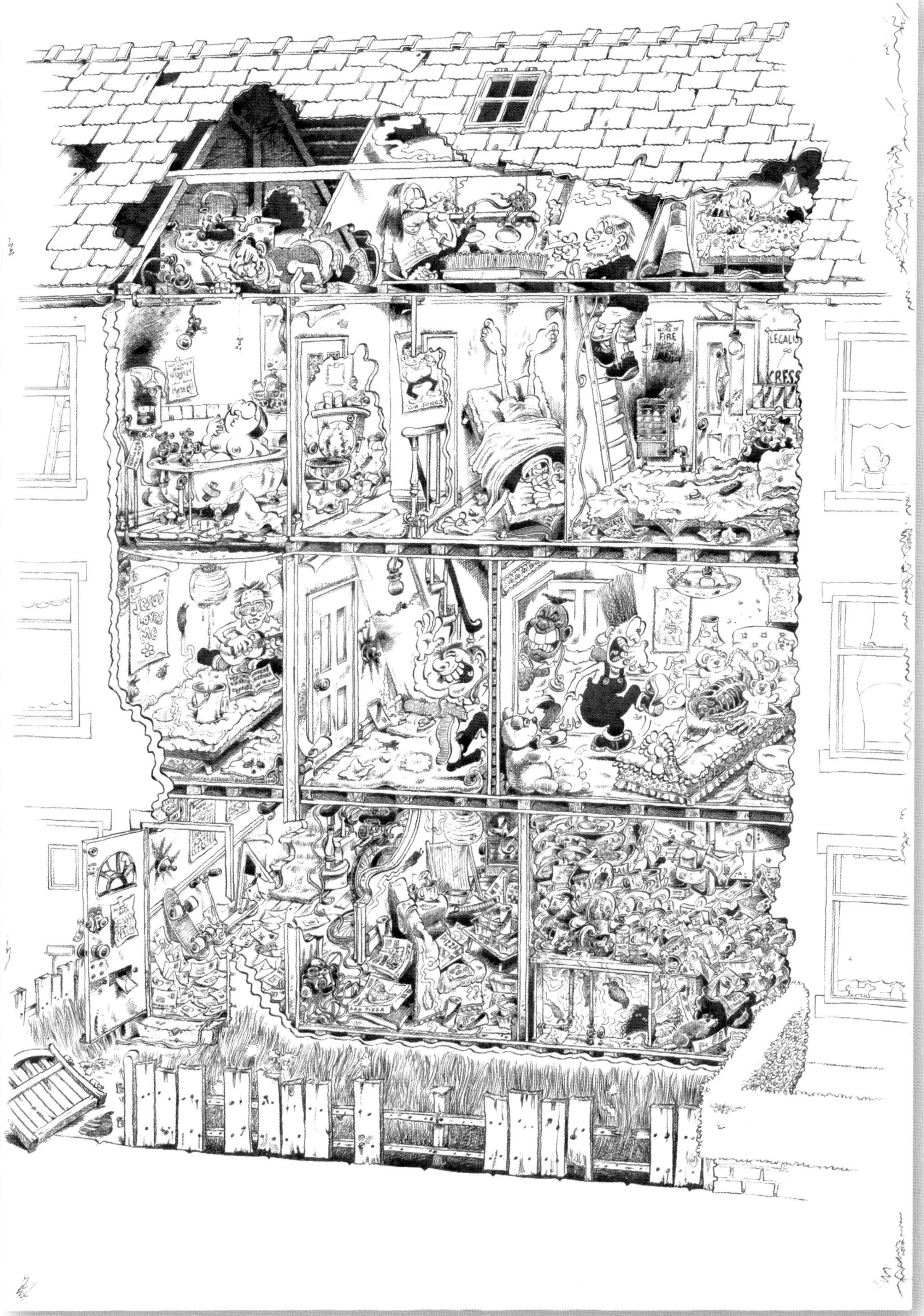
TOM JONES
FIRE
LEGALIS
CRESS
Jesus Loves Me

Above: Thorpy's thirsty family man, 8 Ace. Opposite: A Viz photocall on the stairs at Leeds Poly. Left to right: Graham, Simon, Chris and Thorpy.

animation, but he always assumed he'd end up as an art teacher. However, he drew single frame cartoons in his spare time, and when he was eighteen, in his first term at Aberystwyth University, doing a degree in Visual Art, he sold a cartoon to *Punch*. It was a buzz to see his work in print. He must have bought about ten copies.

It was at Aberystwyth University that Thorpy first saw *Viz*. He especially enjoyed Johnny Fartpants. 'It was fairly crude in those days,' he recalls, 'but it did make me laugh.' He wondered who on earth was behind this strange new comic ('it was a mystery where it came from') and then he saw Chris's advert in *Private Eye*. Thorpy's degree course was mainly painting, but he also drew cartoons for the college magazine. He sent *Viz* a cartoon about a character called Eric Daft. They printed it and paid him a fiver.

'I've never had a proper job. I've never had an interview. I can't think of a job I'd rather have.'

When Thorpy graduated he moved back in with his parents in Pontefract, went on the Enterprise Allowance Scheme and started freelancing for *Viz*. Soon he was doing several pages in every issue, but until he turned up at that party he'd never spoken to Chris – not even on the phone. 'That's one of the appeals of cartoons,' he says. 'You don't have to speak to anybody.' However after that party he started coming up for weekends to work with Chris, sleeping on his floor, and when Chris moved out and got married, he left Pontefract and found a flat in Newcastle. He started off drawing characters like Finbarr Saunders (And His Double Entendres) and Norbert Colon (He's As Tight As A Gnat's Chuff). Nowadays he draws all sorts of strips, including Raffles (The Gentleman Thug), Fru T Bunn The Master Baker (And His Gingerbread Sex Dolls) and 8 Ace (The Thirsty Family Man) and two decades on, he's still hard at it. 'I've never had a proper job,' he says, contentedly. 'I've never had an interview. I can't think of a job I'd rather have.'

By now, Chris and Simon were working with a lapsed botanist called Graham Dury, creator of *Viz* classics like Buster Gonad (And His Unfeasibly Large Testicles). 'Considering what a quiet bloke he is, he took the unusual step of marching up our path at Lily Crescent with a folio full of his cartoons,' recalls Chris. Past experience had taught Chris to be pessimistic. 'I dreaded looking at Graham's cartoons,' he says. 'If somebody said to me "I do cartoons," you knew to avoid them like the plague because they would be shit.' Chris was so desperate to see the back of Graham, he even telephoned Simon to drum up some moral support. 'Can you come over and help me tell this bloke to fuck off?' pleaded Chris. 'We're going to have to get rid of him somehow, and two of us'll be able to pretend to laugh better than one.' [16] Simon came over, as requested, but when Chris finally took a look at Graham's cartoons, he was actually pleasantly surprised. 'They were a bit all over the place, but the drawings were good. They weren't too involved and he obviously had a bit of a sense of humour.' Chris gave him a few back issues and told him to go away and read the *Beano* and the *Dandy* – and keep it simple.

Graham Dury had always drawn cartoons but they were really only doodles, vaguely inspired by cartoonists like Robert Crumb. As a kid, he read *The Beano* and *The Dandy*, plus a comic called *Topper*. 'It was the *Financial Times* of comics,' recalls Graham. 'You felt slightly better than your mates reading it, because it was bigger.' As he got a bit older, he grew into American comics like *Mad* and Gilbert Shelton's *Fabulous Furry Freak Brothers*, and in 1984 he discovered *Viz* while visiting his girlfriend, who was a student at Newcastle Poly. Graham was studying botany at Nottingham University. He was also doing occasional cartoons for the student magazine, so he got in touch with

Chris. His first *Viz* strip was called Victor And His Boa Constrictor. He freelanced for the next three years, travelling to Newcastle for a weekend every month or so to work with Chris. They hit it off, and in 1987 Chris asked him to move to Newcastle and work for *Viz* full time.

By now, Graham was midway through a Doctorate at Leicester University – a potentially world saving PhD in Genetic Engineering, investigating the introduction of drought-resistant genes into commercial crops. However some opportunities are simply too important to pass up, so he packed it all in to work for *Viz*. 'The planet's doomed, all because of me,' he says. 'Famine in Africa – it's all my fault.' Actually, his PhD wasn't really going anywhere – and anyway, he thought he'd probably end up doing something scientific again after a few years. 'I'll get this out of my system and I'll give it two or three years,' he thought. 'If I can just make a half-decent living for two or three years, that'll be fine.'

Seventeen years later, he's still here. 'I never dreamt I'd be doing it full time.' However even after all these years, he still doesn't qualify as a proper Geordie. 'My wife's a Geordie and me kids are Geordies but I'm not and they tell me constantly,' he says. 'If you're not a Geordie, you're not a Geordie – and that's that.' Maybe being once removed from Tyneside gives his cartoons that extra edge.

'I'll get this out of my system and I'll give it two or three years. If I can just make a half-decent living for two or three years, that'll be fine.'

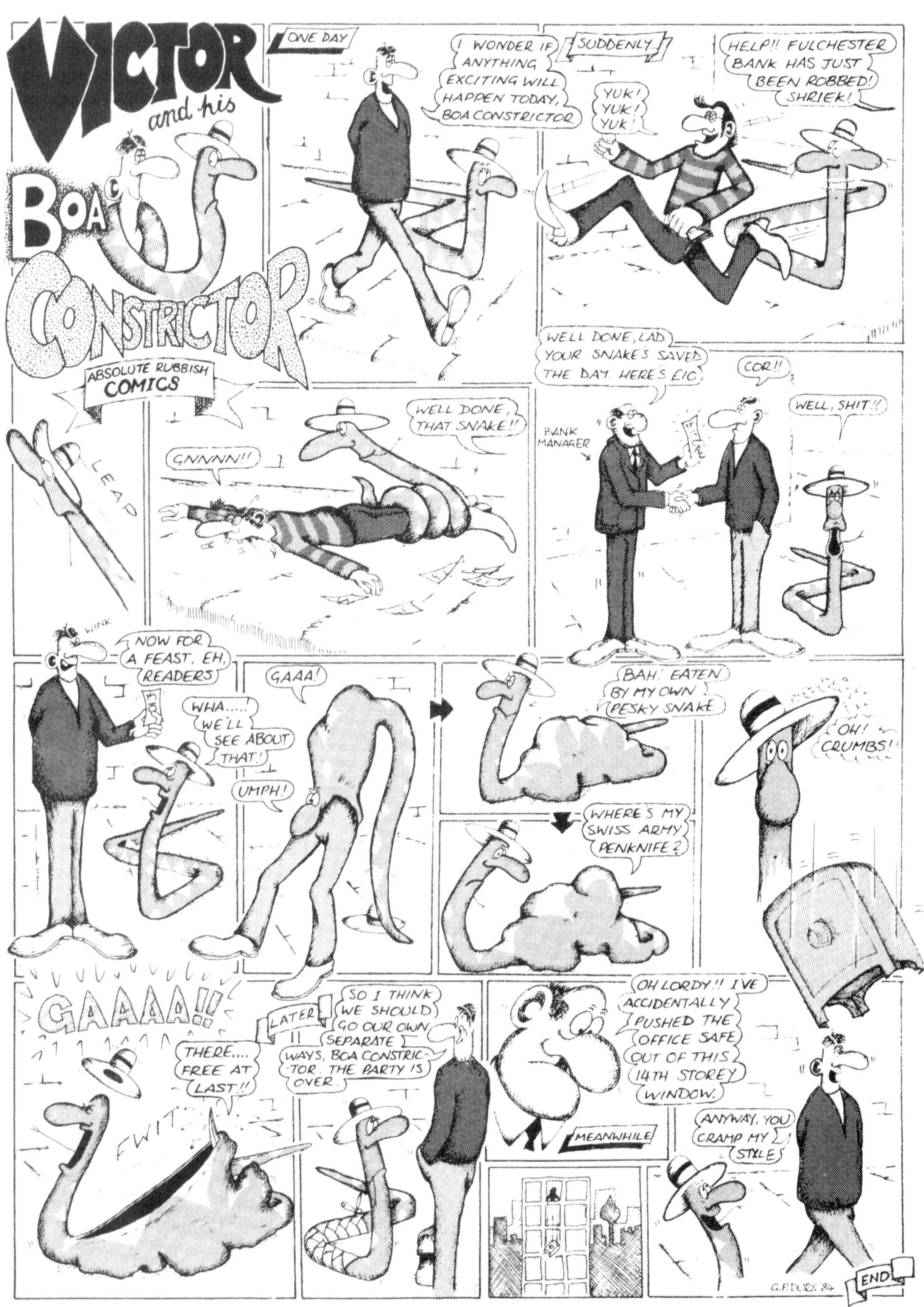
VICTOR and his BOA CONSTRICTOR
ABSOLUTE RUBBISH COMICS
ONE DAY
I WONDER IF ANYTHING EXCITING WILL HAPPEN TODAY, BOA CONSTRICTOR
SUDDENLY...
YUK! YUK! YUK!
HELP!! FULCHESTER BANK HAS JUST BEEN ROBBED! SHRIEK!
LEAP
GNNNN!!
WELL DONE, THAT SNAKE!!
BANK MANAGER
WELL DONE, LAD. YOUR SNAKE'S SAVED THE DAY. HERE'S £10
COR!!
WELL, SHIT!!
WINK
NOW FOR A FEAST, EH, READERS
WHA.....! WE'LL SEE ABOUT THAT!
UMPH!
GAAA!
BAH! EATEN BY MY OWN PESKY SNAKE
OH! CRUMBS!!
WHERE'S MY SWISS ARMY PENKNIFE?
GAAAA!!
THERE.... FREE AT LAST!!
FWIT
LATER
SO I THINK WE SHOULD GO OUR OWN SEPARATE WAYS, BOA CONSTRIC-TOR. THE PARTY IS OVER.
OH LORDY!! I'VE ACCIDENTALLY PUSHED THE OFFICE SAFE OUT OF THIS 14TH STOREY WINDOW.
MEANWHILE
ANYWAY, YOU CRAMP MY STYLE
G.P. DURY. 84
END

Graham is self-effacing about his artwork. 'I'm not a particularly good artist,' he says. Yet a lot of modern cartoons are actually far too arty. Each frame is too busy and the detail obscures the jokes. Graham's style is brisk and lively, and although the drawing always does its job, it never gets in the way of the gags – and what a wealth of gags. Graham draws loads of *Viz* favourites, including Spoilt Bastard, Cockney Wanker and Ravey Davey Gravy as well as those *Viz* superstars, the Fat Slags. Seems it was a good job Chris and Simon didn't tell him to fuck off that first time after all.

With Graham and Thorpy working alongside Chris and Simon, the comic became even better. 'It definitely did enthuse us,' says Chris. 'It made us a lot more productive.' The artwork for each strip was still drawn by one person, but now most of the scripts were written en ensemble. It made for even funnier strips if they all bounced ideas off each other. Chris and Simon still sometimes wrote alone, but Graham and Thorpy ended up doing almost all of their writing together. They found it a lot easier than writing on their own. Chances were, at least one of them would be on form, and inspiration tends to be contagious. It was also useful to test drive the jokes, rather than shoving them straight into a strip. 'You don't know whether something is funny unless somebody else laughs at it,' says Graham. 'When we're writing stuff and nobody laughs, you don't write it down.' Sometimes they still had to write at home, especially if they were still a few pages short on the night before a deadline, but it was a lot harder to tell if they'd written anything funny until they brought it into work the next day.

Thirty-two pages every two months is a lot of comic for four cartoonists, but most other wannabes who wrote in simply weren't up to scratch. 'We did get an awful lot of stuff sent in, but an awful lot of it was completely wide of the mark,' says Graham. 'They thought that all it had to be was crude and badly drawn.' A lot of the stuff they did themselves was crude, but it was very well drawn, and very funny. And with so few freelancers able to follow suit, they had to do virtually everything themselves. As each deadline loomed they'd often end up working eighteen-hour days, weekdays and weekends too. 'We used to work crazy hours,' says Simon. 'We used to be there until God knows what time in the morning, and right through the night.'

Opposite: Graham's first Viz *cartoon. This page: Buster Gonad and the Fat Slags.*

Thanks to these long nights, John Brown got his 32 pages on time, and Virgin published the thirteenth issue of *Viz* in August 1985. 'I couldn't believe it when they started producing it once every two months,' says Brian. 'I just didn't think they had it in them.' They proved him wrong, but there were times when they cut it tight. 'They really had desperate deadline problems,' says Steve. 'Like any creative people they will leave things until the last minute.' Once, instead of sending the magazine to Bristol, where it was now printed, they ran so short of time that they had to drive there, working on the artwork as they went. 'They were still putting the page numbers on in the car in the back seat while they were on the way to Bristol because they were so far behind,' says Steve. 'The only way they manage to get around that now is by slicing the deadline up. They aim to get the magazine done in sections and they have a section deadline more frequently rather than having one big deadline for the whole magazine.'

John was delighted with the comic, but not everyone he knew was thrilled. 'Look what I've got here!' he told guests at a dinner party given by his future wife. 'I'm going to make my fortune on this. It's absolutely fantastic.' The other dinner guests were appalled. 'They didn't know what to do,' says John. 'They just looked embarrassed.' But their embarrassment didn't sway him. 'I had a lot of people who didn't understand it and saw it only as a smutty, pathetic,

In Loving Memory
The day his fourth successive girlfriend died in tragic circumstances young Paul Green began to wonder whether he would ever find true love and happiness.
SORRY MATE! I DIDN'T SEE HER
OH NO! THAT'S THE FOURTH GIRLFRIEND I'VE LOST IN AS MANY MONTHS
PUT 746R

SORRY MATE! I DIDN'T SEE HIM
OH PETE. I LOVE YOU. TALK TO ME PETER

SORRY MATE. I DIDN'T SEE HER!
OH POL! IF I HAD USED WORDS, PERHAPS YOU WOULD HAVE HEARD ME. THE MEDIUM OF DARNCE WAS JUST NOT SUITABLE IN THIS SITUATION.
KOMAL RESTAURANT
A827 K

As Brad breathed his last breath, Judy made a solemn promise to him...
OH BRAD! I WILL ALWAYS LOVE YOU! THERE WILL BE NOBODY ELSE... I PROMISE!
SORRY MATE!... I DIDN'T SEE HIM!
CROAK!

This page: 'Sorry, mate! I didn't see her.' Anvil Springstien, a regular in Viz Photo Love stories. Opposite: TV heart-throb Sean Bean appeared in a Viz photostory.

puerile comic, and some of those people were quite close to me, but that's their problem. I had no doubts.'

He was similarly unperturbed by public carping. 'Yes, I got flak,' he says, 'but I had absolute evangelical right on my side, so I couldn't give a fucking toss. I'm sensitive to criticism, but not over *Viz* because I was right and they were wrong.' Events soon bore him out. 'The last one that they'd done had sold 4,000 copies,' says John. 'The first one Virgin did sold about 11,000.' It still wasn't for sale in major retailers, but it sold very well in Virgin shops, as well as independent outlets. And the feedback was very good. John got a letter from a reader near Perth who went to Glasgow once every two months, just to buy a copy.

Back in Newcastle, the feedback was even better. 'Everybody seemed to be reading it,' says Thorpy. 'Everybody had a copy.' Chris got a postcard from Nicaragua, sent by Billy Bragg. By 1987, circulation was up to 40,000, and during the next six months sales went through the roof. In December 1987, *Viz* outpunched *Punch*, and in May 1988 it overtook *Private Eye*, becoming Britain's best-selling humorous magazine. Eventually, it even outstripped *Woman's Own*. 'The best thing was overtaking the women's weeklies,' says Chris. 'For a while we thought we were going to have to put some knitting patterns in.' [17] By the summer of 1988, circulation had leapt to 500,000 as the *Viz Holiday Special* (featuring a

> 'Now the bastards don't even pay you at all. I never even got a cup of tea last time.'

photo love story starring Harry Enfield) was reprinted an astonishing nine times.

By now, the photo love story had become a familiar feature of the comic, as much of a *Viz* institution as its mock tabloid scoops. An adept piss take of those cheesy romances in girls' magazines like Jackie, the pictures were posed by local amateurs. 'You only needed three expressions,' says Colin Davison, who took the photos. Yet *Viz* rarely sent up anything unless it could do it just as well as the genuine article. Colin is a commercial photographer, and his proficient snapshot epics were a match for the real thing.

Local comedian Anvil Springstien has played the same role in these romantic spoofs for 20 years. He always drives the car that runs over one of the young lovers (once, he even ran over two in the same story) and he always says the same thing. 'Sorry mate, I didn't see her.' His salary always used to be two cans of Red Stripe, but lately he's had a pay-cut. 'Now the bastards don't even pay you at all,' he says. 'I never even got a cup of tea last time.'

Colin never paid anyone either. 'A couple of sandwiches and a couple of pints and that was your lot.' And even though a few folk need their arms twisting (especially if they've agreed to do it on a drunken Saturday night and have forgotten all about it by Sunday morning) for most readers it's a prestige gig, like a cameo in a hit sitcom. People who work for *Viz* tend to be less keen, but they all have to do it at least once, as a rite of passage. Thorpy played an axe murderer as his initiation. 'It's a miserable way to spend a Sunday,' he says, but it has its moments. Once, they were shooting a photo story outside a local church, featuring a *Viz* vicar, complete with dog collar, when the real vicar appeared and chased them away like naughty schoolkids.

There were a few fringe benefits. Hunky movie star Sean Bean appeared in a story, and *Viz* production manager Stevie Glover got into bed with Harry Enfield (in a purely artistic capacity) in a guesthouse in Whitley Bay. Asking people to appear in photo stories was a great way to meet women. Colin met his wife this way – today they have three kids. *Viz* weddings have become his speciality – he photographed a friend's wedding in the style of a *Viz* photo love story, and when Chris got married Colin was his best man.

One of these photo stories, 'Too Young To Love', gave *Viz* its first real taste of Fleet Street outrage. It was a faithful replica of a standard yarn – boy meets girl, they fall in love, but everyone says they're too young, so they run away to London. The only difference was, in this version the boy and girl were both toddlers. It was the bit where they were offered drugs that fired the tabloid furore, even though the kids' parents weren't at all put out. 'The mother of the little girl, she knew what was going on and she thought it was a huge joke,' says Brian. The publicity did *Viz* no harm, especially when the comic came off the shelves. 'That increased their sales enormously,' says Steve. 'When the next issue came out, everybody had heard about it and they were all curious.' In fact, most hacks secretly enjoyed *Viz*, whatever their editors told them to write about it. 'The hypocrisy of it was quite amusing,' says Chris. 'The tabloids were getting stuck in and saying it was disgusting – hypocritically, because the journalists would actually think it was great.

TOO YOUNG TO LOVE
Their parents called it 'Puppy Love', but despite her tender years Camilla Johnson knew her love for Brian would last forever. And she intended to prove it...
I'LL SEE YOU TONIGHT DARLING. AND REMEMBER, I LOVE YOU, BRIAN
CAMILLA. DADDY AND I THINK YOU'VE BEEN SEEING A LITTLE TOO MUCH OF BRIAN LATELY. PERHAPS IT WOULD BE BEST, IF...
OH MOTHER!
I THINK MUMMY'S RIGHT DARLING
YOU JUST DON'T UNDERSTAND. BRIAN AND I ARE IN LOVE, AND ONE DAY WE'LL BE MARRIED
IN LOVE AT YOUR AGE. YOU'RE TOO YOUNG TO KNOW THE MEANING OF THE WORD
I DO LOVE BRIAN AND ALWAYS WILL. I DON'T CARE WHAT YOU SAY
Camilla left, slamming the door behind her.
JUST LEAVE HER, SHE'LL BE ALRIGHT. SHE'S JUST SO YOUNG, THAT'S ALL
OH I DO HOPE SO
21

HI KIDS. I'M PUSHING DRUGS. WANNA BUY A BOTTLE OF HEROIN?
WELL, ERM...

Previous pages: The controversial themes in 'Too Young to Love' sparked tabloid 'outrage' and a further increase in circulation. This page: Sales continue to rocket.

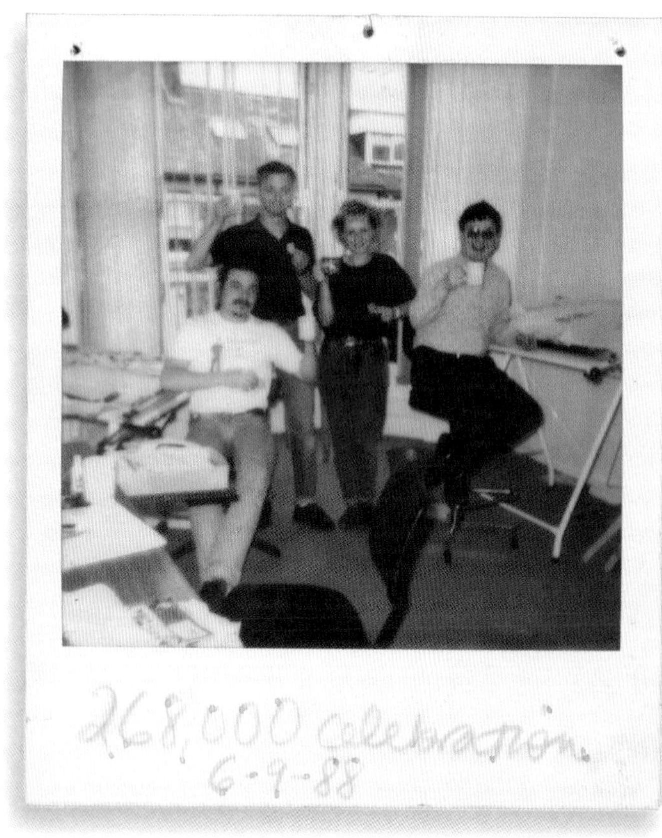

'I personally thought it would reach 400,000, but I thought if I put 400,000 in, everybody would think I was mad.'

Monarchists were more sincerely shocked by the comic's coverage of the Royal Family. A Mrs Stella Shacklady even sent a copy of one *Viz* royal exclusive ('The Queen Is A Fruitcake Claims Former Palace Man') to Buckingham Palace. 'If such a thing was written about me or any of my family, we would be entitled to take the writer to court for slander or defamation of character,' said Mrs Shacklady. 'The Queen is not in a position to do this and I think that such articles should be stopped.' [18] 'This is not the first time that this particular publication has been brought to our attention,' replied the Palace. 'I must explain, however, that in our experience, any public protest or action taken against such articles only serves to give them wider publicity.' [19] Among many other (entirely fictitious) accusations, the article asserted that Her Majesty dressed as Napoleon and barked like a dog.

In 1987, after just a handful of issues with John Brown and Virgin, Virgin Books was sold to another publisher, WH Allen, and John Brown decided to set up on his own. He persuaded Virgin to let him take *Viz* (they retained a 20 per cent stake in the comic) and he persuaded *Viz* to go with him. 'That was a bit of a risk,' says Chris. 'He was asking us to jump ship.'

By now, *Viz* was selling more than 20,000 copies per issue. What's more, it was selling out, prompting reprints – something practically unheard of for a magazine. In his business plan, John predicted *Viz* would end up selling 250,000 copies per issue. 'I personally thought it would reach 400,000,' he says, 'but I thought if I put 400,000 in, everybody would think I was mad.' They thought he was mad to put 250,000, but in fact he was far too cautious. Within a few years, it was selling five times that figure.

Brown's first office was a far cry from the comfort of Branson's Virgin HQ. 'When you to spoke to him on the phone it was all echoey because he hadn't got any furniture,' recalls Chris. Yet for *Viz*, the working relationship was actually a step up. At Virgin, John had to juggle all sorts of projects. Now he just had two – Virgin's inflight magazine, *Hot Air*, and *Viz*. 'When John set up John Brown Publishing, *Viz* became his main focus of attention,' says Simon. 'Once he had the time to devote to it, the sales just absolutely rocketed.' By now, circulation was virtually doubling with every issue.

The comic's relative longevity also helped. Most magazines are thrust onto the national market straight away, without any preparation apart from a few internal dummy issues. By the time most readers discovered *Viz*, it had already been up and running for a decade. Even the first national issue only appeared after a local gestation of almost six years. 'It was eight years before anybody else had ever heard of it,' says Andy Inman, who was now distributing the comic full time. 'It was only two years that

It's the BIG question!

Has Fergie got a FAT ARSE?

Ever since her marriage to Prince Andrew a cloud of controversy has surrounded the Duchess of York's bottom. In factories, shops, pubs and clubs all over Britain the question is being asked. "Has Fergie got a fat arse or what?"

Well now's **YOUR** chance to join in with the debate of the decade, as we invite you to vote in our special postal ballot. All you have to do to register your opinion is fill in the coupon below:

YOU DECIDE

● *OPINION page 33*

To: The Queen, Buckingham Palace, London

Dear Your Majesty

I do / do not* think that Fergie has got a fat arse.

Signed ....

*DELETE AS APPLICABLE

The Royal Family have always provided the comic with rich fodder.

MAD AS A HATTER!

The Queen is losing her marbles. That is the unofficial word from Buckingham Palace as Her Royal Highness begins her 37th year on the throne.

This incredible claim is being made by Roger Thompson, a former Palace employee who says he is desperately worried about Her Majesty's health. Sacked from his job at the Palace for stealing cutlery — a crime which he strenuously denies — Thompson has decided to speak out and make his concerns public, for the Queen's own sake.

"I never stole that cutlery", Roger told us. "It was all a big cover-up, and I took the blame to protect the Queen. Everyone inside the Palace knew that she'd been stealing it herself.

at the Palace. "You see, she was convinced that the chef was trying to poison her and steal the Crown Jewels. I know it sounds crazy, but it's true. At meal-times she would refuse to eat a thing. Eventually she started going out in her royal carriage to buy Chinese take-aways, then she'd take them to the Tower of London and eat them with her eyes firmly fixed on the Crown Jewels".

CUCUMBER

The Queen's unusual behaviour was beginning to cause some embarrassment in public.

The Queen is a fruitcake claims former Palace man

past me on all fours, barking ferociously. I followed her down to the kitchen where I found her underneath a table — feeding small bits of cheese to mice".

DUNGEONS

On another occasion the Queen summoned Mrs Thatcher to the Palace and told her to invade France. The Prime

According to Roger steps are now taken to avoid situations like that. "For most of her public appearances, they use a double — that woman who looks like the Queen usually stands in for her. The Queen herself spends most of her time in her bedroom, watching game shows on TV. She wears

Viz House Lily Crescent
Newcastle upon Tyne NE2

Dear ______________________ Date_______1984

☐ Thankyou very much for writing

☐ Thankyou for the money

☐ Sorry for the delay in replying

☐ Unfortunately your letter has been lost in the post

☐ Enclosed is a copy of Viz Comic No. 11

☐ Enclosed is a copy of Viz Comic '20 Fantastic Hits'

☐ Enclosed is more than one copy of either one or of both of the above comics, as requested

The following issues of Viz Comic are still available from this address:

☐ Viz Comic '20 Fantastic Hits' (the "best" of Vizzes 1, 2, 3 and 4)

☐ Viz Comic No. 11

priced 50p each (including P+P). Cheques etc. payable to 'House Of Viz'. No coins please. Unfortunately all the previous issues of Viz, numbers 1 to 10 are all sold out.

Make sure you get a copy of the next Viz Comic - issue 12 - by sending 50p (including P+P), and your copy will be sent to you as soon as it is ready.

Thanks again for getting in touch. I hope that you enjoy your comic or both your comics or that you will enjoy either or both your comics if and when you order and receive them.

☐ Best wishes, Chris Donald

HOUSE of VIZ

GREEN FORM

To: Arthur Matthews
Drogheda
Co. Louth Ireland

Date: 19.11.86 Viz Ref: $ G70

From: VIZ COMIC LILY CRESCENT NEWCASTLE UPON TYNE NE2

DESCRIPTION of Artwork/Material required:

Script and assorted artwork: 'BILLY'S PAGE' Pd 789672 e sent 2/1/87. + BF (L) T SHIRT 30 00

AS APPROPRIATE * Delete as appropriate.

Purchase Price: 30 00 Sterling

RIGHTS PURCHASED See Overleaf

ARTWORK/MATERIAL PERMISSION	x	IF OTHERS specify here:
ALL RIGHTS		

G1 Please read carefully the section indicated overleaf then COUNTERSIGN and RETURN ONE COPY TO US.

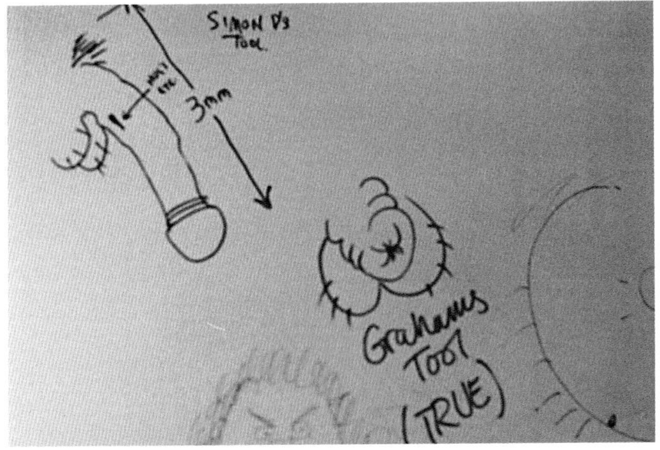

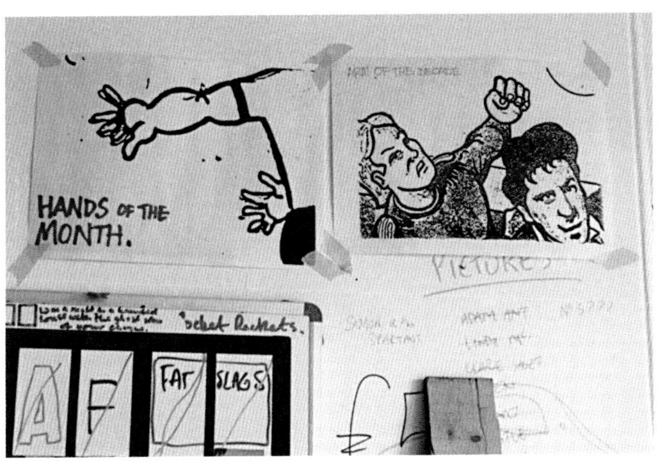

'Chris was always very keen to make it like an official office.'

Opposite and left: More examples of Chris's obsession with forms. Below: Office wall graffiti.

it went from 12,000 locally to a million nationally.' Chris told Andy his annual turnover would be £25,000. In his first year, he turned over £250,000.

Finally, Chris felt confident enough to move the comic out of his parents' house and into a grown-up office, next door to the Newcastle Conservative Association. He even took on a secretary. 'Chris was always very keen to make it like an official office,' says Thorpy. 'He'd stick up office rules, which we all treated with a certain amount of amusement.' He even put up some motivational slogans, a decade before David Brent. Think Before You Ink. Is It Funny? If It Fails, It Costs Us Sales. That kind of thing.

You can take the boy out of the DHSS, but you can't take the DHSS out of the boy. At a time when most trendy magazine offices were awash with cocaine and champagne, the *Viz* office was merely awash with colour-coded memos. Chris once joked that his ambition was to bury himself in his own red tape. 'The *Viz* office is a temple of temperance,' Chris told the launch issue of *Loaded*. 'Of the four editors, two don't drink.' [20]

Yet whether these rules and regulations helped or hindered them, *Viz* went from strength to strength. The artwork of its four cartoonists was distinct yet complementary, and the scripts they wrote together created a coherent house style that was instantly recognizable as *Viz*. With four funny people working together in one room, all firing jokes at one another, the comic found an extra gear.

Suddenly, *Viz* was everywhere and, for once, marketing had nothing to do with it. 'There was never any advertising,' says Simon. 'It was all word of mouth.' But that's always by far the best sort of advertisement, and it meant *Viz* retained a speakeasy chic, even after it became a bestseller. 'People needed to discover *Viz* for themselves,' says John. 'Even when it was selling nearly a million copies, you felt that there were a large amount of people who thought *Viz* was just for them.' In fact, it was for almost everyone, but twenty-something men enjoyed it the most. By 1991, two-thirds of 18–35 year olds were reading the comic, even though it was still classified as a 'specialist' publication. No wonder *Viz* was now valued at £25 million.

This page: More office views. Opposite: Yet another one of Chris's forms.

FORM

OFFICIAL ENQUIRY/MESSAGE/REQUEST REQUIRING A REPLY FORM

For the attention of .... Time/date message received ....

Message taken by .... Describe, in not more than 4 words, how urgent you think this message is ....

Message from .... of .... Tel/Fax no. ....

THE MESSAGE

....

....

....

....

....

....

....

....

* *If the message is attached on a separate sheet, or if another sheet/fax/etc. accompanies this message, tick this box* ☐ Other sheet attached

---

THIS SECTION TO BE USED BY THE PERSON REPLYING TO THE ENQUIRY

REPLY AS FOLLOWS

....

....

....

....

....

....

....

....

Signed .... Dated ....

THIS SECTION TO BE USED ONCE THE ENQUIRY HAS BEEN RESOLVED BY THE PERSON WHO RELAYS THE REPLY ABOVE TO THE PERSON WHO MADE THE ENQUIRY IN THE FIRST PLACE

There we are now. Everything's sorted out. Signed .... Dated ....

YACHT CLUB

Opposite: Simon, John Brown, Chris, Thorpy and Graham show off their ton of money.
Above: The lucky winner.
Left and below: Viz *cartoonists become proper artists at London's exclusive Vanessa Devereux Gallery.*

There were a couple of funny PR stunts. The reader who bought the millionth copy won a ton of money – a huge pile of pennies, actually only worth a few thousand quid. The winner was an unemployed eighteen-year-old girl from Liverpool. There was also a fake fine art show at London's exclusive Vanessa Devereux Gallery. 'We put out a story saying "the *Viz* boys have decided that they're giving up *Viz*, and they're just going to do fine art – they're going to become proper artists",' recalls John. In a couple of days, they knocked out a couple of dozen pictures. Graham painted a portrait of Eighties Welsh Elvis, Shakin' Stevens. Chris contributed a mixed media piece entitled *Chocolates? Maltesers!* This meisterwerk consisted of a Malteser box and a Milk Tray box, glued to a white canvas. Chris claimed it subverted the relationship between life, art and advertising. It was priced at £500 to £1,500.

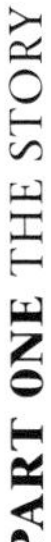

And now the merchandising kicked in. There were *Viz* annuals, computer games, even fruit machines. Think of a souvenir, from crockery to casual wear, and it seemed you could buy it with the *Viz* logo on it. And people did. In December 1989, recalls Andy, one local record shop was selling more *Viz* stuff than actual records. *Viz* had become a brand. Steve's *Viz* character, Orson Cart, was snapped up by a top publisher, for whom he did eight children's books. Johnny Fartpants declined an offer from Harp to advertise their beer, but when Tennent's asked the Fat Slags to appear in their ad campaign, Sandra and Tracey were less fussy. *Viz* asked for the fee Mel Smith would have got, because he was fat and funny too.

In the end, they settled for the same rate as Frank Bruno, but decided to give their share to charity. 'We've got more money than sense already,' [21] said Chris, who treated himself to a signal box and three old train stations. One was converted into a home for his family. Another won an award from National Railway Heritage, after his conversion enabled it to reopen as a restaurant. *Viz* also sponsored nearby non-league football team Blyth Spartans. For an editor who'd started out publishing juvenile soccer programmes and trainspotting periodicals, it was a boyhood dream come true.

It was the perfect sort of fame. The characters became public figures, rather than their creators. 'Nobody knew who we were,' says Graham. '*Viz* was very famous but we weren't and we never wanted to be and still don't.' Roger Mellie and Billy the Fish both landed their own TV series on Channel 4, with voices by Peter Cook and Harry Enfield. Fat Slags and Sid the Sexist films soon followed, but Channel 4 declined to show them, after finding 270 words and phrases in these animations that they thought might cause offence. It didn't matter. They were still released on video, and won awards. This time, the voiceovers were provided by Kathy Burke and Bob Mortimer, plus Caroline Aherne and Simon Day, subsequent stars of that *Viz*-like sketch series, *The Fast Show*. Their *Fast Show* colleague, Charlie Higson had an even closer association with *Viz*. He did a strip called Jelly Head in the Eighties. 'Every bloody comedy programme on the telly owes something to *Viz*,' says Andy, 'just as much as Oasis owe the Beatles or Primal Scream owe the Stones.'

'*Viz* was very famous but we weren't and we never wanted to be and still don't.'

Above: Steve's books were a hit with children. Right and below: Non-league Blyth Spartans were sponsored by Viz.

A selection of animated adventures from the comic.

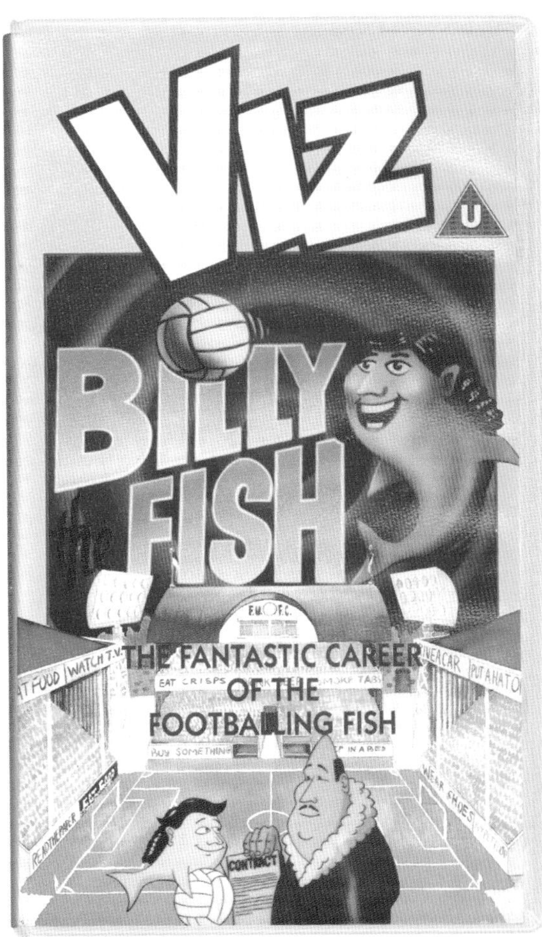

VIZ OFFERS PO Box 232, Melksham, Wilts. SN12 7SB
T-SHIRTS
CANT DECIDE WHICH T-SHIRT TO BUY? THEN BUY THEM ALL! TOP QUALITY NON SHRINK COTTON POLYESTER MIX SHIRTS (BLACK ON WHITE UNLESS OTHER-WISE STATED) SIZES M, L OR XL
ONLY £7·00

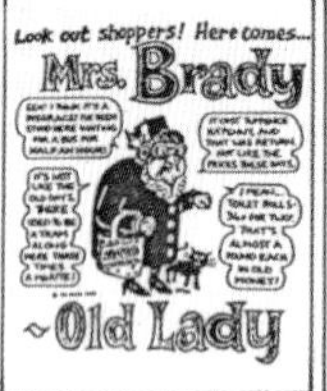

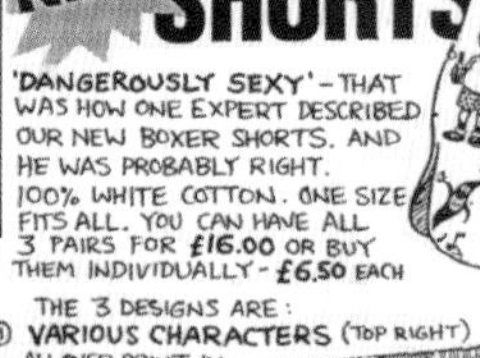

COME TO THE SHOPS DEAR
FUCK OFF!
it's Shakey
RUDE KID (RKT)
IT'S SHAKEY (SKT)
SEXY NEW BOXER SHORTS
'DANGEROUSLY SEXY' - THAT WAS HOW ONE EXPERT DESCRIBED OUR NEW BOXER SHORTS. AND HE WAS PROBABLY RIGHT. 100% WHITE COTTON. ONE SIZE FITS ALL. YOU CAN HAVE ALL 3 PAIRS FOR £16.00 OR BUY THEM INDIVIDUALLY - £6.50 EACH
THE 3 DESIGNS ARE:
① VARIOUS CHARACTERS (TOP RIGHT) ALL OVER PRINT IN BLACK AND BRIGHT YELLOW.
② BUSTER GONAD (LEFT) ALL ROUND PRINT, BLACK + RED
③ JOHNNY FARTPANTS (RIGHT) COMPLETE WITH PUMP CLOUD ON REAR! BLACK ON WHITE WITH GREEN PINSTRIPES

This page: Money-spinning merchandise included T-shirts, boxer shorts and records. Johnny Japes and his Jesticles were in fact XTC's Andy Partridge and John Otway.

Opposite: Big down under - Viz even produced a special edition for Australian readers.

Bags of Fun with Buster
The hit VIZ pop record by
Johnny Japes and his Jesticles

MC BILLY VANILLI ICE CREAM 'T' Featuring the F.U. POSSE
SINGALONGA FULCHESTER UNITED

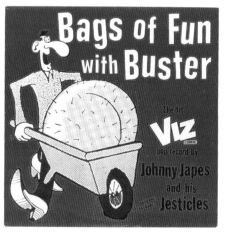

EVERY TWO MONTHLY ISSUE ONE NOVEMBER/DECEMBER 1989
NOT FOR SALE TO MINORS
VIZ
WITH ADDED TOILET HUMOUR
NZ - $3.85 inc GST
MAKES OTHER MAGAZINES LOOK CRAP $2.50
BRITAIN'S BEST SELLING PILE OF SHITE HAS ARRIVED IN AUSTRALIA
ARE YOU SEXY?
FIND OUT ON PAGE 9
FREE FLEXI DISC INSIDE
AFTER 25 YEARS WE NAME PRESIDENT KENNEDY'S KILLER!
Meet SID THE SEXIST
THE FAT SLAGS
and many more
DO YOU LIKE CRICKET, PET? COS I FANCY HAVING A CRACK AT A COUPLE OF BOUNCERS LIKE YOURS
BIG DOWN UNDER
BUGGER ME! I'M ON THE AIR
ROGER MELLIE
THE MAN ON THE TELLY
GIRLS!
HOW TO GET THAT GUY

$2.50
NZ $3.85 inc. GST
IMPROVE YOUR GOLF -after the Bomb
VIZ
WITH NEW 'TWO WAY' LEMON FRESHNESS
EVERY EIGHT WEEKLY ISSUE 2
NOT FOR SALE TO MINORS
INSIDE...
BEATLES RE-FORM
-NEW LP PLANNED
RETURN OF THE BOTTOM INSPECTORS
BARE YOUR BOTTOMS!
PLUS LOTS MORE
OH CRUMBS!
HELLRAISER!
'THAT'S ME' SAYS OLIVER REID
PASSION & POOL in
MMM! IT'S REALLY HARD
A cue for LOVE
SEE IF YOU CAN GET IT INTO THE HOLE
TERROR ON PAGE 28!
The Hand from Outer Space
Free inside: 4 page MAD DOCTOR pull out

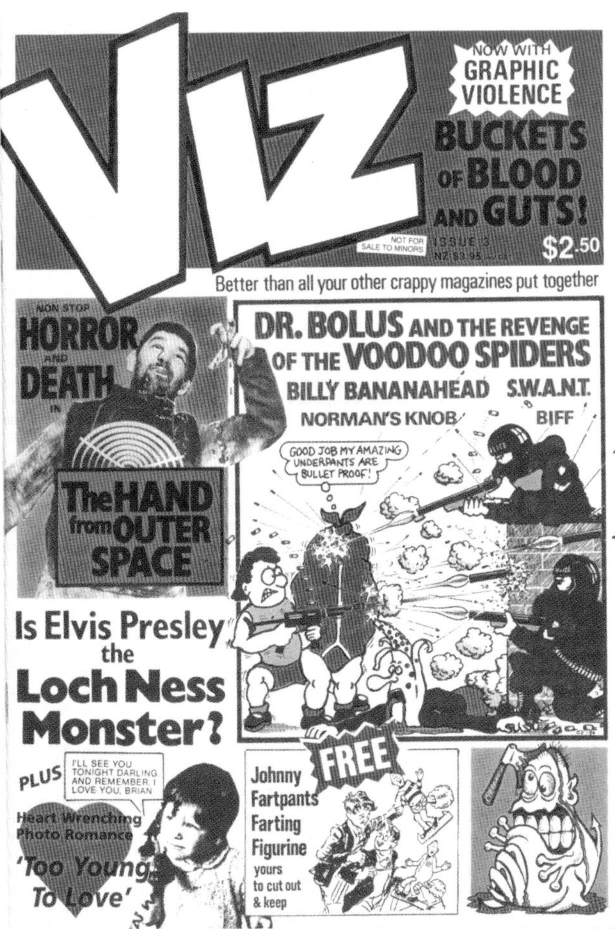
VIZ
NOW WITH GRAPHIC VIOLENCE
BUCKETS OF BLOOD AND GUTS!
NOT FOR SALE TO MINORS
ISSUE 3
$2.50
Better than all your other crappy magazines put together
NON STOP HORROR AND DEATH IN
The HAND from OUTER SPACE
DR. BOLUS AND THE REVENGE OF THE VOODOO SPIDERS
BILLY BANANAHEAD S.W.A.N.T.
NORMAN'S KNOB BIFF
GOOD JOB MY AMAZING UNDERPANTS ARE BULLET PROOF!
Is Elvis Presley the Loch Ness Monster?
PLUS
I'LL SEE YOU TONIGHT DARLING AND REMEMBER I LOVE YOU, BRIAN
Heart Wrenching Photo Romance
'Too Young To Love'
FREE
Johnny Fartpants Farting Figurine
yours to cut out & keep

ISSUE 4 Not for sale to minors
VIZ
EXCLUSIVE
IS PRINCE EDWARD SOFT?
~We ask him
The magazine for anyone who's got $2.50
With The Brown Bottle
Sid the Sexist The Liquidizer
& more!
WHAT? NEY TITS ON THE COVER?
OFFICER! THERE'S A BOMB IN THAT GENTLEMAN'S UNDERPANTS!
SHUT UP, BASTARD! YOU'RE UNDER ARREST!
DID SOMEBODY SAY RUDE WORDS?
We've got a great RUDE WORD COMPETITION
PICK UP YOUR PHONE & WIN A DOLLAR!
Plus~ THE SHAKIN' STEVENS FACT..FILE

And the *Viz* gene was now visible in all sorts of genres completely unconnected with the comic, from advertising to tabloid journalism. Indeed, the red tops were becoming increasingly difficult for *Viz* to parody, since they were now rapidly becoming *Viz* parodies of themselves.

Even the Armed Forces weren't immune. When *Viz* ran a cod recruitment ad, the Royal Marines responded by forking out £16,500 for a proper advert in the comic. 'It sparked our advertising department to look into who reads *Viz*,' revealed a Marines spokesman. 'It found the readers were generally males in the 15 to 24 age group – just the sort of lads we are looking for. The Navy does not endorse *Viz's* policy of taking the mickey out of everything, but the ad was considered good commercial sense. We are looking for extremely fit lads who are hard as nails and can live in a trench for a week. These lads are not going to be reading the *Daily Telegraph*.' [22]

Left: Cod recruitment advert. Below and opposite: Award-winning subscription renewal letters.

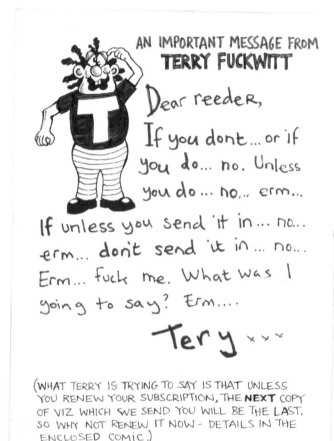

The comic's success spawned loads of imitators, but none of them was much good. 'They were terrible,' says Chris. 'They had nothing going for them.' *Viz* readers agreed. These titles only sold a fraction of what *Viz* was selling, and although their covers were vaguely similar, the contents bore no comparison. 'They'd focused on all the wrong aspects of what *Viz* was about,' says Simon. 'They were all about swearing.' What made *Viz* sell a million was the people who created it, and the chemistry between them. To try and replicate this specific formula was completely futile. You might as well say all you need to duplicate the Beatles or the Stones is a drum kit and a few guitars. Everyone can recognize *Viz* humour, but that doesn't mean anyone can do it. 'They had the ingredients,' says John. 'They just didn't have the chef.'

Chris's only worry was that these lame rivals might damn his creation by association. Having spent a decade trying to fight their way into the biggest newsagents, *Viz* was now forced to share precious shelf space with insipid wannabes, in a special section called Adult Humour. It was a sign of *Viz's* newfound clout that it prompted newsagents to create a whole new category, but since Adult is newsagentspeak for porn, this meant it often ended up buried among all the girlie mags on the top shelf. This anomaly must have resulted in some extremely disappointed customers, since unless you find Felix And His Amazing Underpants sexy (and if you do, you must be very odd indeed), *Viz* really isn't remotely pornographic. Indeed, it's actually far less racy than the laddish monthlies it helped to inspire, which ended up stacked beneath it on the more respectable middle shelf.

Though some retailers remained sniffy, celebs queued up to praise the comic. 'My wife and I find the two-monthly wait for *Viz* to poke its way through our door almost

'My wife and I find the two-monthly wait for *Viz* to poke its way through our door almost unbearable. We're now thinking of having a letter-box cut.'

S2

VIZ SUBSCRIPTIONS
freepost (SW 6096)
frome, Somerset
BA11 1YA

Dear Subscriber,

Remember me? I'm the girl who puts your Viz comic in the envelope every 2 months. I wrote to you last time begging you to re-new you subscription. But I haven't heard from you, and so unless you re-new it now the enclosed comic will be the last one I send. I am sealing this envelope with tears, because I have been crying ever since you didn't reply.

I fancy you loads (if you're a man) and I really, desperately want to send you the next six issues of Viz. So please please please a million pleases send off the tear-off form below.

All my love and kisses

Sally

xxxxxxxxxxx
xxxx xxxxxxx

P.S. I am not very tall, but have a nice figure. I am 17 next month. Please send me a photo of yourself for my birthday (along with your cheque and completed subscription form).

SPECIAL OFFER - Re-subscribe now and receive one issue free (7 for the price of 6).

Please complete and return to:
Sally, c/o Viz Comic Subscriptions, Freepost SW6096, Frome, Somerset, BA11 1YA or phone our charge card hotline FREE on 0800 581409.

Name: (block capitals please) ....
Address: ....
....Post code: ....
Daytime telephone number: ....

Dear Sally,
Please extend my subscription to Viz Comic forthwith, commencing with issue ....

I enclose a cheque/postal order payable to John Brown Publishing Limited for £..............
Please debit my Mastercard/Visa/American Express/Diners Club card for £....................

Card Number: | | | | | Expiry date: | | |

Signature: .... Date: ....

(Six issues, currently a year's supply costs £7.50. Extra copies of each issue to the same address cost £6.00, e.g. 2 copies of each issue for a year, send £7.50 + £6.00. 3 copies of each issue, £7.50 + £6.00 + £6.00 etc.)

Overseas rates: Six issues £11.50. Extra copies £9.50.

* We regret that photographs sent to Sally cannot be returned, and individual correspondence cannot be entered into.

It's a laugh a minute. Fun and games at the office.

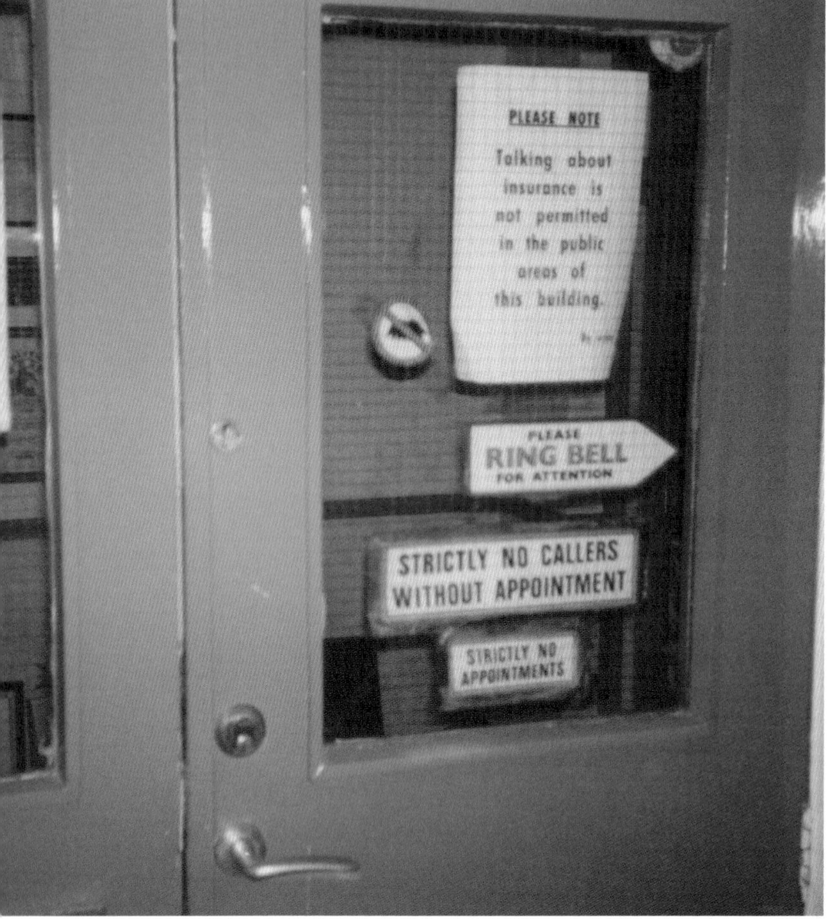

unbearable,' declared Michael Palin. 'We're now thinking of having a letter-box cut.' Glam rock (and road safety) icon Alvin Stardust dropped into the office, and Goodies legend Tim Brooke-Taylor turned up at a book signing. Roger Daltrey was honoured to be teased in *Viz* (it didn't do Noddy Holder any harm either) and Paul Weller drove across London to collect a signed copy of Roger's Profanisaurus ('the definitive reference volume of English obscenities') so he had something to read on tour. 'A rich and deeply compelling book,' wrote Terry Jones, 'which time and again brings the reader face to face with the nature of the human condition.' Jimmy Nail expressed an interest in playing Sid the Sexist in a sitcom. Auberon Waugh likened *Viz* to Rabelais, and the Bottom Inspectors to George Orwell's critique of Stalinist Russia. Even Jilly Cooper was a fan.

Not everyone was quite so keen. *Viz* also attracted a few death threats from religious fanatics and, in 1990, the comic fell foul of the United Nations, after running a strip called The Thieving Gypsy Bastards, triggered by a childhood trauma of Graham's. 'He had a washing machine stolen off him when he was nine, and he'd thought the gypsies had stolen it,' said Chris. 'He'd managed to contain himself for so long, until it all came out in that cartoon.' [23] *Viz* didn't realize that since gypsies are classified as a race, a fictitious strip about imaginary gypsies might be misconstrued as racism. They got complaints from forty gypsies, one of whom referred the matter to the UN. However by now the tabloids were finding it impossible to hide how much they really enjoyed the comic, and one of them came to their aid. 'The *Sun* found out that the gypsy who was pursuing us was up in court on a charge of handling stolen goods,' reveals Chris. 'They just waited until he was convicted then ran a big story and we were

'We never like upsetting people. If something goes in, it's got to be funnier than it is offensive.'

vindicated.'[24] Impartial as ever, *Viz* also did a strip called The Nice Honest Gypsies, just to be fair.

Some targets actually seem to enjoy the attention, much to Chris's frustration. 'You put people like Janet Street-Porter in the cartoons to really offend them, and then they ring up and want to buy the artwork,'[25] he complains. But most of its subjects are sensible enough to let it lie. 'The comic's like a schoolboy sticking his tongue out at somebody,' says Graham. 'You just ignore it.' And like a cheeky schoolboy, *Viz* is far more interested in having fun than in causing offence. 'We never like upsetting people,' says Graham. 'If something goes in, it's got to be funnier than it is offensive.'

Sometimes irate parents complain, after buying the comic for their children by mistake or finding it in their bedrooms. 'One woman rang us up and said it was hardly surprising there were lesbians and AIDS around with publications like *Viz* on sale,' says Simon. 'We told her she was right and we'd shut the magazine down next day.'[26] However, there's really not a lot in *Viz* that children can't easily find for themselves elsewhere. 'My kids read it,' says Graham. 'My eldest is ten and he loves it.' When the comic was banned from a few student unions, *Viz* merely responded with a campaign of their own to get it banned themselves. It was a cunning plan, but it didn't really work. Unfortunately for its critics, *Viz* is simply far too funny.

Journalists who rarely ventured beyond the Groucho Club now travelled north to witness the crazy antics at Britain's most controversial comic. Yet creating cartoons of any kind tends to be pretty studious business, however outrageous the content, and most hacks returned to London distinctly underwhelmed. 'People were constantly disappointed when they came to the office and found that we were all so bloody boring,' says Chris.

Maybe the more badly behaved the cartoon the better behaved the cartoonist. The one time that *Viz* hired some strippers for their Christmas party, they meekly paid them off before they'd had a chance to take off any of their clothes. Despite the profusion of naughty words in the comic about women's rude bits (or maybe even because of them), production manager Stevie Glover sensed the staff were slightly awkward when she breastfed her baby in the office. 'When I first left school, I was a matron in a boys' boarding school,' she says. 'I think it's the same job.' Thorpy describes cartoonists as people who don't get enough fresh air or daylight, and he's probably right. 'I just presumed that everyone was going to be a big mental Geordie,' says *Viz* designer, Wayne Gamble. 'It couldn't be further from the truth.'

Some people still assume that everyone at *Viz* must spend their whole time getting pissed or stoned, or holding all their editorial meetings down the pub. However it doesn't work like that. As with any line of work, if you don't put in the hours, you don't produce the goods. For all they have in common with their randy, violent creations, these scholarly scribes might as well be medieval monks illuminating sacred manuscripts. 'The long hours of absolutely obsessive dedication it takes to build this sort of humour are lost on the readers,' says Steve. 'Often the actual humour itself is about the creepy obsessiveness of the people who've actually made it.'

It's this obsessiveness that keeps them heads down, hard at it. They rarely give interviews. They hardly ever appear on telly. 'They've never got the acknowledgement,' says Andy, 'and the only reason they didn't get the acknowledgement is because they didn't go out there and ask for it, like every other cunt.' And the reason they don't ask for it because they don't want it. They're happiest being left alone to draw their cartoons.

Another controversial cartoon hits the pages.

The tabloids started off trying to whip up controversies about *Viz*. Now they're fulsome in their praise. The *Sun* called *Viz* 'a beacon of light in an increasingly drab, public relations driven, right on world'.[27] Yet once the red tops were won over, the broadsheets embarked on a tedious debate about whether *Viz* was sexist. Most concluded that it probably wasn't, although the correct answer was Who Cares? There is vulgarity in *Viz* and there is sexism,' says Chris. 'We don't set out to be sexist. We set out to be funny. If it's funny but sexist at the same time, that doesn't really bother us.' [28]

'The comic didn't pontificate at all,' says Graham. 'It never told people how to live their lives. It just poked fun at people, and I think that's probably still true today.' 'It's self criticism,' says Steve. 'When they take the piss out of people who smoke and drink and throw up on the pavements on a Saturday night, they're talking about themselves as well.' And anyway, crude caricatures are what cartoons are all about. 'They're about broad strokes and skipping the detail,' says Steve. 'It's all that stuff which is unfashionable in intellectual society. They say that you shouldn't jump to conclusions about people, you shouldn't stereotype people, you shouldn't lump them together and classify them as a group or whatever, but that's exactly what people do all the time.' Anyway, a lot of stuff in *Viz* has hardly anything to do with the real world. It also inhabits another universe, with hardly any connection with the here and now. This is a style personified by Davey Jones, creator of surreal flights of fancy like the Vibrating Bum Faced Goats. 'You never know what you're going to get from Davey,' says Thorpy. 'It's unlike anything else.'

Davey Jones always wanted to be a cartoonist. Even when he was a kid, he wanted to draw for the *Beano*, although he never thought he'd be able to turn it into a full-time career. 'I always fancied doing it,' he says, 'but I didn't think that's how you made your living – I thought you had to have a job as well.' From the age of nine, he was drawing his own cartoons and comic strips. He collected comics as a kid (he's still got them all today), but by the time he was old enough to send his own strips in he'd come across a comic he liked even better than the *Beano*. This was *Oink*, a comic Thorpy used to draw for before he went to work for *Viz*. Davey had already drawn a few strips for *Oink* when he saw *Viz* in a paper shop in Hereford, where he used to live. It was 1986, he'd just left school and *Viz* had just gone national. He might never have seen it otherwise. Davey liked *Viz* even more than *Oink*. He sent in a strip, Vlad The Impaler And His Cat Samson – cheerful chap impales kindly old lady on sharp spike and steals her purse to buy a slap up feast. Chris asked for more, and in 1987 he came up with Roger Irrelevant. *Viz* printed that strip too, and the next one. Davey was on his way.

16-year-old Davey Jones (far right) wins the 1983 Young Cartoonist of the Year Award. The boy in the centre is Joel Morris, lead singer of Candidate, one of the creators of the Framley Examiner, *and now a regular contributor to* Viz.

Above: Davey's first published cartoon in Oink. *Below: His* Viz *debut.*

THERE'S NOTHING THAT YOUNG VLAD MORE LIKES ~ THAN SKEWERING FOLKS ON WOODEN SPIKES!

VLAD THE IMPALER AND HIS CAT SAMSON

I WONDER WHAT'S UP WITH THAT KID.

BOO HOO

(SNIFFLE) MY BALL HAS GOT STUCK IN THE BRANCHES OF THIS TREE!

HO, HO, THAT PUT A STOP TO HIS CRYING!

CRUMBS! I'VE JUST REMEMBERED, IT'S VIZ COMIC DAY! I'D BETTER GET DOWN TO MY LOCAL NEWS-AGENT OR NEAREST BRANCH OF VIRGIN RECORD STORES, PLUS MANY OTHER RETAILERS THROUGHOUT THE COUNTRY, RIGHT AWAY!

D. JONES

OH NO! LOOK AT THAT QUEUE! THIS CALLS FOR A CRAFTY DODGE!

NEWS AGENT

Q HERE

I SOON GOT THEM TO SEE MY 'POINT' — EH, READERS? (CHOCKLE)

NEWS AGENT

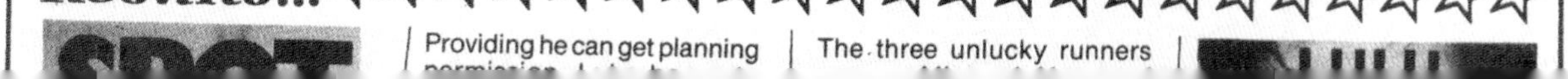

Results...☆☆☆☆☆☆☆☆☆☆☆☆☆☆☆☆☆☆☆☆☆☆☆☆☆☆☆☆☆

Providing he can get planning

The three unlucky runners

IRRELEVEMBUARY

(Between ~~Oc~~ September & October)

‘You feel like you’re getting away with something that can’t last. I’m still waiting for someone to tell me to stop.’

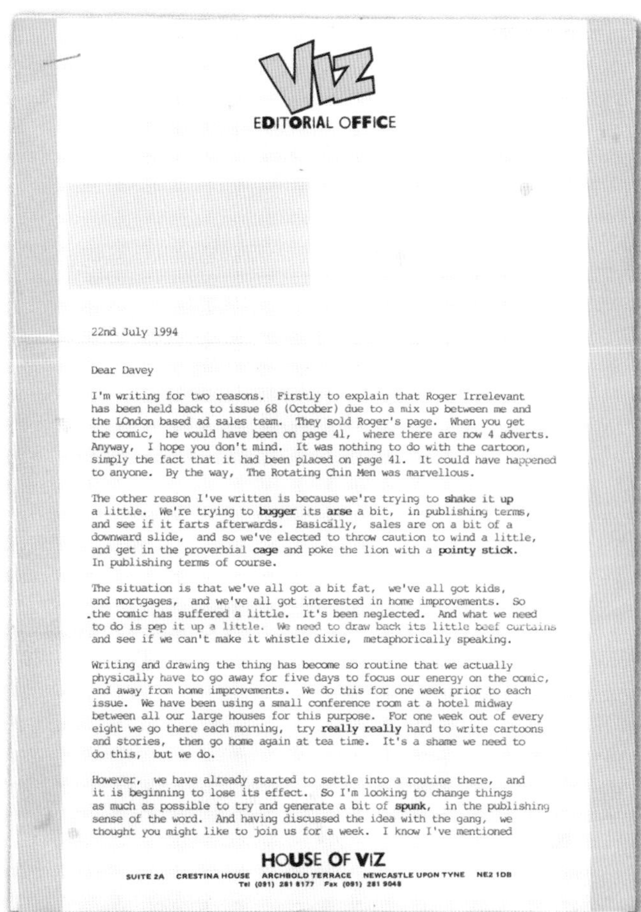

VIZ

EDITORIAL OFFICE

22nd July 1994

Dear Davey

I'm writing for two reasons. Firstly to explain that Roger Irrelevant has been held back to issue 68 (October) due to a mix up between me and the LOndon based ad sales team. They sold Roger's page. When you get the comic, he would have been on page 41, where there are now 4 adverts. Anyway, I hope you don't mind. It was nothing to do with the cartoon, simply the fact that it had been placed on page 41. It could have happened to anyone. By the way, The Rotating Chin Men was marvellous.

The other reason I've written is because we're trying to **shake it up** a little. We're trying to **bugger** its **arse** a bit, in publishing terms, and see if it farts afterwards. Basically, sales are on a bit of a downward slide, and so we've elected to throw caution to wind a little, and get in the proverbial **cage** and poke the lion with a **pointy stick.** In publishing terms of course.

The situation is that we've all got a bit fat, we've all got kids, and mortgages, and we've all got interested in home improvements. So the comic has suffered a little. It's been neglected. And what we need to do is pep it up a little. We need to draw back its little beef curtains and see if we can't make it whistle dixie, metaphorically speaking.

Writing and drawing the thing has become so routine that we actually physically have to go away for five days to focus our energy on the comic, and away from home improvements. We do this for one week prior to each issue. We have been using a small conference room at a hotel midway between all our large houses for this purpose. For one week out of every eight we go there each morning, try **really really** hard to write cartoons and stories, then go home again at tea time. It's a shame we need to do this, but we do.

However, we have already started to settle into a routine there, and it is beginning to lose its effect. So I'm looking to change things as much as possible to try and generate a bit of **spunk**, in the publishing sense of the word. And having discussed the idea with the gang, we thought you might like to join us for a week. I know I've mentioned

HOUSE OF VIZ

SUITE 2A CRESTINA HOUSE ARCHBOLD TERRACE NEWCASTLE UPON TYNE NE2 1DB
Tel (091) 281 8177 Fax (091) 281 9048

Despite his schoolboy success, Davey never considered going to art school. He even had to retake his Art O Level, although God knows why when you look at his realistic yet inventive artwork. Instead, he went to Manchester to do a philosophy degree, but when he finished college he moved to North Wales, where his parents came from, and began doing regular stuff for *Viz*. He started doing Gilbert Ratchet and Tinribs, plus loads of similarly bizarre strips, like Plankton Boy, The Bereavement Beavers and Mickey’s Miniature Grandpa.

For the next six years he drew cartoons in his flat in Beaumaris on Anglesey and sent *Viz* a couple of pages per issue. It was a pretty solitary existence. He only tended to meet other cartoonists once a year, at the *Viz* Christmas party. ‘That’s a good thing if you’re not very comfortable knocking on doors,’ he says. ‘You just do it all by post.’ This isolation also helped him develop a distinctive style. With no formal training, and hardly any personal contact with his colleagues, no one ever told him how to do cartoons, and so he did what all decent artists do – he found his own voice. Even today, his drawing style is curiously old-fashioned, especially for a bloke who’s still only in his thirties, but the scripts are something else.

In 1996, Davey told Chris he fancied living in a city again. ‘Why don’t you try this one?’ said Chris, so he moved up to Newcastle. He started coming into the office and found he really liked it. *Viz* has always taken solo cartoons from freelance cartoonists, but most of the regular strips are done in house, and though the artwork for each of these is generally done by just one person, the script is usually written by the entire team. ‘It’s just getting your head to work in a slightly different way,’ says Davey. ‘Everyone sits around and talks about it and chips stuff in and I think that works pretty well.’ Davey didn’t chip in much stuff at first, but he soon began to relish this ensemble way of working. ‘You feel like you’re getting away with something that can’t last,’ he says, but eight years later, he’s still there.

Lately he’s started doing improbable adventure stories featuring real people, from showbiz stalwarts like Rod Stewart (And The Island of Death) to historical figures such as Oswald ‘Mind My Brolly’ Mosley (The Blackshirt Funnyman). More recent targets include Janet Street-Porter Crusoe (And Her Researcher Friday) and Old Mother Teresa (The Scream of The Calcutta Slums). ‘I’m crap at doing caricatures,’ he says. ‘I can’t get a likeness.’ But his caricatures are actually perfectly recognizable. And although Saturday night archetypes like the Fat Slags and Sid the Sexist hog the headlines, Davey’s weird fantasies are just as big a part of *Viz*. As a child, he always dreamt of getting a job that involved drawing and not getting up early in the morning. And unlike most of us, he’s achieved his childhood ambition.

‘I’m still waiting for someone to tell me to stop.’

Opposite: Davey’s page for the 1993 Viz Calendar. *Above: Chris invites Davey to get more involved, in publishing terms. Below: Old Mother Teresa.*

BY GUM! I'VE GOT SOME CORKING NEW BIBLES FOR ME MISSION HOSPITAL
OLD MA TERESA'S MISSION HOSPITAL
THEY'LL DO ME TERMINALLY ILL PATIENTS A WORLD OF GOOD

As Chris became more busy, producing *Viz* books and other spin-offs, many of the strips he'd created were drawn by other members of the team. Thorpy adopted Big Vern, Billy the Fish and Mrs Brady (Old Lady), while Graham turned his hand to Biffa Bacon, Terry Fuckwitt (The Unintelligent Cartoon Character) and Roger Mellie (The Man on The Telly). Freelancers Simon Ecob and Lew Stringer took on two of his other classics, Jack Black and the Pathetic Sharks. However, these cartoonists were used to drawing one another's strips as deadlines loomed, and so the comic stayed much the same. Chris's only complaints were that Thorpy didn't know anything about football (a bit of a handicap in a strip about a goalkeeper) and that Graham made Roger's feet too big. 'The mice have been in,' he'd tell the others, when they discovered the last minute alterations he'd made to their artwork.

In 1999, Chris hung up his boots. 'I'd been talking about leaving for ages,' he says. 'Everyone knew I was fed up and I didn't want to work there any more.' *Viz* was moving offices and acquiring state of the art computers. It all felt a long way from making Letraset headlines on an old card table in his boyhood bedroom in Lily Crescent. 'It was all getting more businesslike,' he explains. 'There wasn't the same smell of Cow Gum any more.'

For a while, he carried on coming in two days a week, but then an issue went to press without him and it didn't seem to matter. 'I wasn't there at all at the deadline and they did perfectly well without me.' And so after twenty years at the helm, he finally stopped coming in altogether. 'Quitting has been a bit like leaving school – the same kind of relief,'[29] he said, when he left, but *Viz* has been rather more lucrative than attending Heaton Comprehensive. Chris now lives in a former hotel near the handsome Northumbrian market town of Alnwick, and works part time in a local bookshop. 'Unlike their granddad – who once shared an outside lavatory with nine other families – my three children have six lavatories to choose between. When your entire family can visit the lavatory at the same time and you've got a bog to spare, you know you've made it.'[30] The creator of a comic famed for its toilet humour, this seems a fitting epitaph for his youth's work. He doesn't regret leaving, but he still sends things in from time to time. 'I had an idea for a Top Tip the other day.'

John thought *Viz* would fold when Chris quit, but he was pleased to be proved wrong. 'Not only did it not collapse, in some ways it got better,' he says. To all but the most obsessive reader, the comic remained remarkably similar, though that actually confirmed how much influence Chris has had, rather than how little. Chris's greatest gift was creating new characters rather than cultivating them, and like the first issue of *Viz*, the essence of his creations was usually all there in the first strip. Like a Tyneside Walt Disney, he's invented a cartoon style so fertile that it can carry on reproducing itself without any input on his part. 'He's a genius,' says John, 'a comic genius.' Works of genius usually outlive their makers, and so *Viz* continued in much the same vein, as Simon, Graham, Thorpy and Davey took over as co-editors, along with new recruit, teenage wunderkind Alex Collier.

Below: Thorpy, Simon, Chris and Graham.

'It was all getting more businesslike. There wasn't the same smell of Cow Gum any more.'

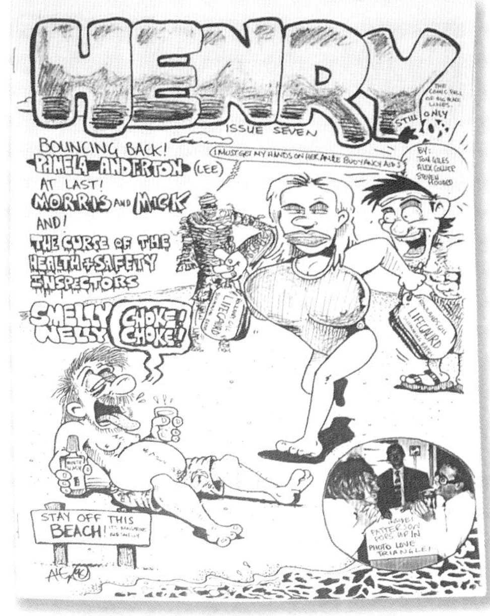

Above: Alex Collier's teenage comic, Henry. *Left: Geoff Brewer, Alex's supportive and influential art teacher, appears in this strip about the rise and fall of* Henry.

'I had this vision in me head of them all smoking and flushing people's heads down toilets.'

The first time Alex Collier read *Viz* was at his mate Hayley's house when he was twelve. Hayley's dad used to hide it under his bed. 'It was just the best thing ever,' says Alex. 'It was like the *Beano*, but it made you laugh.' The first strip he read was Simon's Snowman, in which a boy befriends a supernatural snowman whose hobbies include boozing, car theft and casual sex. 'It was fucking brilliant,' says Alex. 'It was just so rude and funny.'

Note to parents: if you've got a magazine that you really want your children (and their friends) to read, hide it under your bed.

Alex had seen *Viz* in the shops, but he'd never even flicked through it. He presumed it must be porn because it was on the top shelf, but after he read Hayley's dad's copy, he was hooked. 'I always wanted to work for *Viz*, from the first time I saw it,' he says. 'I never thought I'd actually ever work there. I just really wanted to get some

DEAR VIZ

Hi! My name is Alex Collier, and I am 15 years of age, anyway I am a big fan of VIZ and drawing cartoons myself.

I started a comic at school three years ago, and it is getting better every issue, I have included a special recent edition, and some past strips of "HENRY", The main cartoon. Alongside this I have done cartoons and comicstrips for a company based in Newcastle, which will be published soon, and also got a comic strip printed in the REDDWARF magazine, amongst other stuff

I Hope you like the Stuff I have sent you, and havent fallen asleep yet, but I really want to do my job experience with you. It isnt untill around the last week of October (no actual date known yet) By which time I will be 16.

Iam not expecting to do drawings for you, but to see what gos into making the funniest comic in the world (next to the Beano of course) I Hope you could do this

Best Wishes

Alex (ALEX COLLIER).

24 August 1995

Dear Alex

Thanks very much for sending us your work for possible inclusion in Viz. We appreciate the effort you have made.

Unfortunately we didn't think your work was quite right for publication and hope you're not too disappointed. We get lots of unsolicited cartoons and scripts every day and very rarely find one which is suitable.

Thanks once again for taking the time and effort to send it to us.

Yours sincerely

Susan Patterson

pp Chris Donald
EDITOR

Opposite: Alex's letter applying for work experience at Viz.

Above: Alex's rejection letter. A few years later, he was a full time member of staff.

Below: Tasha Slappa's first appearance in print in the Henry *strip 'Big Fat Dirty Pervy Teacher'.*

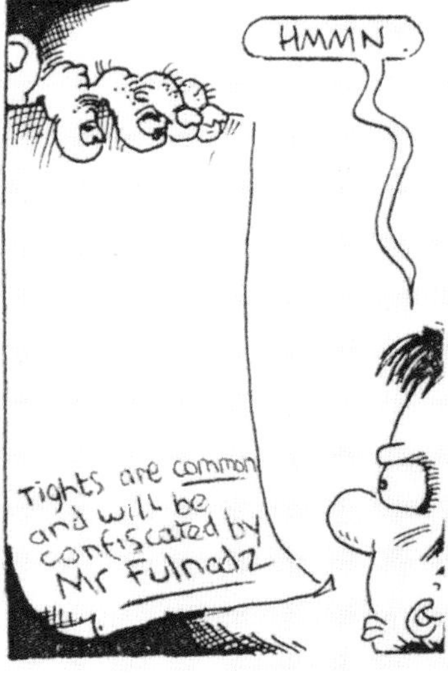

work published in it.' Mind you, he hardly thought there was a career in it. 'It was just a kind of hobby. I didn't think it was possible to make any money out of it or have it as a job. It was just something I did for a laugh in me spare time.'

Yet for someone having a laugh in his spare time, Alex was already pretty focused. He'd been drawing cartoons ever since he could remember, and by the time he first read *Viz* he was already drawing his own comic strips. His parents were both artists, so he never ran short of encouragement, or supplies. In 1995, he sent a strip in to *Viz*, but they rejected it. Still, he was only fourteen at the time. 'I was a bit disappointed but it didn't stop me,' he says. Because by now, Alex was already editing his own comic.

Like Steve, Chris and Simon, half a generation earlier, Alex lived in quite a smart area, but went to quite a rough school. However, it was also a very good school, with an inspiring art teacher called Geoff Brewer. Geoff encouraged Alex to make his first comic, called *Henry,* with two schoolfriends, Tom Giles and Stephen Howard. They printed a few dozen copies on the school photocopier and sold them for 20p. Strips included Big Fat Dirty Pervy Teacher ('we weren't allow to put that one in at first') and Pamela Anderton And Her Huge Jugs, about a blonde starlet with two gigantic flagons. 'My humour didn't get any better,' says Alex. But it was already very funny. Over five years, he published nine issues, each one better than the last. 'If some teachers got on our tits, we'd do stuff about them,' he says, but though one teacher made a point of never buying a copy, most of the staff and pupils loved it. And all the while, he kept reading *Viz* strips, for business as well as pleasure, learning to recognize the way their structure worked.

After he'd done his GCSEs, Alex decided to stay on for A Levels, but anyone who wanted to go into the sixth form had to do some work experience first. By now, after half a dozen issues, *Henry* had really found its feet, so in 1996 he sent a copy to *Viz* and they invited him in for a week. He was a bit nervous on his first day. 'I had this vision in me head of them all smoking and flushing people's heads down toilets.' But like every other visitor before and since, he found *Viz* surprisingly sedate. It doesn't matter if it's Tintin or Johnny Fartpants – drawing cartoons for a living takes a lot of work. Alex picked up lots of useful tips, like the importance of scripting strips in advance, but the most important lesson was confidence. Rubbing shoulders with the people behind the comic made his dream seem real.

'If some teachers got on our tits, we'd do stuff about them,'

He still didn't think he'd ever get a full-time job there, but he did start to believe that if he worked hard enough, one day his work might actually be published in *Viz*.

Alex carried on dropping in to the office to shove his latest cartoons under people's noses. Everyone was very friendly, but though Simon was the most encouraging it was Chris who took the trouble to go through his first *Viz* strip, frame by frame, and give him detailed notes on how to bring it up to standard. By now Alex was in the sixth form, doing A Levels, but his heart wasn't really in it. 'I was doing Maths, Arts and Design and drawing for *Viz* as a hobby on the side, and by the end of it, after two years, it was the other way around.' By the time he sat his A Levels, he was hardly ever in school, and spending almost all his time at *Viz*. He decided to take a year out before he went to university, and went down to London to see John Brown about a job, but by then he'd already had over a dozen strips published in *Viz*, so John said that after everything he'd already done, he might as well work for him in Newcastle. He joined the staff of *Viz* in 1998.

Alex was still only in his teens, almost a generation younger than the others. At first he felt timid in the writing sessions, but he gradually got the hang of it. He discovered most suggestions simply don't work, whoever's making them, and learnt not to take it personally when the others didn't find something funny. He discovered that creating comedy is always a process of trial and error. It's like doing the lottery – you need to buy an awful lot of tickets to get even a few winning numbers. This comic hothouse honed his talents, and made his work sharper and stronger, and over the next five years he came up with contemporary characters like Tasha Slappa, Rat Boy, Boyz R Uz, Anna Reksik, Billy No Mates and Pop Shot. Unlike Graham and Thorpy's timeless creations, they were all about the modern world. 'Our references are to things that were on the telly in the Seventies,' Chris explained, a few years earlier. 'Mud, Sweet and John Noakes. The fourteen year olds with baseball caps turned round, who listen to raves, haven't heard of John Noakes.'[31] Alex didn't wear his baseball cap turned round, but he had heard of John Noakes – and he knew a bit about raves as well.

By 2001, John Brown Publishing had become a thriving business with a host of titles. 'It was all getting a bit much for me,' says John. 'I was rich and yet I was working harder than I wanted to.' And then a man called James Brown (no relation) approached him and asked to buy three of his magazines: *Bizarre*, *Fortean Times* – and *Viz*. James had read *Viz* since his teens. He used to sell the comic in Leeds, while Chris sold his fanzine in Newcastle. He'd since made his name as the founding editor of *Loaded*, the pioneering lads' mag with some of the same *Viz* chutzpah. 'He always used to say that we were one of the influences for *Loaded*,' says Chris. His company, I Feel Good, paid John Brown £6.4 million for *Viz*, *Bizarre* and *Fortean Times*. 'It took three minutes to convince the brokers,' said James. 'I read them two cartoons, and when they had finished laughing, they said OK.'[32]

I Feel Good was backed by Dennis Publishing, and chaired by Felix Dennis, who now publishes *Viz*. Although Felix Dennis is a multi-millionaire, with a string of international titles, he's probably the perfect publisher for *Viz*. Expelled from several schools, he played in various rock bands and worked as a park attendant and gravedigger for Harrow and Pinner County Councils, before joining an underground magazine called *Oz*.

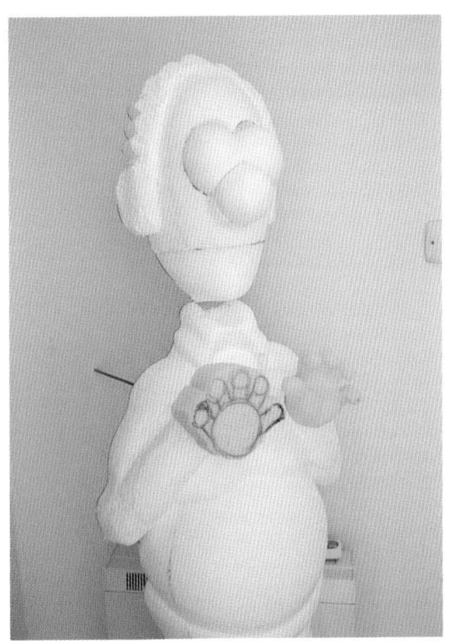

A selection of exhibits from the magazine's 20th Anniversary Exhibition, including a Damien Hirst-style Billy the Fish (top) and Sid the Sexist's 'I Speak Your Tits' Machine (left, under construction).

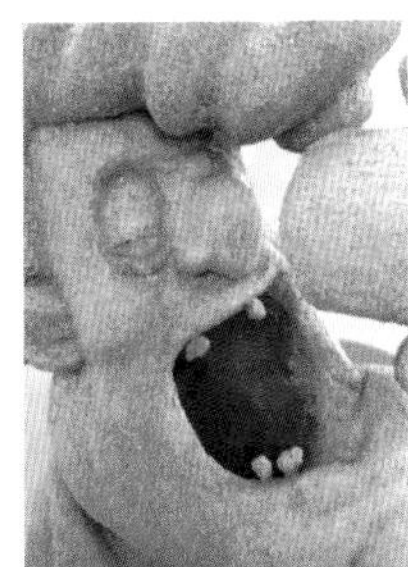

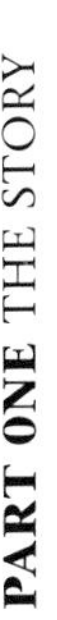

In 1971, Felix Dennis, co-editor Jim Anderson and founding editor Richard Neville were all sent to prison after the longest obscenity trial in history, having pleading not guilty to the charge that they had conspired to produce a magazine which would corrupt the morals of young people, and had intended to 'arouse and implant in the minds of these young people lustful and perverted desires'. They were all acquitted of this charge, but found guilty of four lesser charges. Neville was sentenced to 15 months, Anderson got a year and Dennis got nine months. These convictions were subsequently quashed on appeal, after the verdicts were found to be unsafe because of a serious and substantial misdirection of the jury by the judge, Michael Argyle, QC. Ironically, Neville, Anderson and Dennis hadn't edited the offending issue of the magazine, but had handed it over to a group of schoolkids. The case became a *cause célèbre*, and if it hadn't been for this trial, and the liberal outrage it generated, it's debatable whether comics like *Viz* ever could have been published. 'You are younger than the other two,' Argyle told Dennis, justifying his shorter sentence, 'and very much less intelligent.' He can't have been that daft. In the mid - 1990s, *Business Age* magazine rated Dennis 56th in its annual Rich 500 list. The Queen was 57th.

'A lot of his cartoons are the backbone of *Viz*, but I don't think he really enjoyed doing them. He likes to enjoy himself. He's got a life.'

In 2003 Simon left Viz, after nearly a quarter of a century with the comic, and Alex left with him, to set up a new partnership called Blissna – Geordie slang for excellent. During the past few years they'd pretty much become writing partners, a lot like Graham and Thorpy, so it made sense for them to club together. Some of the stuff they're doing together wouldn't look out of place in *Viz* (a book sending up teenage girls' romances, for instance) but they're also planning a sketch show and doing a new game show for Tyne Tees TV. Drawing cartoons had been Simon's boyhood dream, but the quiet seclusion of comic art never entirely suited his gregarious nature, and after twenty-four years it had all become a bit of a bind.

'A lot of his cartoons are the backbone of *Viz*,' says Andy, 'but I don't think he really enjoyed doing them. He likes to enjoy himself. He's got a life.' Simon always had outside interests, and when the comic went from six issues a year to ten, there wasn't a lot of time left over to pursue them.

Alex had always shared Simon's interest in TV, so he felt much the same. 'I'm not bothered about performing,' he says, 'but I really want to write a film or a sitcom or something like that.'

Simon was adamant it would be business as usual at *Viz*. 'Graham, Thorpy and Davey have been the backbone of the magazine's output since the mid-1980s,' he announced. 'I'm sure most readers won't notice a change.' But although *Viz* looks much the same, it was still a milestone for the comic. With Jim long gone, and Chris now departed, Simon was the last founder to leave, and with Alex leaving too, there were now no Geordies at this Geordie mag. Nevertheless, Newcastle United still feels like a Geordie football club even when virtually every player on the pitch is foreign, and maybe *Viz* is much the same. Perhaps the biggest difference is that Graham, Thorpy and Davey are all graduates, unlike Chris, Simon or Alex.

Chris and Simon have always been the public face of *Viz*, and it's hard to see who'll replace them. 'Davey does go out but Thorpy and Graham basically don't socialize,' says Simon. 'Thorpy goes to the pub at the end of his own street for a pub quiz once a week. He spends the rest of his time in his house or in the office, and Graham is much the same. They're both family guys. They've got three kids each.' Yet although they're nudging early middle age, Graham and Thorpy's humour feels forever young. 'When we got married and had kids we stopped going out drinking so much, and going out drinking's where you often see a lot of the stereotypes and the characters,' says Graham, 'but when people go out socially they go out for a laugh and a carry-on – and that's effectively what we do all day at work.'

For a decade now, sales have been in slow but steady decline, but the staff don't seem that bothered. After all, if sales had ascended to their present level, rather than descending to it, the publishers would probably be delighted, since the current six-figure circulation is still extremely healthy for a publication of this kind. And anyway, it was never going to sell a million for very long. 'In the early days, it was probably the shock value that sold it as much as anything, but you can't shock people forever,' says Graham. 'You've got to make them laugh.' And though it no longer seems so shocking, he reckons there are just as many laughs in *Viz*. 'I don't think it was as funny when it was selling a million as it is now.'

But *Viz* has become a venerable British institution, and there's nothing fans of any institution like more than harking back to the good old days. Mark E. Smith out of indie band The Fall was the first to say *Viz* wasn't as funny as it used to be, and that was way back in 1986, just after the comic first

Life imitating art. Simon signs his art 'Shiloe' here, his name from the Bumph Club – *see page 13.*

went national. *Viz* responded by putting his criticism on the cover, but the contents really didn't bear it out. After all these years, *Viz* is even funnier, and one of the funniest things in it today is the comic art of John Fardell.

Like most cartoonists, John Fardell had drawn cartoons ever since he was a kid. At primary school he made his own comic with a schoolfriend ('every break time, if we could stay in, if it was raining') and at secondary school he drew caricatures of his teachers – all over his exercise books. 'They were very tolerant really,' he says. 'I did some quite outrageous pictures of some probably quite nice teachers.' He went to the local comprehensive, and then on to Middlesex Polytechnic, to do a performing arts degree.

He first saw *Viz* when his brother gave him an annual for Christmas. 'I found it really funny,' he says. 'You don't often see kids sitting down with a *Dandy* or *Beano* or Tintin book and actually laughing out loud.' By then he'd left college and was working as a freelance illustrator, mainly doing pictures of pubs and selling them to landlords. He simply picked a part of London where he hadn't been before, went into every single pub, showed the landlord his drawings and asked them if they'd like a picture. Most said no but a few said yes, and he usually did several pictures a week, at around forty quid a time. It wasn't glamorous or lucrative, but it wasn't bad training. 'My drawing did get better,' he says. 'It's quite a good way to learn to draw.'

Viz didn't take the first thing John sent in, but hawking pub pictures door to door makes you tough enough to face rejection. 'When you've been refused commissions by hundreds of pub landlords, it takes quite a lot to completely discourage you.' He created The Modern Parents for *Viz*, and the first one he sent in, they printed. Then he sent them The Critics. *Viz* printed that one too. 'I should have gone to art college and learnt how to draw better,' he says. 'It's taken me years and years to get my drawing to a better standard.' But studying performing arts rather than fine art gave him some great source material for both these strips, and so does living in Edinburgh, where he's spent the last twelve years. 'The details have to be right,' he says. 'That's the trick to all the humour which works.'

John Fardell's Modern Parents.

Viz's ill-fated foray into the charitable world of otter sponsorship. Most of the otters died.

It was ME!

DUDLEY ZOO rolled out the red carpet for Viz Ottery winner Lesleyanne Avery last week as she enjoyed a 10-bottle-of-champagne day out of a lifetime.

"Winning the Ottery is a dream come true for me, but I'm not going to let it change my life," she told us as she was picked up by Turdbridge, the Viz chauffeur. The Croydon PDSA worker was then whisked 125 miles to Dudley in our £170,000 Bentley, quaffing five bottles of vintage champagne and guzzling 1 lb of Bombay mix on the way.

At the zoo, she was introduced to Rosie the Viz otter by keeper Richard Brown, and spent over four minutes looking at her. Then it was time to head back to the Bentley and make a start on the return journey, her sixth bottle and the rest of the nibbles. Back home, all ten bottles empty, Turdbridge helped the now incoherent and nauseous jackpot winner back to her front door, where she made repeated pathetic attempts to get her key in the lock.

"It's a day I'll never forget," she slurred, adding "Thank-you Viz!" as her legs finally buckled underneath her.

We would like to thank ***Dudley Zoo*** *for the loan of their otter and their hospitality, and* ***Bentley Motors*** *for the loan of their car. Bentley would like all Viz's kebab-noshing unemployed readers to know that their cars are available for about 170 grand each, or two for 320.*

Ottery Extra Latest...

The Viz *Ottery Extra* prize of a day with the otter keeper at Newquay Zoo has unfortunately had to be withdrawn. "We saw the article and we don't find this sort of thing very amusing," a zoo spokesperson told us. "This is not something we wish to be involved with."

THE ROYAL ZOOLOGICAL SOCIETY OF SCOTLAND

Certificate of Sponsorship

in recognition of the generous support given to the Royal Zoological Society of Scotland by

Viz Comic

through sponsorship of

the oriental small-clawed otters

as part of the Animal Sponsorship Scheme

1st September 2001 to 31st August 2002

EDINBURGH ZOO DIRECTOR HIGHLAND WILDLIFE PARK

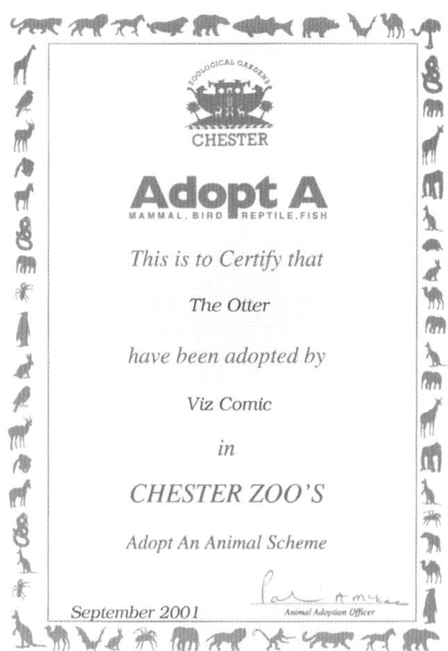

ZOOLOGICAL GARDENS CHESTER

Adopt A

MAMMAL, BIRD, REPTILE, FISH

This is to Certify that

The Otter

have been adopted by

Viz Comic

in

CHESTER ZOO'S

Adopt An Animal Scheme

September 2001

Animal Adoption Officer

Constructing the Bus of Fools in 2001, a pyrotechnic spectacular for New Year's celebrations in Newcastle.

'It leaves a vapour trail over everything. There's a *Viz*ness about this town.'

With Chris, Simon and Alex all gone, *Viz* is now more dependent on outside contributors like John Fardell. Yet finding them is another matter. Virtually everyone who contributes to *Viz* started off sending something in on spec, but as in any lottery, winning entries are few and far between. When the comic was selling a million, they used to get dozens of speculative submissions every day, even though almost everything was drawn in-house. Now they only get about half a dozen a week, but the number of new discoveries is still the same – about half a dozen a year, if they're lucky. There's no shortage of people out there who can draw, but really good writers are in such short supply that they now write some strips in house, and farm out the artwork to outsiders. One of these hired hands is a churchwarden who also draws for conventional comics. *Viz* started out mocking these sort of mags. Now it employs their artists, at a rate of several hundred pounds a page.

Yet most of the old working practices remain. Most of the strips are still produced in the same way, with one person doing the drawing, and everyone mucking in on the script. And the staff still do their utmost to avoid any tedious meetings about the future direction of the magazine. 'That's always a chore,' says Davey. 'They don't really make any sense to any of us. It's just a lot of pie charts and graphs.' They used to have a graph in the office charting the declining circulation, but in the end that got too depressing, so they took it down. What made *Viz* so funny in the first place was that it had clearly never been anywhere near a focus group, and market research is still treated with healthy contempt. 'A lot of that stuff is bollocks,' says Davey. 'You can't do that kind of analysis. It's people making jobs for themselves.' *Viz* has never tried to second-guess its readers, and it never will. As Graham says, 'The only thing that's ever determined whether something goes in the comic is if it made us laugh.' And that's precisely why it's lasted. 'In every issue, there are still four or five strips that make me shit myself laughing, and that's twenty-five years later,' says John Brown.

Twenty-five years later, it may be a bit unfair still to dismiss *Viz* as schoolboy humour, but it is fair to say that the comic has always been mainly made by, and for, young men. 'It is a peculiarly male pursuit,' says Stevie Glover, the only woman in the office. *Viz* does have a few female fans, but after all this time, it still has no female cartoonists. Like making lists and collecting things, drawing comics tends to be a boy thing. Perhaps most women are simply too well adjusted to put in all those lonely hours. 'The people who produce it are male, and we do it mainly to amuse ourselves,' says Chris. 'Women mature early. Men never mature. I hope to remain immature for the rest of my life.'[33] Yet as the *Sun* said,

toasting the comic's twentieth birthday, in a world full of women's magazines, what's so wrong with a men's comic?

Wisely, *Viz* has always resisted the temptation to move to London, where it would surely lose its Northern flavour. 'A lot of the characters are very obviously Geordies,' says Wayne, the *Viz* designer. 'You can tell from their accents.' And even if you're not from round here, being here has an effect on who you are. 'It's a city which has a very definite and defined image,' says Wayne. 'Living here you can't avoid it. It's in the bricks. It's in the very make-up of the city. You're constantly aware of it as an outsider. You can't go anywhere without being reminded you're in Newcastle.' And you can't go anywhere in Newcastle without being reminded of *Viz*. On New Year's Eve, 1999, a busload of *Viz* effigies was burnt here to celebrate the new millennium. '*Viz* is a bigger part of Geordie culture than the RSC coming up here for a season,' says Anvil Springstien. 'It leaves a vapour trail over everything. There's a *Viz*ness about this town.'

Not everyone in Newcastle is thrilled that characters like Sid the Sexist and the Fat Slags have become local heroes. 'A lot of people took great offence, but that was the whole point of it as far as I'm concerned,' says Brian. 'You could take offence, but if you went down the Bigg Market on a Saturday night you could see exactly what they were talking about – it's there to this day.' When the Fat Slags were in their prime, there were 77 pubs around the Bigg Market, and you could buy a blow job for just two quid – a blow job, in this instance, being a cocktail of vodka, whipped cream and Tia Maria. No other British city has a higher concentration of pubs in such a small area. A normal Saturday night in the Bigg Market feels like New Year's Eve.

The price of cocktails has risen with inflation, but not a lot else has changed. 'You look at the Bigg Market of a night – it's just big gangs of lads and lasses,' says Anvil. 'They all go out and they drink like there's no tomorrow, and it's like every gang of lads and every gang of lasses is a hen party or a stag party.' And whatever the weather, they're usually wearing next to nothing. How do you spot a Londoner in Newcastle? He's the only one wearing a coat. Yet far from damaging its reputation, *Viz* has helped turn Newcastle into an international party town. 'We're a tourist destination now,' marvels Anvil. 'At the weekend, it's full of frigging tourists.'

And the *Viz* effect isn't confined to Tyneside. 'It's had an effect on what, twenty years ago, we were calling alternative comedy,' says Anvil. Back in the Eighties, alternative comedians were telling people how to vote and what to think, and PC punters were booing words like cunt and even girlfriend. Comedy today is less politically correct, and it was *Viz* that led the way. It's never been remotely pious. It wouldn't know how to be po-faced. 'It invented laddism,' says Phil. 'I'm sure it did.'

2001/2

After all, what other comic could publish a book called *The Joy of Sexism* – and get away with it? Or celebrate its twentieth birthday with a Johnny Fartpants Wheel of Fartune and a Sid the Sexist I Speak Your Tits machine? Today's stand-ups have finally learnt from *Viz* how to take the piss without preaching, but it's taken them a generation to catch up. 'It managed to sneak in under the radar by looking so childish,' says Steve. 'If it had been more professionally produced it would have set alarm bells ringing earlier, but it was a stealth attack on the establishment and it wasn't taken seriously for a long time.'

Viz still isn't taken terribly seriously (thank God) and, although it's had a glossy cover for ten years now, it's still the same rough and ready comic underneath. Despite the shiny wrapper, inside it's still a fanzine – riotous, unruly and reassuringly ragged around the edges. 'The way we do it's no different, really,' says Thorpy. 'We're still just having a laugh.'

There's still the occasional controversy, although these spats are often created by the papers, rather than simply reported by them. 'The cover of *Viz* gives you a pretty good idea of what the content is going to be like,' says Chris. 'It only becomes an issue when the media start waving sticks at it.'[34] And even *Viz* humour has its limits. 'We might sometimes be offensive, but we've never made jokes about disability,' he says. 'That just wouldn't be funny.'[35] In fact the gags in *Viz* are far tamer than the sick jokes you hear in any office. Even in the early days, the 'four-letter comic' headlines were mainly a media myth. 'There wasn't actually that much swearing in it,' says Graham. 'People got this impression that it's full of filth and it's absolutely not.' A lot of *Viz* humour has always been remarkably innocent, from Balsa Boy to Playtime Fontayne. Today, the lewdest things in it are the ads.

There'll never be another comic quite like *Viz*, and even if there is, it won't happen the same way. Twenty-five years ago, nobody had a computer and few had video recorders. There wasn't even much on telly – just three channels, all of which shut up shop around midnight. Like their grandparents, 1970s' kids really did make their own entertainment, even if it consisted of swigging cider in bus shelters rather than playing with hoops and sticks. Kids' comics had a captive audience – there really wasn't a lot else going on – and the punk fanzines followed suit. And when a few Geordies crossbred a comic with a fanzine, they spawned the virile mongrel that is *Viz*. Perhaps the Internet will make this whole process a thing of the past. After all, it's now far easier to set up your own site on the World Wide Web than it once was to print a few dozen homemade magazines, and sell them in your local pub.

Yet even if *Viz* doesn't last forever, and there's nothing to replace it, it'll still have far more to say about modern Britain than any number of highbrow publications. 'If the future generations look back on the literature of the age, they'll more usefully look back to *Viz* than they would, for instance, the novels of Peter Ackroyd or Julian Barnes,' said Auberon Waugh, 'because *Viz* has got a genuine vitality of its own which comes from the society which it represents.'[36] Waugh was right, as usual. It's always the populist art forms that tell us most about the world we live in. And, more to the point, they're usually more entertaining too. 'We pride ourselves on the fact that you're no cleverer when you've read *Viz*,' says Graham. 'You might have had a few laughs but you've not learnt anything.'

'I've heard many people say that *Viz* has only got one joke which it repeats endlessly,' writes Steve Bell, creator of the *Guardian*'s daily cartoon strip, IF. 'This is true, but only in the same sense that Poussin painted a lot of one-track abstruse shepherd gags. For the begetters of *Viz* are true classicists of the toilet form. What is striking about their work is not its grossly explicit over-the-top rudeness but its classical restraint.'[37] After all, as Bell points out, Rubens was a tit and bum man, too.

In the end, the only difference between high and low culture is how long it's been around. An awful lot of stuff that's revered today was dismissed as pap when it first appeared. William Hogarth's bawdy engravings would look very much at home in *Viz* – especially his *Rake's Progress* or *Marriage à la Mode*. Hogarth portrayed lads on the pull, getting pissed and chasing tarts – Sid the Sexist and the Fat Slags in frock coats and powdered wigs. Today there's a statue of Hogarth in Chiswick, calling him the father of modern painting. Maybe one day they'll put up a statue of Chris and Simon and their pals in Jesmond, calling them the kid brothers of modern comics. Hogarth was born in 1697. His statue finally went up in 2000. Which means *Viz* fans should only have to wait about another three hundred years.

'We pride ourselves on the fact that you're no cleverer when you've read *Viz*. You might have had a few laughs but you've not learnt anything.'

The misleading cover on this compilation of Viz cartoons ensured it became a bestseller in 2004.

THE VERY BEST OF
WAKEY SHAKEY!
VIZ
THE SEXIST
BOOK
Roger's
PROFANISAURUS
with a foreword by TERRY JONES
the Ultimate
SWEARING DICTIONARY
WHAHEY
VIZ
ON VIDEO
18
RUBBER
THE
ROGER
MELLIE
£1.75
MC BILLY VANILLI ICE CREAM 'T'
Featuring the F.U. POSSE
Bags of Fun
with Bust
DESPERATE SID'S
PIE EATERS' CLUB
Roger Mellie's
AD BREAK
VIZ
ON VIDEO
18
SID THE SEXIST

PART TWO **THE CHARACTERS**

THE FAT SLAGS

'I can remember the day we wrote the first Fat Slags strip,' recalls Thorpy. 'Usually an idea for a cartoon comes out in the course of conversation, but that was a deliberate attempt to come up with a strong character.'

'It's very unusual that that happens,' agrees Graham, who draws the strip, and writes the bulk of the scripts with Thorpy. 'Normally something comes to you and you think, ooh, that'll make a good character. You'll see somebody or something, but this was done the other way. We actually sat down and actively tried to think of a character.' And they came up with a couple of grotesque crackers – Sandra and Tracey, aka the Fat Slags.

No other comic strip divides the Great British public quite like the Fat Slags. Some people swear by them. Other people swear about them. Even Simon, creator of Sid the Sexist and Millie Tant, had his doubts about the title. But it's surely no coincidence that sales hit their seven-figure peak shortly after Sandra and Tracey first appeared. And although a lot of women can't stand them, plenty of other women enjoy them – and some even cheer them on. To their critics, they reveal how men really view women. To their apologists, they're girls on top, beating the blokes at their own game. And to their fans, they're simply the funniest thing in the entire comic. When visiting football supporters chant 'We're only here for the slappers', you know they're paying homage to the Fat Slags. 'The Fat Slags are feminist icons because they are not men's stereotypical women,' says John. 'They're heroines.'

Not everyone is that enthusiastic. In 1997, the Independent Television Commission received over 300 complaints about

Sandra and Tracey, the Fat Slags, make their first appearance in issue 36, summer 1989.

Left: Production polaroids taken during the making of the first Fat Slags animated video. Overleaf: The very first sketches made of the Fat Slags.

a Fat Slags commercial for Lucozade, objecting to the word 'slag' and the 'negative, stereotyped portrayal of the overweight.' The bad language complaint was upheld. 'It's the same old story – it's ironic, it's satire, stop being humourless and live with it,' wrote Katherine Viner in the *Guardian*. 'But by accepting the irony, we are also accepting the premise on which the Fat Slags is founded: that women who enjoy sex are slags, that "slag" is an acceptable term to describe a woman, that women who are fat and enjoy sex are disgusting.'[42]

'Women who are happy with their size and who go out and dominate men in order to achieve their own objectives can be quite amusing in certain exaggerated comic book situations,' responded Chris, in a letter to the paper. 'The Fat Slags were, at the outset at least, accurate caricatures of real people.'[43] But the most persuasive response came from a female fan. 'I am a frequent reader of the magazine and I have never been offended by its portrayals of women,' wrote Ivy Garlitz of Felixstowe. '*Viz* shows women in a critical light, but it exposes its male characters in equally critical ways. For all its sexist comments (towards both sexes) it makes valid points about modern Britain.'[44] And whether you approve of them or not, a Saturday night stroll around Newcastle's Bigg Market should convince you that San and Tray's antics really are rooted in reality. 'It hit home because it's true,' says Brian Sandells, owner of the Kard Bar in Newcastle. 'I could see exactly what they were talking about and I think everybody can.' Which is why it's so ironic that, like their creators, Graham and Thorpy, the Fat Slags aren't from Tyneside at all. 'Graham always thought they were from Nottingham and I always assumed they were from Leeds,' says Thorpy.

Oh well, at least Sid the Sexist is a Geordie through and through.

7.5
130

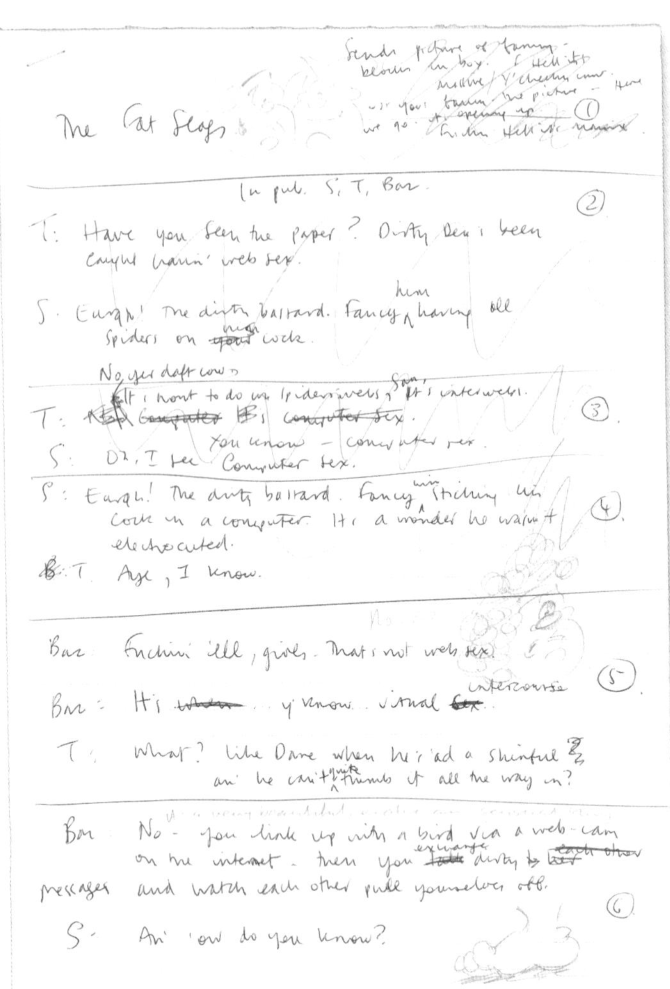

The Fat Slags (1)

In pub. S, T, Baz. (2)

T: Have you seen the paper? Dirty Den's been caught havin' web sex.

S. Eurgh! The dirty bastard. Fancy him havin' all spiders on his cock.

No, yer daft cow. It's nowt to do wi' spiders webs, San, it's interweb. (3)
T: It's computer sex.
S: Oh, I see. You know – computer sex.

S: Eurgh! The dirty bastard. Fancy stickin' his cock in a computer. It's a wonder he wasn't electrocuted. (4)

T. Aye, I know.

Baz Fuckin' 'ell, girls. That's not web sex. (5)

Baz: It's … y'know … virtual intercourse.

T: What? Like Dave when he's 'ad a skinful an' he can't quite thumb it all the way in?

Baz No – you link up with a bird via a web-cam on the internet. Then you exchange dirty messages and watch each other pull yourselves off. (6)

S: An' 'ow do you know?

Baz: Ow do I know? I've got a computer, me. (7)
Baz: I do web sex all the fuckin' time.

Baz: That's me handle.

Baz: I was havin' it last night with some bird in Adelaide. Juicy Lucy 9368. (8)

Tay: Ooo?
S: That's a fuckin' stupid name.

Baz: That's the point, see. It's anonymous. Everybody has to pick a nom de plume. (9)

S: A what?
Baz: A handle. I'm Dirk Diamondcutter 712.

S: Well I'm jealous. You having web-sex is like cheating on me. (10)

T: Aye, not to mention your

Baz: … her out of this. She'd have my knackers on a plate if she knew I was watching some Aussie tart flick her bean.

Above: Extracts from a script for a recent Fat Slags strip. Below: Preparatory sketch and finished T-shirt produced for Blyth Spartans football club.

JOHNNY FARTPANTS

'The idea was, it was going to be the ultimate *Viz* character,' says Simon, 'in that it was very much like a British comic and yet it was about schoolboy humour which had never been in print.' It also established a way of working that still thrives at *Viz* today, with one person doing the drawing, and everyone else collaborating on the script. 'That was the first time that more than one person had actually worked on a cartoon,' says Chris. 'Previously everybody did their own cartoons on their own.' Maybe that was one of the things that made this cartoon such a hit, but there was something else as well. 'It's funny because it's taboo,' says Simon, who created and drew Johnny. 'Twelve-year-old kids all find farts and toilets and willies very funny, but because they're told not to laugh at them they never grow out of it. What we've done is provide a joke for people who never realized others think these sort of thoughts as well.'[45]

Right: Cover artwork for the Johnny Fartpants 'Old Gold Rope' compilation, published May 2000.

Below: A cut-out dress-up doll, printed on the back page of issue 29, April 1988.

FREE! JOHNNY FARTPANTS FARTING FIGURINE

Here is your chance to put the pumps in Johnny's bottom!! Our artist has prepared a picture of your favourite guffing boy-blunder for you to colour, stand up and dress in a choice of three fantastic costumes.

Here's what to do...

1. Using crayons or coloured pencils colour-in Johnny, his outfits and his gas-clouds.
2. Cut roughly around him then paste onto an empty cornflakes packet. Now cut him out carefully, fold back his base at the dotted lines and cut a slot along the line marked 'A'.
3. Cut out Johnny's outfits and choose the one you want him to wear first, now put it in place and fold back the tabs.
4. Now cut out and choose a pump (you can use your own favourite guff-noise by filling in the blank gas-cloud provided), slip the thin end of the pump under Johnny's clothes and through the slot 'A' until it is firmly in place.
5. Stand your 'Stand-up 3-D Farting Figurine' anywhere you wish and remember you can change his costume any time you like.

HONK!

QUACK!

!

ANO-ROD

A

EIGHT ACE

'The inspiration for Eight Ace was a man Simon saw in his local off-licence,' says Thorpy, who draws the character. 'He went up to the counter and all he said was "Eight Ace". The shopkeeper just handed over the beer and the man handed over his money. No other words were exchanged. Somebody in the *Daily Telegraph* likened Eight Ace to Prometheus out of Greek mythology, because he's tragically going through the same process every day. Only Eight is drinking cheap beer and wetting his trousers rather than pushing a rock up Mount Olympus.'

Top: Eight Ace makes his first appearance in issue 74, October 1995.
Opposite: Finished cartoon and traced drawings for a dialogue-free strip in issue 126, summer 2003.

ACE LAGER
Sunny Delight
ACE LAGER
PATEL'S 24 HOUR
ACE LAGER

ROGER MELLIE
HELLO, GOOD EVENING AND WELCOME
THE MAN ON THE TELLY

IT'S A BUSY DAY FOR ROGER. HE'S GOT A MEETING AT T.V. CENTRE
AH HELLO ROGER. THIS IS MR WEST, HEAD OF DOCUMENTARIES
YES. WE WERE JUST THINKING ABOUT A TITLE FOR YOUR NEW SERIES, ROGER

BUT I THOUGHT WE'D ALREADY SETTLED ON 'BASTARD WORLD IN ACTION'...
ERM. NO ROGER..
WELL, I THINK WE DECIDED THAT WAS A BIT TOO SIMILAR TO 'WORLD IN ACTION', ON I.T.V., ACTUALLY

YEAH, I SEE WHAT YOU MEAN. HMM! DIFFICULT ISN'T IT.... HOW ABOUT 'PANOR-FUCKING-RAMA' THEN?
NO ROGER. GAVIN AND I WERE THINKING THAT WE SHOULD CHOOSE A TITLE WHICH FITS THE SHOW...

AND I THINK WE DECIDED ON 'UK TODAY'. IT'S SIMPLE AND HAS A CATCHY RHYME TO IT AS WELL!
...SO DOES 'ARSEHOLE NEWS AND BASTARD VIEWS'. HOW ABOUT THAT GAVIN?

NO, SORRY ROGER. WE DON'T WANT ANYTHING VULGAR. IT'S AN EARLY EVENING SHOW. A NEWS DOCUMENTARY, Y'KNOW. I THINK WE SHOULD TRY TO KEEP IT CLEAN, OKAY
OH YEAH! OF COURSE. I CAN SEE THAT...

SO WHY NOT JUST KEEP IT SIMPLE? HOW ABOUT 'CUNT'?

I THINK YOU'D BETTER GO TO THE STATION CONTROLLER'S OFFICE, ROGER. HE WANT'S TO SEE YOU.
HMM!
I THINK IT'S ABOUT LAST NIGHTS NEWS HEADLINES. HE'S HAD SOME COMPLAINTS. WE'LL SORT THIS TITLE OUT LATER.

LATER...
YOU WANTED TO SEE ME? I SUPPOSE IT'S ABOUT THE SHODDY CAMERA WORK ON LAST NIGHTS NEWS. WE OUGHT TO GET SOMETHING DONE ABOUT IT...
CONTROLLERS OFFICE
NO ROGER. I'VE GOT A COMPLAINT HERE FROM 10 DOWNING STREET. IT'S ABOUT SOMETHING YOU SAID. I DON'T SUPPOSE THE PHRASE "MARGARET TWATTING THATCHER" RINGS A BELL?

Above: An early Roger Mellie strip from issue 7, drawn by Chris in 1981.

Right: Viz boxer shorts camera ready artwork, 1988.

Opposite: A later strip, drawn by Graham.

I'VE GOT A
BIG COCK

ROGER MELLIE

The inspiration for Roger Mellie actually stems from a specific incident. Chris & Co had been invited along to the local television station to talk about the comic, when they overheard a presenter called Rod Griffith swearing in the canteen. It was the incongruity of hearing this mild-mannered professional curse that inspired the creation of Roger Mellie – the most badly behaved anchorman in the history of British broadcasting. However any resemblance between fact and fiction finished right there in that TV canteen. 'Roger Mellie isn't like Rod Griffith,' assures Simon. 'Rod Griffith was actually a really nice guy. He wasn't a fanny rat like Roger Mellie.'

ROGER MELLIE
THE MAN ON THE TELLY
4.00 am. AT TOM, THE DIRECTOR'S HOUSE...
ZZZZ!
TOM THE DIRECTOR

DRING! DRING!.. DRING! DRING!..
EH!?..WASSAT!?

ER...ERM... HELLO!?
ROGER! DO YOU KNOW WHAT TIME IT IS?
WHAT THE HELL DO YOU WANT?

I'M IN TROUBLE, TOM. BIG TROUBLE
GOD! WHAT'S HAPPENED, ROGER?
ARE YOU IN PRISON OR SOMETHING?
WORSE THAN THAT, TOM... THEY'VE PUT ME IN THE FUCKIN' SAUCE CLINIC

I'M FACING UP TO IT, TOM. I'VE GOT A PROBLEM, BUT I CAN'T DO IT ON MY OWN I NEED YOUR HELP... YOUR SUPPORT. PLEASE

DON'T WORRY, ROGER. I'LL BE OVER FIRST THING IN THE MORNING. YOU CAN RELY ON ME

THANKS, TOM. THAT'S GREAT. WE'LL HAVE A CHAT... SORT THIS THING OUT, ONCE AND FOR ALL, EH? LOOK FORWARD TO SEEING YOU...
OH, JUST ONE THING, TOM...

DO ME A FAVOUR AND BRING A BOTTLE OF KETCHUP IN Y' POCKET, WILL YOU?
...I'M FUCKIN' CHOKIN' FOR A DRINK

NEXT MORNING...
WELCOME TO THE BETTY FORD-CAPRI CLINIC FOR PISSED UP CELEBS £3000 per WEEK

...AND THIS IS ME!
BLOOAGH!

HI, ROGER. NICE TO SEE YOU. HOW ARE YOU FEE...
FUCK THE SMALLTALK, TOM. COME ON, LET THE DOG SEE THE RABBIT

WOR! THANKS, TOM, EH! I KNEW I COULD COUNT ON YOU. LET ME NECK THIS TWAT FIRST, EH? WE CAN HAVE A CHIN WAG LATER. THANKS AGAIN, MATE.

EH!? YOU FUCKING CUNT... WHAT'S THIS?
SORRY, ROGER. BUT IT'S FOR YOUR OWN GOOD
YOU'RE HERE TO DRY OUT

NO... THE DOCTOR SAID I COULD HAVE ONE OR TWO... HONEST... FOR MY BREAKFAST... JUST TO GET ME GOING
LOOK, ROGER. THE FIRST STEP ON THE ROAD TO RECOVERY IS ADMITTING YOU'VE GOT A PROBLEM

OH, I ADMIT THERE'S A PROBLEM, TOM... THREE FUCKIN' GRAND A WEEK AND THIS PLACE HASN'T EVEN GOT A BAR!..
THAT'S THE PROBLEM

I MEAN, FUCK ME, TOM. EVERYONE IN T.V. LIKES THEIR POP. IT GOES WITH THE TERRITORY

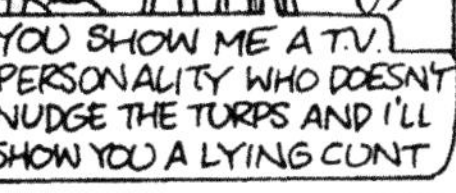
YOU SHOW ME A T.V. PERSONALITY WHO DOESN'T NUDGE THE TURPS AND I'LL SHOW YOU A LYING CUNT

BUT I'M A PRO, TOM. I DON'T LET IT INTERFERE WITH MY WORK
OH, NO? WHAT ABOUT THE 50 TAKES TO SAY 'HELLO, GOOD EVENING AND WELCOME'?
A CASE IN POINT, TOM. WE GOT IT IN THE CAN EVENTUALLY.

YEH! BUT IT TOOK 20 MINUTES AND THE SHOW WAS GOING OUT LIVE!
I CAN'T HELP BEING A PERFECTIONIST
ROGER! YOUR EYES ARE GLAZED, YOUR SPEECH IS SLURRED, AND YOU SHAKE VISIBLY IN FRONT OF CAMERA

WELL, WHAT'S THE FUCKIN' P.R. DEPARTMENT FOR? PUT IT OUT I'VE GOT PARKINSON'S DISEASE OR SOMETHING, I DON'T KNOW...
JUST GET ME A FUCKIN' DRINK!

NO, ROGER... I CAN'T HELP YOU THERE. NO ONE CAN HELP YOU UNTIL YOU FIRST HELP YOURSELF
YOU'RE RIGHT, TOM...
I NEED TO HELP MYSELF... AND THAT'S WHAT I'M GOING TO DO

COME ON, TOM. LET'S GO BACK TO MY ROOM AND CRACK OPEN A BOTTLE OF LUCOZADE, EH?
HA! HA! HA! THAT'S MORE LIKE IT, ROGER

SHORTLY...

TIME FOR YOUR LETTUCE AND CELERY ENEMA MR. MELLIE
KNOCK! KNOCK!

EEEK!
GNNNGH! GNNGH!

MEANWHILE, AT A NEARBY OFF LICENSE...
QUICK!..
...GIMME A BOTTLE OF THE NEAREST THING TO YOU... AND A FUNNEL

Over 700 rude words & phrases

PRESENTS

Roger's PROFANISAURUS

- *Incomplete & abridged.*
- *An essential glossary of expletives, profanities and sexual euphemisms.*
- *Ideal for use in the home and office.*

Fulchester University Press
Free with Viz issue 87 - not to be sold separately

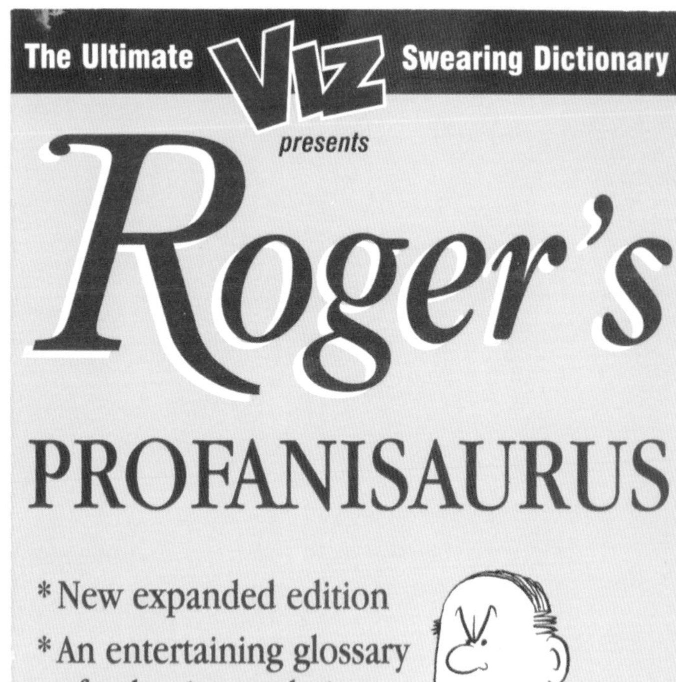

The Ultimate Viz Swearing Dictionary

presents

Roger's PROFANISAURUS

* New expanded edition
* An entertaining glossary of vulgarity, expletives, colourful obscenity and sexual euphemism
* Ideal for use in the home and office

Over 2,250 rude words and phrases

Hundreds more rude words and phrases

Roger's PROFANISAURUS 3

An all new collection of expletives, obscenities & euphemisms

Fulchester University Press
Free with Viz issue 98 - not to be sold separately

This page: Various incarnations of Roger's Profanisaurus *including free cover-mounts from issues 87 and 98, the original best selling paperback version and one of the early updates included in the magazine.*

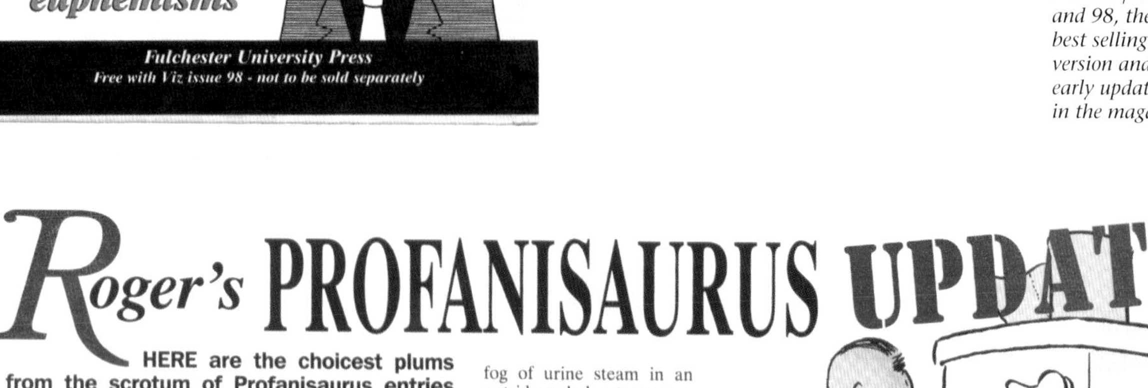

Roger's PROFANISAURUS UPDATE

HERE are the choicest plums from the scrotum of Profanisaurus entries we've received for this issue. Thanks to everyone who sent one in. Send all your entries to Ribena de Farquah-Toss, Viz Comic, PO Box 1PT, Newcastle upon Tyne, NE99 1PT or send them elecrolytically to profanisaurus@letterbocks.com

me descend to her ladygarden. After fifty years of widowhood, I found her to be considerably aroused. It was like being hit in the face with a clown's pie". (from *"The*

fog of urine steam in an outside pub lavatory on a cold winter's evening.

pram fat *n.* See *plum sauce*

put the red lights on *v. Nav.* To have a silent *wank* in bed so as not to disturb the wife. Also *silent running, American Beauty.*

put to the sword *v.* To make love to. *"From the Charing Cross Theatre where I saw Mr. Herbert give his*

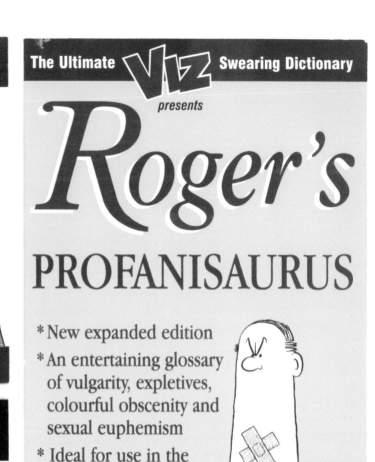

Left: The much expanded, hardback edition of Roger's Profanisaurus, published in 2002.
Below: The original cover rough.

Bottom: Tasteful artwork drawn for a recent update in the magazine.
Overleaf: Script for the animated version of Roger Mellie, signed by Peter Cook who provided Roger's voice.

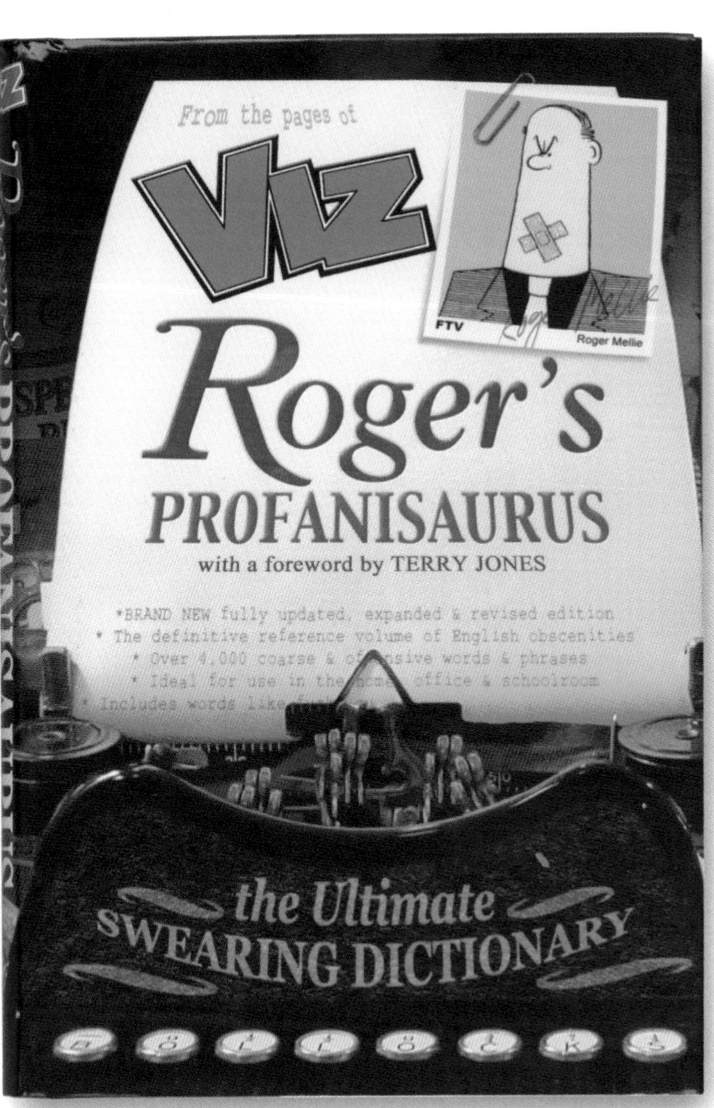

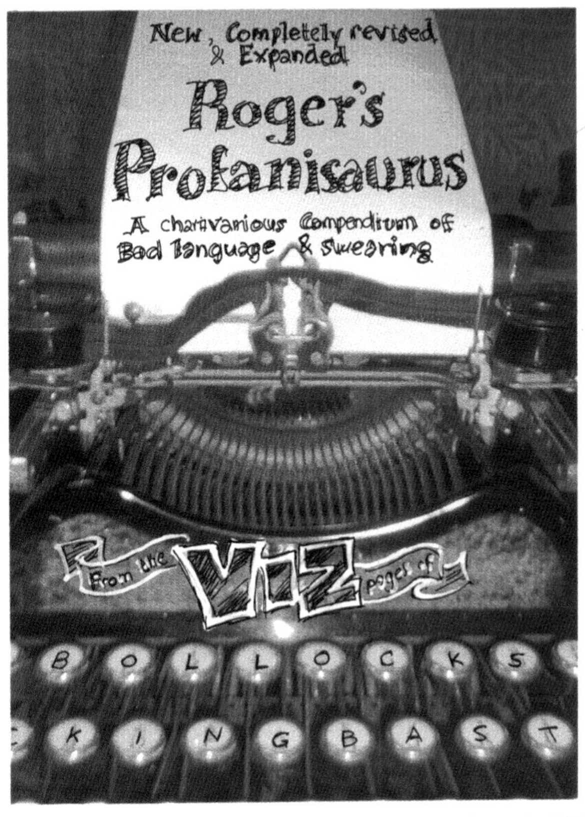

ROGER MELLIE - EPISODES 1-7 DATE 23.05.91 PAGE 1

EPISODE 4 - **"CELEBRITY GOLF"** 3 MINUTES ~~CHANNEL FOUR.~~ 6 MINUTES VIDEO

HI THORPY

01) NARRATOR: Sunday morning. . . .

02) ROGER: (BLEARY BUT ANGRY) Who the fuck's that? Don't you know what day it is?

03) TOM: Roger? It's me, Tom. Have you forgotten? You're supposed to be taking part in Fulchester T.V.'s first Celebrity Golf Tournament today. You should have been HERE at the Golf Club over an hour ago!

04) LADY 1: (SEXILY) Who is it Roger?

05) LADY 2: (LIKEWISE) Oh. . .my toes are getting cold. . .will you warm them up again for me Roger?

06) ROGER: SHUT UP WILL YOU. It's Business. (QUIETLY) Listen Tom. I'm a bit tied up right now. I er. . . .HIT THE JACKPOT last night, and I've erm . . got BOTH my hands full if you see what I mean.

07) TOM: (MOUNTING FURY) I don't care what you're up to, Roger. Everyone's here. Tarby, Brucey. They'll all waiting. AND I've got a whole crew here on overtime sitting doing nothing!

8) ROGER: Okay, okay. Cool it Tom. Don't get excited. Just buy everyone a couple of drinks, relax, and I'll be there in twenty minutes.

09) NARRATOR: Two Hours Later. . .

Mr Logic pages from the Viz calendars for 1993 and 1994.

Mr Logic wants to know, upon which train he ought to go,
But BR staff don't have the brains, to know about the times of trains.
And they couldn't give a fuck anyway.

OCTOBER

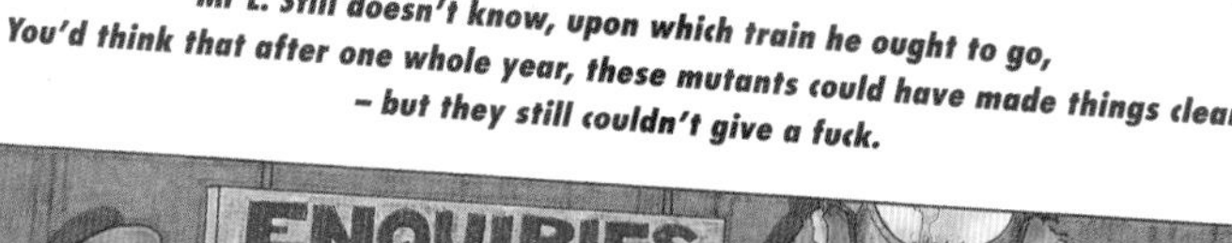

Mr L. Still doesn't know, upon which train he ought to go,
You'd think that after one whole year, these mutants could have made things clear
– but they still couldn't give a fuck.

October

MR LOGIC

'Mr Logic was a very simple one to do,' explains Simon, the strip's creator. And one of the reasons he was so simple is because Simon based him on his big brother, Steve. 'We always thought that he sort of modelled himself on Mr Spock,' says Simon. 'He looks at every situation very logically, which has been absolutely his winning trait in his career because he's got a great imagination, but he's also got tremendous technical and engineering ability.'

So just how similar is Steve Donald to the character in the comic? 'Obviously, Mr Logic is an exaggerated version,' says Simon, 'but not by a lot, it's got to be said.' Simon's exaggerating too, of course – any actual similarity is really very slight. Although Steve is well aware of his resemblance to Mr Logic, it was still quite a surprise to discover he'd inspired the character – especially as he first found out along with millions of other people, when Chris told Terry Wogan on his chat show on peaktime TV.

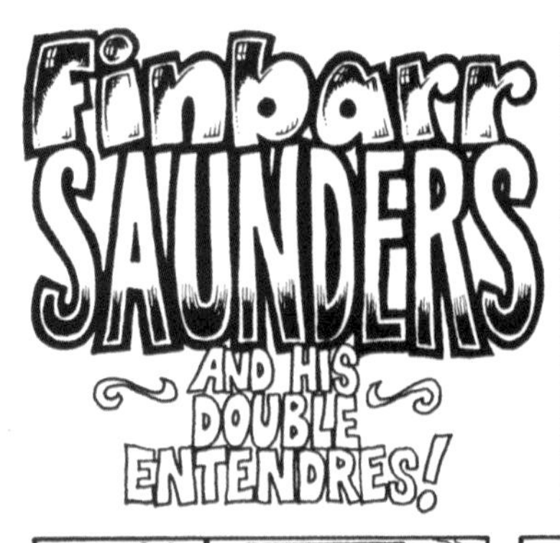

Issue 28 1 page.

FINBARR SAUNDERS

'Finbarr is just a cross between a small boy and Sid Boggle out of *Carry On Camping*,' says Thorpy. 'He is one of the few characters who never says anything. He just makes noises to indicate where the jokes are supposed to be. Mary Whitehouse once said that double entendres are the cheapest sort of humour. Mind you, she also once told an audience from the Festival of Light that she was being palmed off by the Director General of the BBC, so she didn't mind going for the odd cheap laugh herself.'

Opposite: Original artwork for an early Finbarr strip in issue 28, February 1988. Above: Point of sale poster from 1988. Left: Computer-coloured style-guide design.

SID THE SEXIST

Like Roger Mellie or Mr Logic, Sid the Sexist was inspired by a real person. And like Roger Mellie and Mr Logic, the real person is actually nothing like the character in the strip. 'We had this friend who was an intellectual guy, a mathematician, and he had a great sense of humour,' says Simon, 'but he was very shy around women. He was a bit older than us and he wanted to ask this girl out and he didn't know how to do it. He wasn't brave enough. And he came round to see me and Chris to sort of seek a little bit of backing. Basically, he was just looking for us to sort of encourage him into doing it.' Chris and Simon did their best. 'You've got nothing to worry about,' they told him. 'Even if she doesn't want to go out with you she'll be flattered that somebody wants to go out with her.' In the end, he decided to ask her out by letter, and having composed a chivalrous little note, he set off to post it through her letterbox. However as he left Chris and Simon's house, this polite intellectual underwent a Jekyll & Hyde transformation. 'Aye lads,' he said, 'so you reckon this is going to pull the totty, or what?'

'When he got into the real world he couldn't be himself, and it was such an obvious thing to play with,' says Simon. 'The guy who wants to be the macho man, and in the public eye has to be seen to be a macho man, but in truth is a mouse.' And so Simon came up with Sid the Sexist. 'He doesn't know what to do,' says Simon. 'He can't actually admit to the world that he's a nice guy because everyone will think less of him for it.'

Simon created the strip, and he's almost always drawn it. He's also the main writer, though everyone else has contributed material along the way. Graham collaborated on the artwork for Sid's book, *The Joy of Sexism*, but lately his main collaborator has been Alex, because, like Simon, he likes going out on the town. And it's out on the town that they often find the inspiration for the next strip. 'A lot of the banter in it is proper banter that he'd have down the pub with his mates,' says Alex. 'He'll sometimes base a story around something that someone said to him down the pub.' Another reason that Alex is an especially useful

The first Sid the Sexist cartoon, from issue 9, November 1982.

collaborator for Sid the Sexist is that like Sid, he's Tyneside born and bred. 'Sid the Sexist is as Geordie as you can get,' confirms Steve. 'Simon knows which road in Byker he lives on.' He's even appeared on his own special edition bottle of Newcastle Brown Ale.

Like Alf Garnett or Loadsamoney, some people laugh with Sid the Sexist as well as at him, but only the most blinkered feminist or chauvinist could fail to see whose side this strip is on, 'Sid the Sexist has done more against sexism than any amount of well-meaning government schemes,' says John. 'You've got, at one stage, thirty per cent of all men aged between eighteen and forty in England reading a character called Sid the Sexist, who makes oafish sexist comments and has oafish sexist attitudes, like a lot of them, and ends up being ridiculed and not being shagged.' And yet even though Sid's virginity remains intact, some lads still look up to him. 'Lots of blokes do love Sid,' marvels Simon. 'It's a bit ironic that their hero is a completely inept virgin.'[46]

Left: In 2002 Scottish & Newcastle produced a limited edition run of Sid the Sexist Brown Ale to raise money for the Sammy Johnson Memorial Fund. Sammy had provided Sid's voice for the animated cartoon.
Below: 1996 saw the publication of The Joy of Sexism.

SID (1)

SID THE SEXIST

19 FEB 1992

JOE (1)

BOB (1)

Character model sheets produced by Simon as reference for animators working on the unbroadcast Channel 4 TV series.

BAZ (1)

HEIGHT COMPARISON

This is to certify that a cheque from

Ronald Hackston

has attained the requisite level of £6.00 sterling and has thus qualified him as a full blown member of

Desperate Sid's
Hairy Pie Eaters' Club

Signed Sidney Smutt

Sidney Smutt,
Life President

For Job application purposes, this certificate is equivalent to 4 GCSEs at grade C or above, and covers the bearer for the ownership of a colour television. It may also be used as full proof of identity as required by immigration officials, customs officers and police. In addition, it serves as a full car, motorcycle and HGV driving licence (including track laying vehicles) in most non-EEC countries.

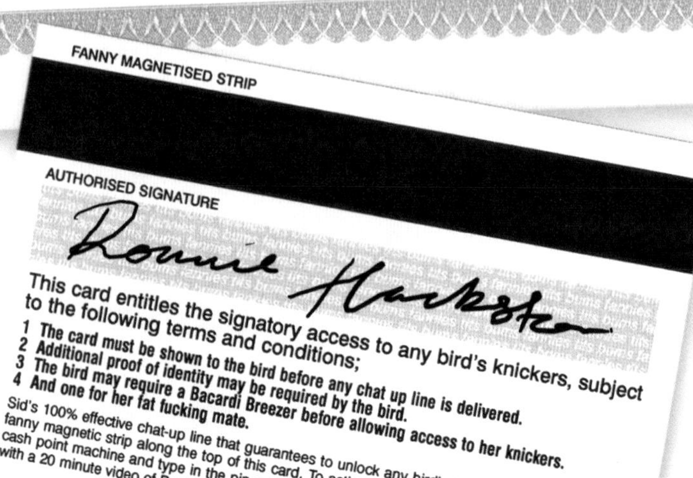

FANNY MAGNETISED STRIP
AUTHORISED SIGNATURE
Ronnie Hackston
This card entitles the signatory access to any bird's knickers, subject to the following terms and conditions;
1 The card must be shown to the bird before any chat up line is delivered.
2 Additional proof of identity may be required by the bird.
3 The bird may require a Bacardi Breezer before allowing access to her knickers.
4 And one for her fat fucking mate.
Sid's 100% effective chat-up line that guarantees to unlock any bird's knickers is encoded in the fanny magnetic strip along the top of this card. To activate it, insert the card into any high-street cash point machine and type in the pin number 69. The phrase will appear on the screen, along with a 20 minute video of Pamela Anderson sucking off Tommy Lee on a yacht.

Original badge, certificate, and member's 'gash card' from Desperate Sid's Hairy Pie Eater's Club.

RAVEY DAVEY GRAVY

Graham has always drawn Ravey Davey Gravy, but as a bloke in his forties with a wife and family, he happily admits that he knows absolutely nothing about the rave scene. Luckily Alex is still in his early twenties, and he was happy to help him out. 'It was always him who'd sit down and write it with us because he knew what they were up to,' says Graham. And when Alex couldn't help, he'd stick his head round the office next door, where Andy Inman handled *Viz* distribution. 'There was a bloke called Darryl who used to work in Andy's office and he used to MC these clubs,' says Graham. 'What are they doing?' Graham would ask him. 'Are they still wearing white gloves?' 'Oh no,' Darryl would tell him. 'That was last week.'

Original artwork for the cover illustration of issue 117, July 2002.

BIG VERN

'Big Vern's surname is Dakin, in honour of Vic Dakin who Richard Burton played in that film *Villain*,' says Davey. 'He's basically an amalgam of every cockney villain out of the Sweeney and he kills himself at the end of every strip. Chris drew him originally, but now Thorpy does it because he enjoys drawing all the bits of brains and skull flying about. Probably a bit too much, come to think about it.'

Left: A recent Big Vern, drawn by Thorpy.
Below: A 1982 strip, drawn by Chris.
Opposite: Computer-coloured style-guide design.

BIFFA BACON

'All my inspiration used to come from watching people,' reveals Chris. 'I started Biffa Bacon after seeing two kids fighting in a train in front of their parents. One of the fathers went up and instead of stopping them whispered to his boy: "Go on son, I'm right behind you."'[38]

Opposite top: Biffa's debut in issue 7, 1981.
Opposite bottom: A more recent strip, drawn by Graham.
This page: Original artwork with colour separation overlay possibly for a Biffa Bacon T-shirt, 1988.

Bottom: The Billy the Fish Football Yearbook, *published in 1990, reprinted the first 35 episodes of the popular/unpopular adventure strip. Right: An uneventful episode from 2003.*

BILLY THE FISH

'Readers' opinions were always split about Billy,' recalls Graham. 'Half of them thought it was shit, the other half thought it was really shit. The *Dandy* and the *Beano* always had wordy stuff like the Shipwrecked Circus that you only read as a last resort when you'd finished everything else, so we thought we'd better have a strip like that. It was also the only strip drawn in grey, which made it look even duller. Recently it ran for nearly a year as a weekly cartoon in the *London Evening Standard* until sharp-eyed editors spotted how shit it was. They still owe us for the last four months' worth.'

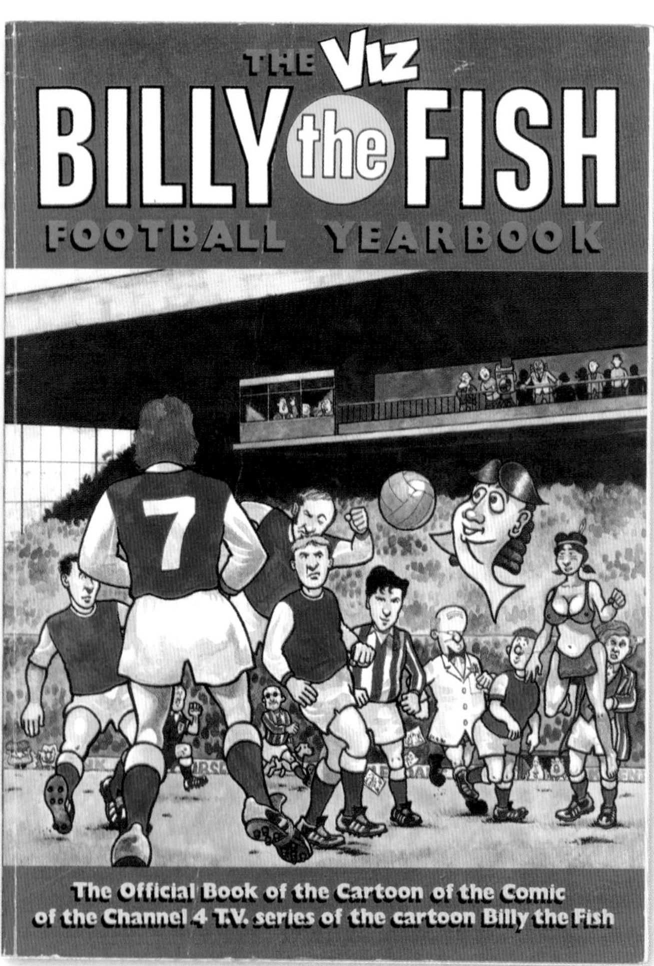

THE VIZ
BILLY the FISH
FOOTBALL YEARBOOK
7
The Official Book of the Cartoon of the Comic of the Channel 4 T.V. series of the cartoon Billy the Fish

BILLY the FISH
THIS SPACE STILL FOR SALE. WHY NOT
E MAIL viz@viz.co.uk for details. CASH PREFERRED OBVI
BORN HALF MAN HALF FISH, GOALIE BILLY THOMSON IS SPOTTED PLAYING IN THE PARK BY FULCHESTER UNITED BOSS TOMMY BROWN BUT IS KIDNAPPED BY GUS PARKER, BOSS OF ARCH RIVALS GRIMTHORPE ON THE EVE OF HIS DEBUT AND REPLACED WITH A BALLOON, WHICH IS SHOT BY UNITED'S UNSETTLED RESERVE KEEPER TERRY JACKSON. MEANWHILE, DISCREDITED HYPNOTIST ROMANO TRIES TO MESMERISE BILLY INTO PLAYING FOR GRIMTHORPE BUT ACCIDENTALLY KILLS HIM. NOTWITHSTANDING, FULCHESTER ARE ABOUT TO WIN THE MATCH WHEN RUTHLESS MILLIONAIRE MAXWELL BAXTER ANNOUNCES PLANS TO DEMOLISH THE STADIUM, BUT HE TURNS OUT TO BE A CARDBOARD FAKE AND BILLY - NOT DEAD AFTER ALL AND AT THE CONTROLS OF A JET POWERED BALL - WINS THE MATCH FOR UNITED. THE REAL MAXWELL BAXTER APPEARS AND EXPELLS UNITED FROM THE LEAGUE, BUT HE TURNS OUT TO BE A CARDBOARD FAKE TOO. COACH SYD PRESTON IS SHOT AND THE REINSTATED UNITED SIGN SHAKIN' STEVENS FOR £½M AND ABSEIL ONTO THE PITCH ONLY FOR THEIR STAR SIGNING TO KNOCK HIMSELF OUT. THEN A PUNCTURED BALL MEANS THAT FULCHESTER'S VICTORY IS ALL DOWN TO THE TOSS OF A COIN. THEY LOSE - BUT IT TURNS OUT TO BE BEST OF THREE SO THEY WIN AND ARE SET TO MEET EUROPEANS BONGO GDAZA. TRAINING IS INTERRUPTED WHEN FULCHESTER'S PITCH IS DUG UP TO REVEAL A FLYING SAUCER - THE PROPERTY OF CHAIRMAN RICK SPANGLE WHO ANNOUNCES PLANS TO FLY THE TEAM TO MARS, HOWEVER, ON THEIR WAY TO GDAZA SYD PRESTON EXPLODES AND BILLY IS FORCED TO SWIM FOR HELP. THE RESCUED TEAM ARRIVES IN THE NICK OF TIME BUT BONGO'S MANAGER TRICKS BILLY INTO SIGNING A CONFESSION OF SPYING AND HAS HIM IMPRISONED IN A MINE. HOWEVER, IT'S ALL A DREAM AND BILLY WAKES TO FIND HE HAS BEEN PICKED TO PLAY FOR ENGLAND, BUT GUS PARKER HAS LAID A TRAP AT WEMBLEY AND HE NEARLY DROWNS. MEANWHILE UTD. FIND THEMSELVES RELEGATED TO THE FOURTH DIVISION. LARGE BREASTED REDSKIN WINGER BROWN FOX AND INVISIBLE STRIKER JOHNNY X SAVE THE DAY BUT BILLY IS EXPOSED AS A HEROIN ADDICT. LUCKILY IT'S A DIFFERENT BILLY AND A WELCOME VICTORY AGAINST REDHURST ROVERS LEAVES UTD. LOOKING GOOD IN THE CUP, BUT DISASTER LOOMS WHEN A SHARK MAKES ITS WAY INTO THE CHANGING ROOMS BATH. REVEALED AS A RELATIVELY HARMLESS NURSE SHARK, THE DANGER PASSES AND FULCHESTER LOOK SET FOR THE LEAGUE CHAMPIONSHIP BUT BILLY IS FORCED TO PLAY ON CRUTCHES AND SCORES AN OWN GOAL. IT LOOKS LIKE GRIMTHORPE WILL SECURE PROMOTION UNTIL BILLY SETS UP BROWN FOX FOR A LAST MINUTE WINNER AND UNITED ARE CROWNED LEAGUE CHAMPIONS. BILLY IS BLACKMAILED BY GUS PARKER AND FACES AN EXPLODING PENALTY IN THE DYING SECONDS OF THE FA CUP FINAL. HE DIES SECURING VICTORY AND IS REPLACED BY HIS OWN SON, BILLY, WHO IS ARRESTED FOR THE MURDER OF HIS FAMILY, SENTENCED TO DEATH, PARDONED ETC ETC. THEN SYD PRESTON RUNS INTO UNITED BOSS TOMMY BROWN'S OFFICE WITH SOME DREADFUL NEWS....
TOMMY! IT'S BILLY THE FISH! SOMETHING TERRIBLE HAS HAPPENED!
SORRY, SYD. WE'VE RUN OUT OF SPACE.
What HAS HAPPENED TO BILLY? IS THIS THE END FOR FULCHESTER? DON'T MISS THE NEXT THRILLING INSTALLMENT OF BILLY the FISH IN ISSUE 129!
VIZ 128

Fulchester United team picture, drawn by Chris for The Billy the Fish Football Yearbook. *Back row (left to right): Discredited hypnotist Romano, a cardboard replica of ruthless millionaire Maxwell Baxter, former Archbishop of Canterbury Dr. Robert Runcie, the late Cardinal Basil Hume, millionaire property developer Winyard Hall, 6-footer Boris McGraw, another cardboard replica of Maxwell Baxter, Samantha Brown, old Alf Higson the boot cleaner. Middle row: evil Gus Parker, boss of arch-rivals Grimthorpe City, Wilf, stumpy Argentinian cheat Diego Maradona, millionaire pop star and chairman Rick Spangle, invisible striker Johnny X, large-breasted redskin winger Brown Fox, the referee, top model Cindy Smallpiece, Mick Hucknall out of Simply Red. Front row: unsettled reserve team keeper Terry Jackson, footballing Siamese twins Wing and Wong Wang, Shakin' Stevens, team boss Tommy Brown, coach Syd Preston, Professor Wolfgang Schnell BSc. PhD., Kylie Minogue, defence counsel Norman Wisdom QC, and blind Rex 'Banana Boots' Findlay and his guide dog Shep. Foreground: Young Billy 'The Fish' Thomson, a ball.*

Below: The final strip drawn for the London Evening Standard *in 2003.*

GILBERT RATCHET
"FIXING STUFF ACROSS THE LAND, WITH A SMILE, A SPANNER, AND A HELPING HAND"

MY OLD TOOL KIT HAS JUST ABOUT HAD IT — BUT I HAVEN'T GOT THE MONEY TO BUY A NEW ONE.
DE-LUXE TOOL KITS

HEY GILBERT! I'VE JUST DECIDED TO GIVE UP BEING A GREENGROCER AND EMIGRATE TO AUSTRALIA. I'LL GIVE YOU 50P IF YOU GET RID OF MY OLD STOCK FOR ME.
CLOSED DOWN

WELL THAT WAS AN EASY 50P — BUT WHAT AM I GOING TO DO WITH ALL THESE VEGETABLES?

WHAT'S WRONG, MR BROWN?

I WAS HOPING TO ENJOY A QUIET PINT AT THIS PUB - HOWEVER, THE LOUD AND OBNOXIOUS BEHAVIOUR OF THAT GROUP OF STUDENTS PREVENTS ME FROM SO DOING.
HMM.

A LARGE WOODEN BOX WITH POTATOES AND TURNIPS PASTED TO THE INTERIOR WILL MAKE AN IDEAL SOUNDPROOF BOOTH WHEREIN YOU CAN ENJOY YOUR DRINK IN PEACE.
EXCELLENT.

REWARD

DAMN IT. I AM A KEEN SEXUAL PERVERT, YET AT PRESENT AM UNABLE TO THINK OF ANY BIZZARE AND PHYSICALLY IMPROBABLE ACTIVITIES WHEREBY TO PROCURE CARNAL GRATIFICATION.

PERHAPS I CAN BE OF SOME ASSISTANCE

I JUST ATTACH A CAULIFLOWER TO THE END OF THIS LENGTH OF COILED STEEL WIRE, AND VOILA!
AN UNUSUAL AND POTENTIALLY STIMULATING EROTIC ACCESSORY!

QUICK THINKING, SON! HERE'S A FIVER FOR YOUR TROUBLE.

LATER..
:SIGH: I'D LOVE A PAIR OF PLATFORM SHOES
SPOT-U-LIKE
HOWEVER, THE ONLY ONES ON SALE IN TOWN ARE MADE OF LEATHER, AND MY STRICT VEGETARIAN PRINCIPLES FORBID ME FROM BUYING THEM.

SO..
HOLD STEADY, PLEASE.

SPLENDID! THESE IDEOLOGICALLY SOUND 'RADISH SOLES' MAKE THE PERFECT PLATFORM SHOE SUBSTITUTES!

HMM. SEVEN POUNDS FIFTY. THAT STILL WON'T BE ENOUGH FOR A NEW TOOL KIT.
HEY, YOU!

THE TABLOID PRESS LEARNED OF MY VEGETABLE - RELATED PROCLIVITIES AND, BECAUSE I AM A PROMINENT GOVERNMENT OFFICIAL, THE STORY MADE HEADLINE NEWS!

THAT CAULIFLOWER OF YOURS COST ME MY REPUTATION...
CRACK

...BUT EARNED ME A LUCRATIVE PUBLISHING CONTRACT. PLEASE ACCEPT THIS SMALL PERCENTAGE.
??

I SAY THERE, YOUNG MAN!

I'M MR BROWN'S WIFE - OR RATHER, HIS WIDOW!
IT APPEARS THAT SOMEONE SEALED MY HUSBAND IN AN AIR-TIGHT BOX WITH A NUMBER OF DECAYING VEGETABLES. HE DIED OF ASPHYXIATION SHORTLY AFTERWARDS.

CONSEQUENTLY, I AM ARRANGING THE CATERING FOR AFTER THE FUNERAL. PERHAPS YOU WOULD SELL ME THESE COURGETTES AND RUNNER BEANS?
I CAN MAKE THEM INTO A CASSEROLE, OR A QUICHE PERHAPS.

WELL, THAT'S ALL THE VEGETABLES DISPOSED OF.
EMPTY
AND NOW I HAVE ENOUGH CASH TO BUY THAT TOOL KIT!

I'M SORRY, GILBERT, BUT AS AN ECCENTRIC SHOPKEEPER I CAN ONLY ACCEPT VEGETABLES IN PAYMENT FOR GOODS!
OH NO! JUST MY LUCK!
SORRY NO CASH! VEGETABLES ONLY!
HA HA HA HA HA

34

GILBERT RATCHET

'There's not a lot to say about Gilbert really,' says Davey, who draws the surreal handyman. 'I suppose he was inspired by Screwy Driver who used to be in the *Dandy*. Mind you, Screwy Driver tended to do less genital mutilation of vicars than Gilbert does.'

Opposite: The first Gilbert Ratchet strip, from issue 44 in 1990.

This page: Original artwork of vicar mutilation from various strips.

This page: Detail of style-guide artwork. Opposite top: Original artwork for the Spoilt Bastard page of the free calendar given away with issue 105, December 2000. Opposite bottom: Typical behaviour in a strip from issue 70, February 1995.

SPOILT BASTARD

'Simon went to primary school with a kid whose mum bought him a pair of running spikes for sports day,' says Graham, who draws Timmy Timpson. 'So we thought a spoilt kid character might have a bit of mileage in it. He's also based a bit on my elder brother who used to behave quite badly when he was younger. I, on the other hand, was a model child.'

TASHA SLAPPA

Tasha Slappa was Alex's first comic strip for *Viz*. When he started it, he was still in the sixth form at school. However he'd already done a week's work experience at *Viz*, and they'd encouraged him to keep in touch, so rather than sending it in, he took it into the office to show it to Simon. 'That was great,' says Alex. 'I can still remember him laughing at it.' Simon passed it around the office, and everyone else laughed too. He got a cheque for £350. He didn't want to cash it. The strip was inspired by a mate of his sister's. 'Virtually everything in the first couple of Tasha Slappa comics had actually happened,' he explains. 'It was all stories that went around school.'

Originally, the character was called Kappa Slappa, but after a couple of strips, the Kappa clothing company complained, although the first Alex knew about that was when he came home from school one day to find an official looking letter waiting for him, forwarded from *Viz*. 'They sent me the legal letter for a laugh,' says Alex. 'They thought that was funny.' It was curiously appropriate that this letter should arrive that day. 'Earlier in the day, I'd been smacked by some bloke wearing Kappa who got on the school bus.'

Alex phoned *Viz*, 'sobbing down the phone', but now they'd had their fun, his colleagues quickly put his mind at rest. He wasn't in any personal trouble. The publishers would sort it out. Alex had to change the name to Tasha Slappa, but thankfully for all concerned, this didn't make any difference to the strip. Tasha could have been wearing any leading brand of sporting leisurewear. Kappa simply happened to rhyme with a girls' name. And anyway, Alex has since shifted his attention to Tasha's mum, who doesn't wear any sportswear whatsoever. 'She's old enough to know better, so it's a lot more fun.'

Right: Poster featuring Tasha produced by Alex for a Newcastle travel agent.
Below: Frame from a recent strip.
Opposite: Full colour Tasha strip from issue 102, June 2000.

Tasha Slappa

MORNING...
MAM- AAH'M GANNIN' TU SCHOOL - WHERES ME BAIT MONEY? -DID Y'NOT GET Y' BENEFIT YESTERDAY?

AYE AH FUCKIN' DID. BUT AH INVESTED IT ON 16 SCRATCHCARDS.
MAM MAN!
WHAT HAVE AH TELT YER? YOUR NOSHA'LL GAN FUCKIN' RADGE! THAT WUH HIS BANDIT MONEY
HAD Y' FUCKIN MOOTH. AH SUPPOSE YULL NOT BE WANTING ANY OF THE WINNINGS THEN

Y' WON?!! FUCKIN' GET IN!
AYE. TWELVE QUID. SUR AH TREATED MESELF AND AH SPLASHED OOT ON TWELVE SCRATCHCARDS F' TO CELEBRATE

OUTSIDE...
IT'S FUCKIN' CHUDDY FOR ME DINNER AGAIN, THEN
HOO TASHA!!

AALREET?
HERE- IT'S A FUCKIN' LUSH DAY, SUR WUZ'RE BUNKIN' OFF SCHOOL T' HANG ROOND THE GEET ESCALATORS IN THE SHOPPIN' CENTER
...ARE Y' COMIN'?

AM AH FUCK. AH'M GANNIN' TO SCHOOL
EH?!
ARE YE A FUCKIN' HIPPY?
NA. IT'S FRIDAY.
SCHOOLS FUCKIN' BLISS ON A FRIDAY

EH?! EH?!! WHAAAT?!
AYE MAN. ITS MRS ROSS TODAY. SHE'S FUCKIN' GREAT MAN - ME FAVOURITE TEACHA
...DEAD FUCKIN' SOFT. Y' CAN TELL HER T' FUCK OFF T' HER FACE AND EVERYTHING, AND SHE'LL NOT DE OWT. SPAT IN HER EYE LAST WEEK. FUCKIN' BELTER

SMASH! CRASH! BANG!
HA HA HAA!
ERM... DO YOU THINK YOU MIGHT, ERM, POSSIBLY, CALM DOWN A TOUCH, PLEASE, NATASHA
FUCK OFF Y' BITCH!
MRS ROSS
GAN ON TASHA! DEE A SHIT DOON HER FRIGGIN' BLOWSE!

SWING!
BOO HOO HOOO!!
UTTER CHAOS
WHERE THE FUCKS SHE GANNIN'? SHE'S AANLY JUST GOT BACK FROM HER LAST NERVEOUS BREKDOON

WHEY SHE MUSTN'T WANT HER FUCKIN' PORSE THEN
GET IN! THATS MY BAIT MONEY
SNATCH!
LET WUH GAN SPEND, THEN

BLISTNA BOB! THERES ABOOT TWO SPOND HERE
EEH! WHAT YER GANNA BUY TASHA?
DINING HALL >
CLASSROOMS <
TOILETS >
AH DIVVINT KNAA. WHATEVER SMELLS THE FUCKIN' NICEST

REGAL KING SIZE TODAY KERRY
HALF ON MAN, DONNA
AYE. TWO SPOND
HOO, Y' DAFTY! THEZ TWENTY LEFT ON THIS STILL!
HERE YE- GI'Z A DRAAAW
OOT ME MITT! YEE DUCK ARSE 'EM

AND SO...
SNIFF SNIFF SNIFF!
MMM. THAT SMELLS FUCKIN' LUSH - AH KNAA WHAT MY BAIT MONEY'S GANNIN' ON - SLURP!

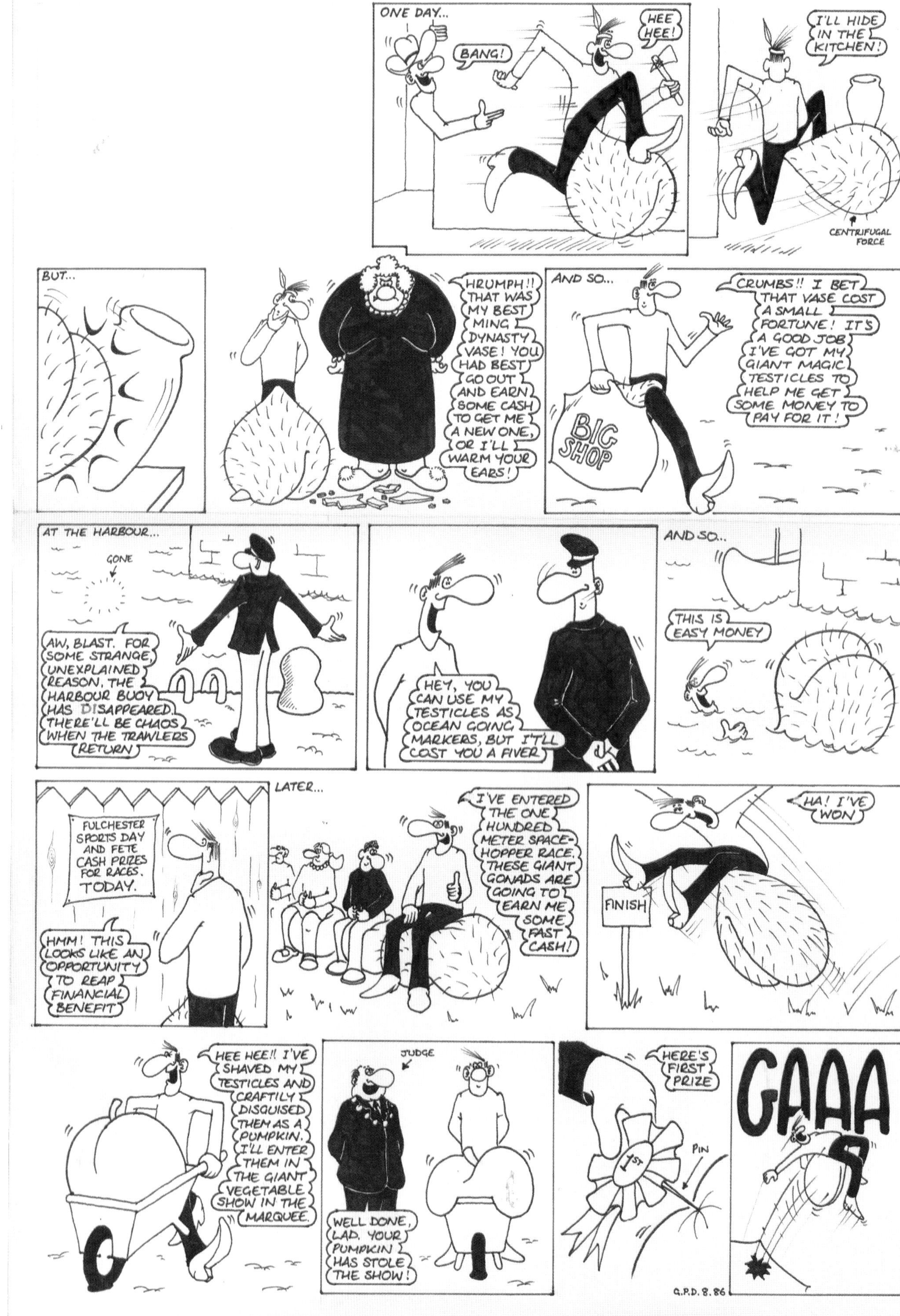
ONE DAY...
BANG!
HEE HEE!
I'LL HIDE IN THE KITCHEN!
CENTRIFUGAL FORCE
BUT...
HRUMPH!! THAT WAS MY BEST MING DYNASTY VASE! YOU HAD BEST GO OUT AND EARN SOME CASH TO GET ME A NEW ONE, OR I'LL WARM YOUR EARS!
AND SO...
CRUMBS!! I BET THAT VASE COST A SMALL FORTUNE! IT'S A GOOD JOB I'VE GOT MY GIANT MAGIC TESTICLES TO HELP ME GET SOME MONEY TO PAY FOR IT!
BIG SHOP
AT THE HARBOUR...
GONE
AW, BLAST. FOR SOME STRANGE, UNEXPLAINED REASON, THE HARBOUR BUOY HAS DISAPPEARED. THERE'LL BE CHAOS WHEN THE TRAWLERS RETURN
HEY, YOU CAN USE MY TESTICLES AS OCEAN GOING MARKERS, BUT IT'LL COST YOU A FIVER
AND SO...
THIS IS EASY MONEY
FULCHESTER SPORTS DAY AND FETE CASH PRIZES FOR RACES. TODAY.
HMM! THIS LOOKS LIKE AN OPPORTUNITY TO REAP FINANCIAL BENEFIT
LATER...
I'VE ENTERED THE ONE HUNDRED METER SPACE-HOPPER RACE. THESE GIANT GONADS ARE GOING TO EARN ME SOME FAST CASH!
HA! I'VE WON
FINISH
HEE HEE!! I'VE SHAVED MY TESTICLES AND CRAFTILY DISGUISED THEM AS A PUMPKIN. I'LL ENTER THEM IN THE GIANT VEGETABLE SHOW IN THE MARQUEE.
JUDGE
WELL DONE, LAD. YOUR PUMPKIN HAS STOLE THE SHOW!
HERE'S FIRST PRIZE
1ST
PIN
GAAA
G.P.D. 8.86

Opposite: Original artwork by Graham for an early Buster Gonad strip.
Right: Sleeve for 'Bags of Fun with Buster' by Johnny Japes and his Jesticles, the not quite hit single produced in 1987.

Below: T-shirt design, 1988.
Bottom: A more recent appearance.

BAGS OF FUN WITH BUSTER

Written and Produced by Andy Partridge, Neville Farmer and Dave Gregory. Featuring John Otway.

Who's that dragging what looks like a pink sack of spanners down the road?
His swollen folly on a supermarket trolley to alleviate the load
Testicular tomfoolery
To the rescue of humanity
It looks a lot of balls to me

Fun and japes and merry frolics
With Buster Gonad's bulbous bouncing ...
Bags of fun with Buster
And his super scrotal cluster

Who's that lad with his cobblers clad in a disguise of some form?
When the cosmic power of a meteorite shower made them swell beyond the norm
Now here he comes to save mankind
His enormous nuts not far behind
And they're not the salted kind

He cures mutes and alcoholics
When they first see his bulbous bouncing ...
Bags of fun with Buster
And his super scrotal cluster
There's bags of fun with Buster
See them shine with evil lustre

Buster! Watch out for that revolving door
Ooh Buster! They look so incredibly sore
Buster! Especially as you drag them through that powerful cleaning agent someone spilled upon the floor
Ooh Buster! Why do you let your sack swing so low?

"Sax swing solo?" Yeah!

Fun and japes and merry frolics
With Buster Gonad's bulbous bouncing ...
Bags of fun with Buster
And his super scrotal cluster

Doctor Who could defeat the Daleks
If he had Buster's swinging space age ...
Bags of fun with Buster
And his double Sputnick thruster
Bags of fun with Buster
Just to stroke them would disgust her
Bags of fun with Buster
If she held them would you trust her?
Bags of fun with Buster
Loads more balls than General Custer
Bags of fun with Buster
Lots more scrots than you could muster

B side
SCROTAL SCRATCH MIX

VIZ 1
TOP OF THE POPS
I DON'T CARE WHAT YOUR NAME IS, YOU'RE NOT BRINGING THOSE IN HERE!
STUD
For further information contact John Brown Publishing, Suite 216, Canalot Studios, 222 Kens
Road, London W10 5BN. Buster Gonad created by Graham Dury. More testicular tomfoole
with Buster in Viz Comic, available from your newsagent, or by subscription. (Send a SAE to V
Info., PO Box 232, Melksham, Wilts. SN12 7SB for full details).

BUSTER GONAD

'I got the idea for Buster from someone I met on a train,' says Graham. 'He had this enormous nose, cowboy boots and his nuts in a wheelbarrow.'

MRS BRADY OLD LADY

'We just sit Graham down and say "right, talk like an old lady," and off he goes,' says Thorpy, who took over the drawing of this strip from Chris. Somehow, Graham can summon up the most antiquated turns of phrase. In full flow, he could almost be the reincarnation of a geriatric woman. Maybe that's why it's one of the strips Thorpy's parents enjoy. 'They occasionally phone up and they'll have read a Mrs Brady and thought that was very funny,' he says, 'but there's bits in Mrs Brady that they probably shouldn't see.'

Right: Original artwork for the Mrs Brady page of the free calendar given away with issue 105, December 2000. Below: Strip produced for a leaflet publicizing the Viz 'Bus of Fools' bonfire, December 2000.

FRANKLIN
MINT

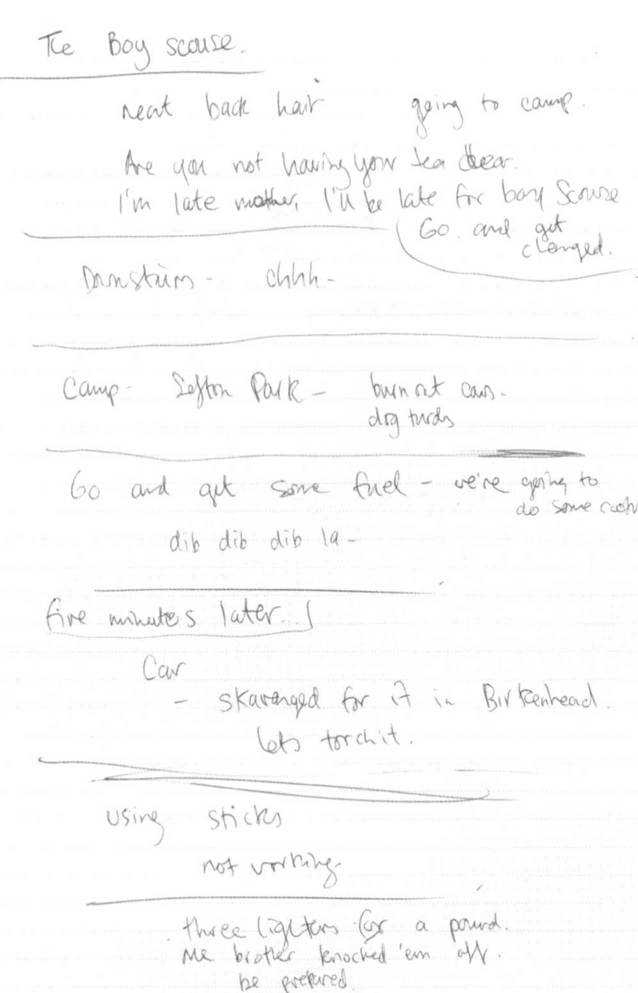

The Boy Scouse.

neat back hair — going to camp.

Are you not having your tea dear.
I'm late mother, I'll be late for boy Scouse
(Go and get changed.)

Downstairs - chhh -

Camp - Sefton Park - burnt out cars.
dog turds

Go and get some fuel - we're going to do some cooking
dib dib dib la -

five minutes later..!

Car
- skavenged for it in Birkenhead.
lets torch it.

using sticks
not working

three lighters for a pound.
Me brother knocked 'em off.
be prepared.

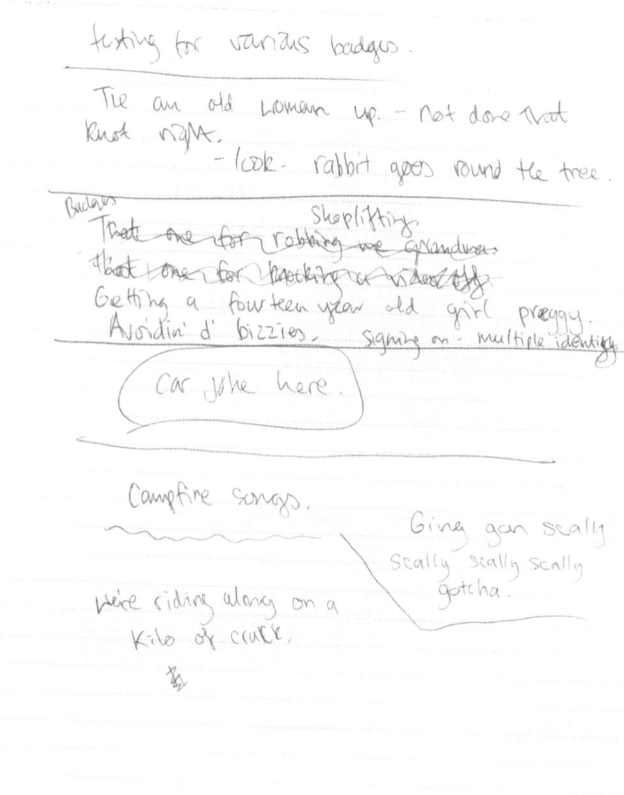

testing for various badges.

Tie an old woman up. - not done that knot right.
- look - rabbit goes round the tree.

Badges
~~That one for robbing me grandma.~~ Shoplifting.
~~that one for knocking a video off~~
Getting a fourteen year old girl preggy.
Avoidin' d' bizzies. signing on - multiple identity.

(Car joke here.)

Campfire songs.

Ging gan scally
Scally scally scally
gotcha.

We're riding along on a
Kilo of crack.

THE BOY SCOUSE

The Boy Scouse was Alex Collier's breezy skit about Scouse boy scouts who steal cars, mug old ladies and earn badges for shoplifting and benefit fraud, but some Liverpudlians failed to see the funny side. Local Labour MP Louise Ellman claimed the strip enforced negative stereotypes of the city, and the *Liverpool Echo* even devoted an editorial to the matter. 'The *Viz* comic strip portraying Liverpudlians as foul-mouthed thieves recycles a tired old joke,' proclaimed the paper. 'If some people find it funny, then let them laugh. It's easy to overreact and actually fuel the stereotyping which has caused

Opposite: *The Boy Scouse plot outline and an illustration produced for the* Liverpool Echo. *This page: The strip which sparked the fuss.*

so much damage and offence to Liverpool people. This is just a cheap attempt by *Viz* to revive its flagging circulation by ripping off Harry Enfield's old sketch characters. That's the firm conclusion we draw about the cartoon.'[39]

Of course by giving such a prominent space to this storm in a stolen teacup, the paper did a fine good job of fuelling the very stereotype it was objecting to, but Alex proved perfectly capable of sticking up for himself. 'I have links with Liverpool and have spent a lot of time there – and I don't think it will really offend anyone,' he told the *Echo*. 'I'm surprised there have been complaints. I always thought Scousers could take this sort of thing on the chin – they're famed for their sense of humour.'[40] *Viz* has taken the piss out of Geordies for years, yet most folk on Tyneside seem flattered by the attention. However it appears some Scousers aren't quite so thick skinned. 'I was going to come to Liverpool for Christmas, but I'm not sure if I'll be welcome after this – there might be a fatwa out on me,' said Alex. 'My grandparents still live in the city and they've seen the article. However, they are unable to comment because they've gone into hiding. Actually, they're out stealing cars.'[41]

I am 6
Bingo & win a yurt.
Play Politically Corre
The G
dian
in G2
Femi
of w
"Fu
RAZZLE

Opposite: Original artwork for the cover of the Student Grant 'Old Gold Rope' compilation issue, Summer 2000.

Above: Excerpt from the computer-coloured version of a strip which first appeared in issue 88, 1998. Right: Point of sale poster, Summer 1995.

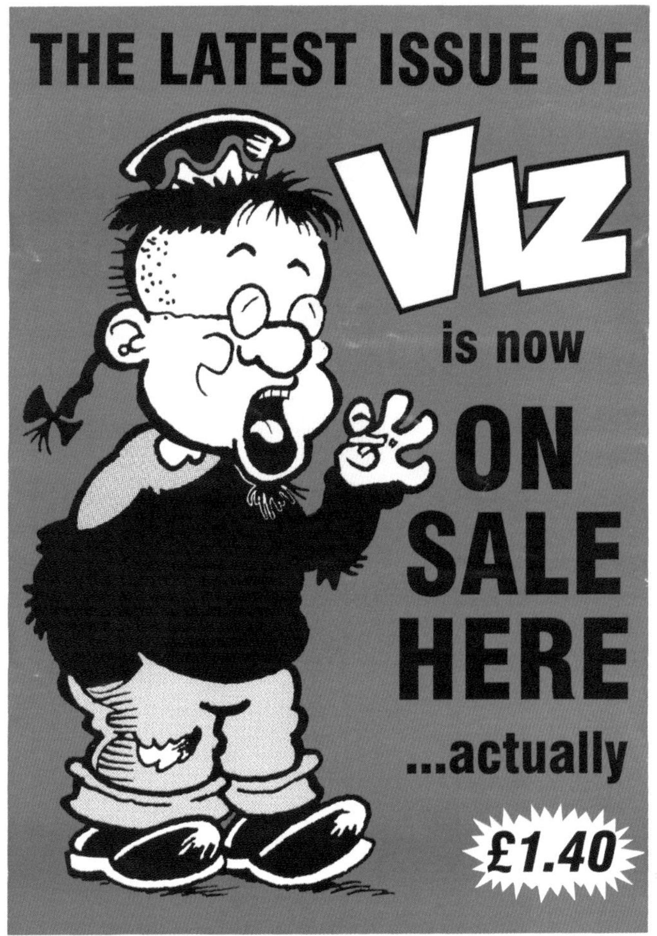

THE LATEST ISSUE OF
Viz
is now
ON SALE HERE
...actually
£1.40

STUDENT GRANT

Thorpy drew Student Grant as a response to *Viz*'s being briefly banned from a few student unions, but it's nearly twenty years since Thorpy left Aberystwyth University, and although Spunkbridge Univeristy is a comic classic, he admits it might be a bit out of date. 'It's probably the sort of students that were at college with us, where nobody was really that bothered about getting a job,' he says. 'Nowadays, they're more worried about their future.'

Original artwork by Simon Ecob for the Jack Black page of the free calendar given away with issue 105, December 2000.

JACK BLACK

'Jack Black's first adventure was called "The Cauliflower Mystery" and Chris traced it out of an old *Whizzer and Chips* annual or something,' says Davey. 'Jack started out as a cheerful boy detective, but over the years sinister ultra right-wing overtones have crept into his character. For instance, he reads the *Daily Mail* and in one episode he had a slap-up tea with Hitler. We've nearly all had a go at drawing him, but now we write the stories in the office and send them away to a lad called Simon Ecob, who can draw like a bastard. The bastard.'

MILLIE TANT

'We'd seen that feminist Andrea Dworkin on the telly,' says Thorpy, 'and we were very unimpressed with her physical appearance, so we decided to do a story about a boot ugly women's rights campaigner. One of our feminist readers didn't see the funny side, however, and wrote to Simon - who drew it - saying that he should "have his cock cut off and stuck up his arse till it came".'

Original artwork of Millie as Britannia, drawn for the cover of issue 118, September 2002.

RAT BOY

Alex's Rat Boy may look like some strange feat of fantasy, but like a lot of the weirder strips in *Viz*, it actually takes its cue from real life. 'There was a bit of a spate of various rat boys around Newcastle,' says Alex. 'There was Rat Boy, there was Spider Boy – there was one called Worm Boy because he used to hide in the grass and make tunnels.' But Rat Boy was the prototype, and the local legends that grew up around him and his imitators became a kind of urban folklore, like a modern remake of Oliver Twist. 'They always break into people's houses and do shits in the corner as their kind of calling card, so that's why Rat Boy had that tail – it's like a big turd coming out of his arse.'

Above: Rat Boy's first appearance on the bagged cover of issue 99, December 1999.

Opposite: Motion-filled frame, 2000.

Below: Computer-coloured style-guide designs.

Sketch and finished postcard featuring Thorpy's 'rubbish' cockney character, Ken.

COCKNEY WANKER

'Thorpy did a couple of half pages about a cockney character in the mid eighties, but they were rubbish,' says Graham, 'so we thought we'd have another go. Cockney Wanker is the lovechild of Mike Reid and Bob Hoskins, and like all Londoners he speaks exclusively in rhyming slang, loves the Queen and punches his wife.'

Right: The 'Cockney Wan-Cab', a London taxi promotion organised by John Brown Publishing. An alternative scheme for a pink cab covered in little hairs – the 'Unfeasibly Large Taxicle' was turned down by the authorities on the grounds of taste.

Left: A sequence from a strip in issue 89, April 1998.

Below: Original artwork for a Cockney Wanker saucy seaside postcard which was given away free with issue 96. The caption read: – 'Gaw! What a laverly pear, Wankah!' – 'Fack your fruit, Shirl. I'm gawpin' at this bird's tits!'

the PONTIFF MAN
THE CAULIFLOWER MYSTERY
BIG VERN'S BACK IN TOWN
BA-BAM!!!
BOOM!
BOOMFF!!
Raffles The Gentleman Thug
SPANG!

PART THREE **THE ART**

Preliminary sketches and unfinished artwork for the abandoned cover of the 2005 annual The Hangman's Noose.

THE HANGMAN'S NOOSE
A Hearty breakfast of
old rope from

Preliminary sketches and finished artwork for the final version of The Hangman's Noose.

Finished fold-over cover and original obscene artwork for issue 96.

Crop marks are only approx. Sid wants to be q close to left so that thumb can cover his gut-stick. Feel free to lose the starfish if it makes the picture confusing.
N.B. Speech balloons ought to be at an angle with the card.
erm... That's it.
NUDIST BEACH
172
Graybags or Davey - can you rub out the pencil on the NUDIST BEACH sign? Ta.
Thumb should cast a bit of shadow onto flap picture, d'you reckon?

Preliminary sketches, mock up and final cover of issue 113.

Finished pencil drawings for 'The Joy of Banging' in the 'Fat Slags Gold' issue.

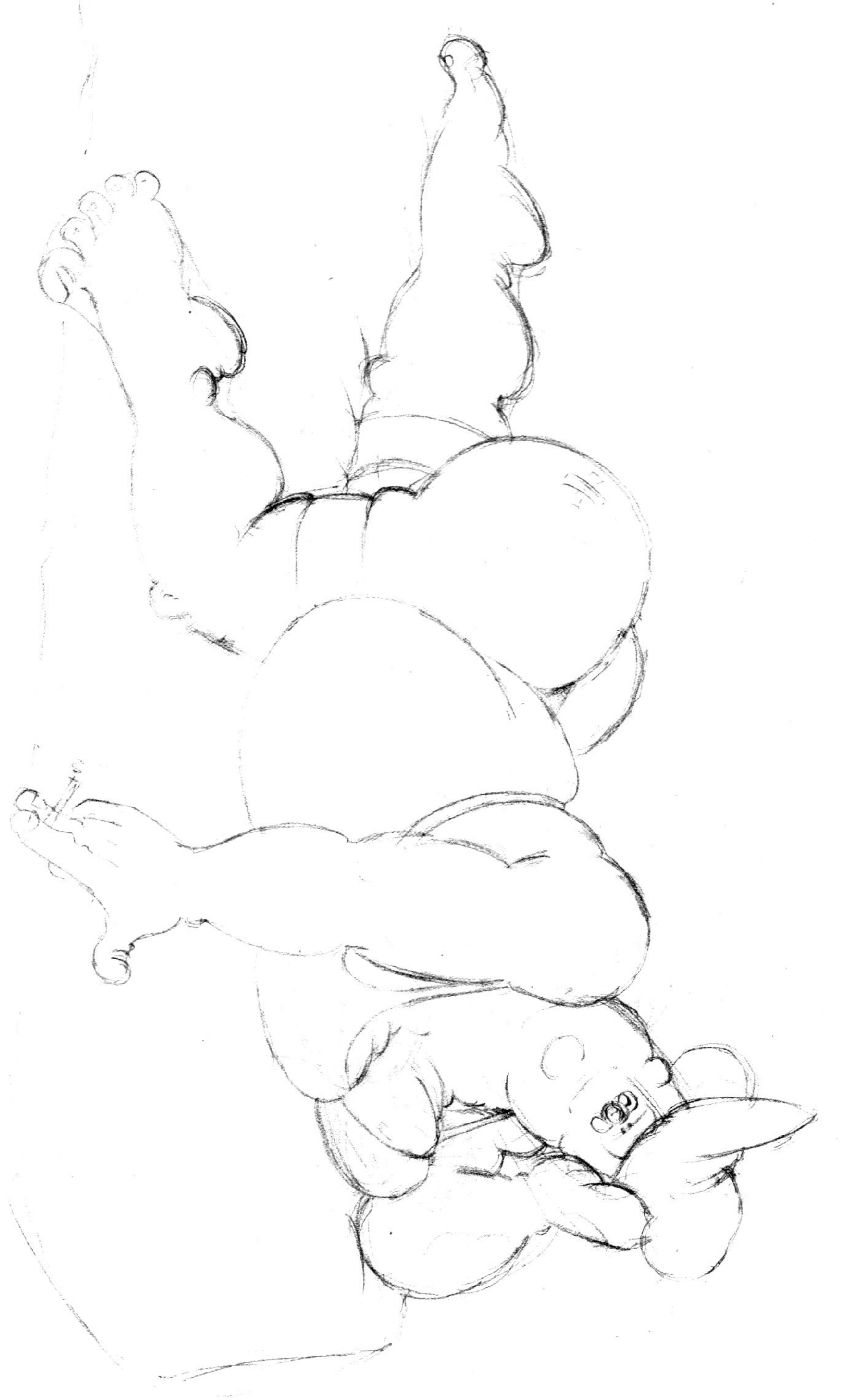

This page, opposite and overleaf: Preliminary pencil sketches for a Fat Slags 'glamour' spread in Front *magazine.*

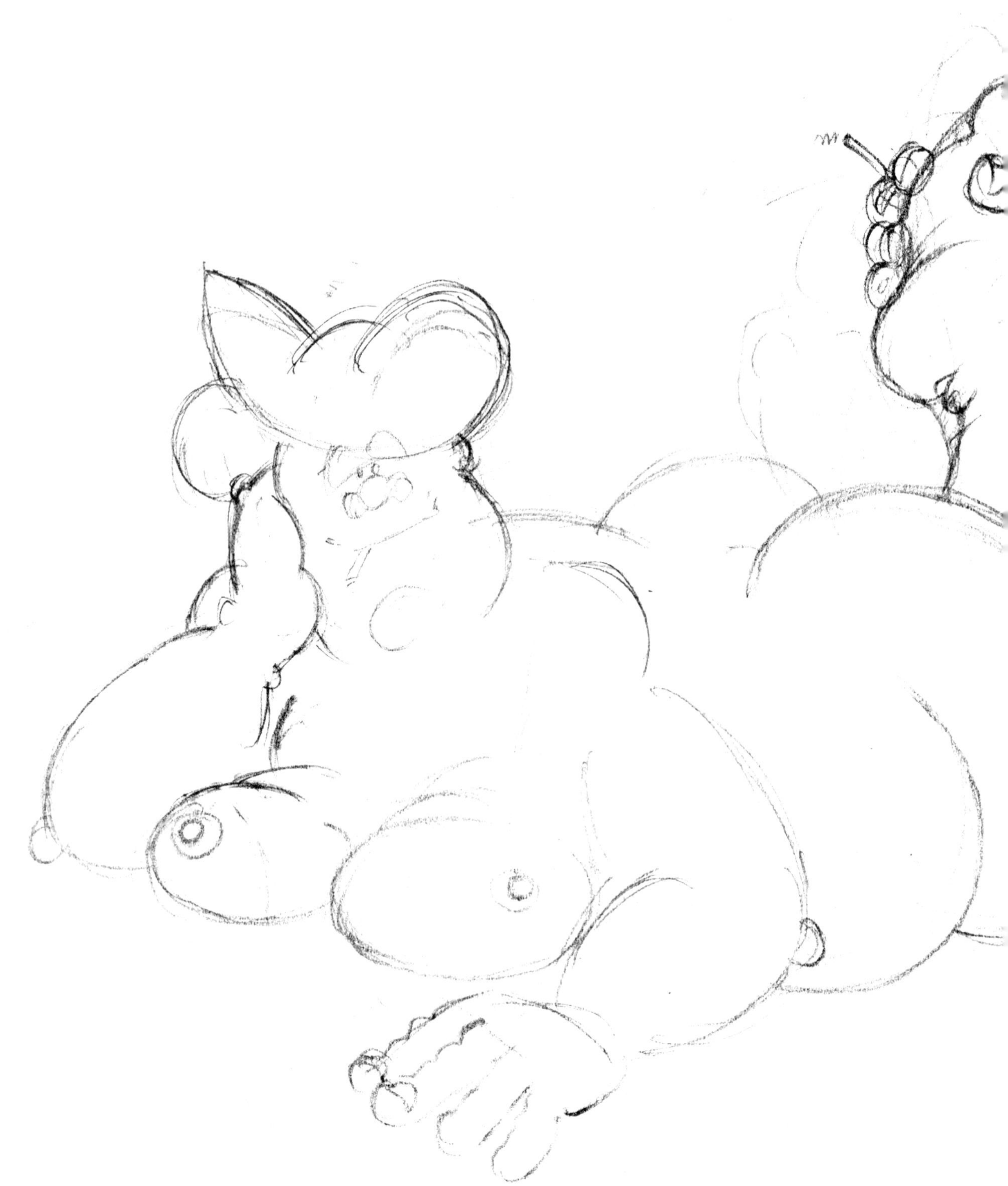

BNM - IMAGINATION

Various stages in the production of Tyson, a cartoon strip based on the antics of the ear chomping heavyweight boxer.

Preliminary sketches, finished ink drawings and computer-coloured artwork of 8 Ace for 'The Viz Style Guide'.

Original sketch, artwork and finished cover of issue 122.

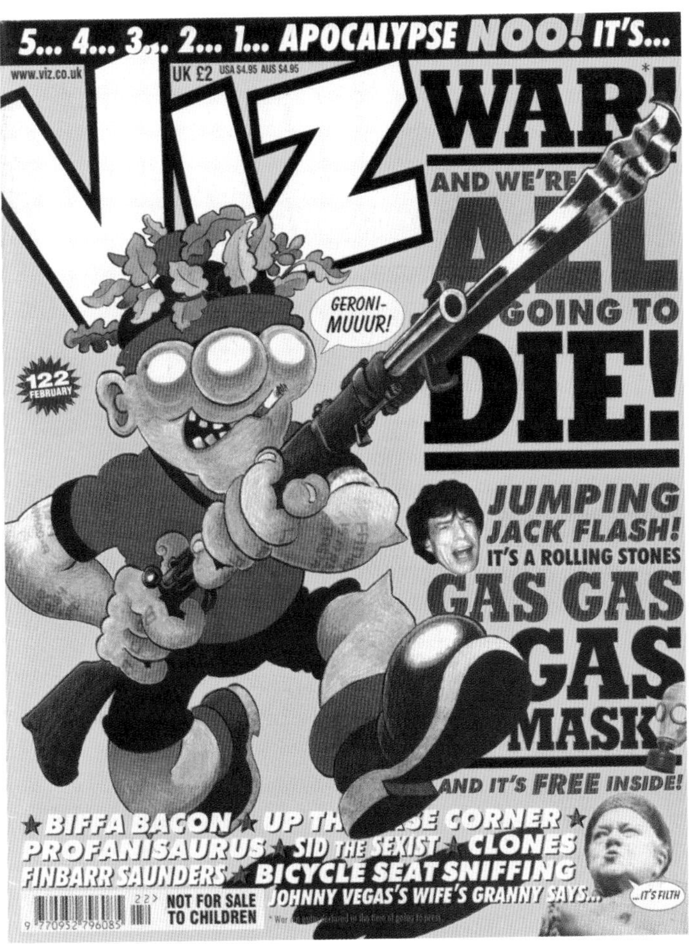

BILLY NOMATES.

Opposite: Pencil sketches of Billy No-Mates and his genitals.
This page: An unused strip, Jack the New Lad.

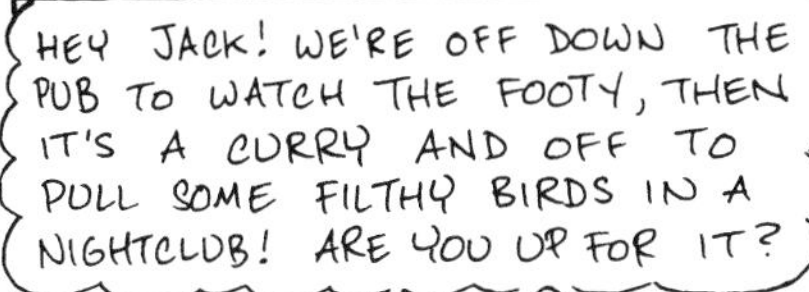

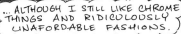

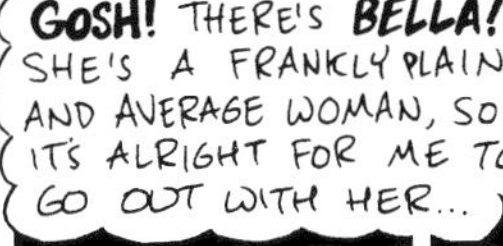

Preliminary sketches and finished artwork produced for the 2004 Blyth Spartans Sportsman's Dinner Auction.

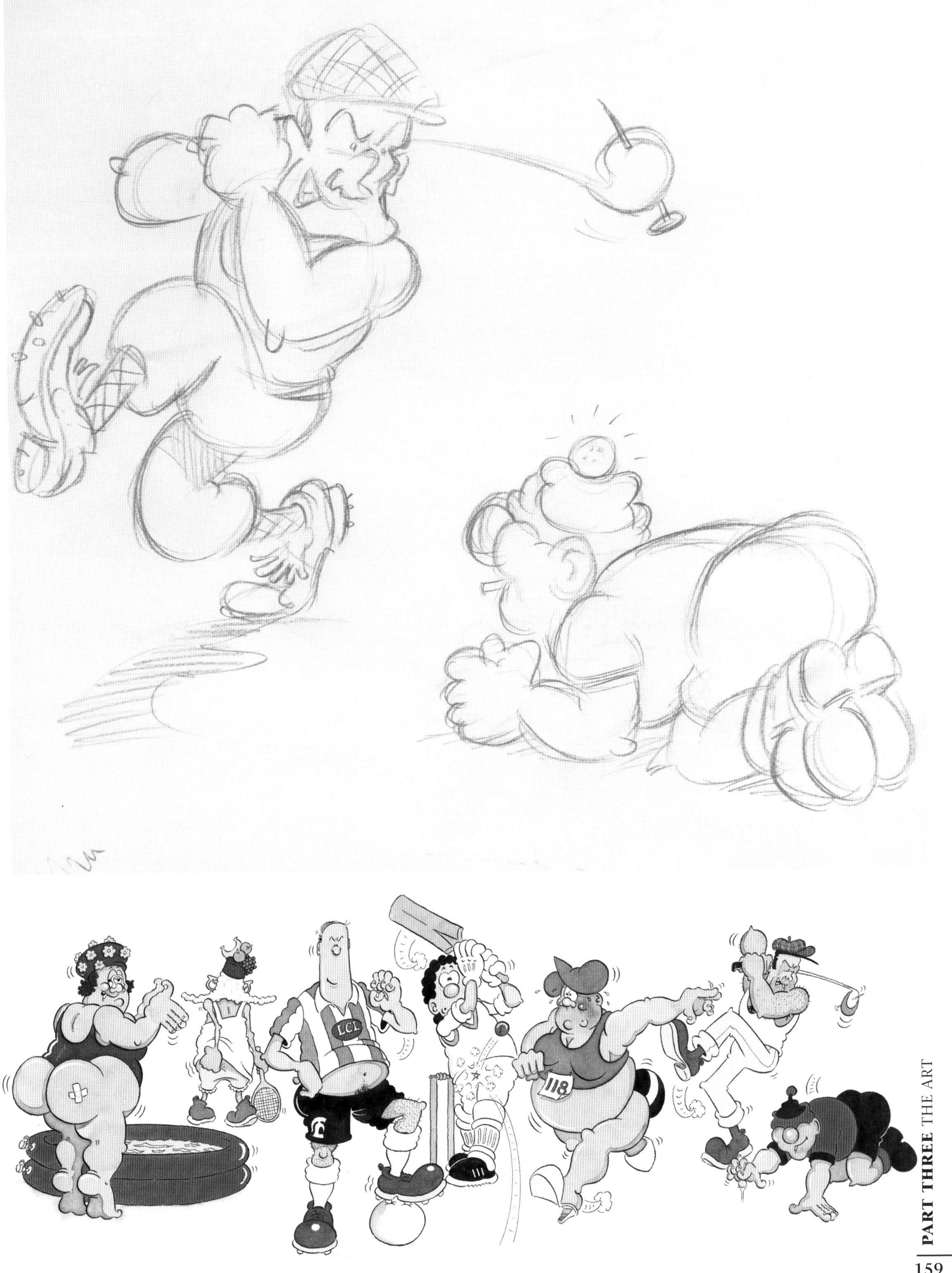

LCL
118

Preliminary sketches, original artwork and finished cover of the 2003 annual The Bag of Slugs.

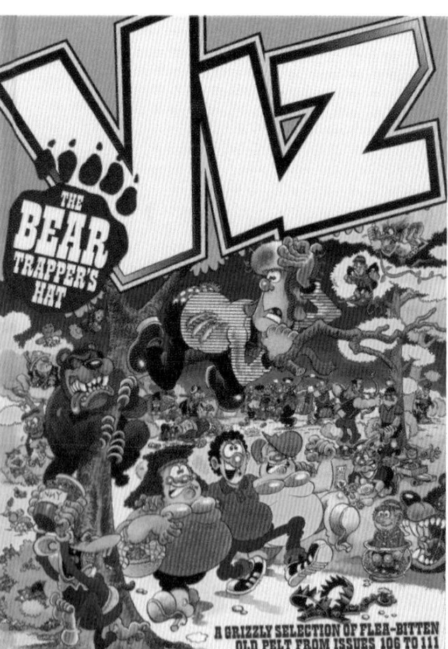

Preliminary sketches, original artwork and finished cover of the 2004 annual The Bear Trapper's Hat.

To Santa.

Various pencil sketches and finished artwork of Roger Mellie.

This page: Pencil sketch, finished drawing and computer-coloured artwork of Roger Mellie for 'The Viz Style Guide'. Opposite: A rough layout from a Roger Mellie cartoon.

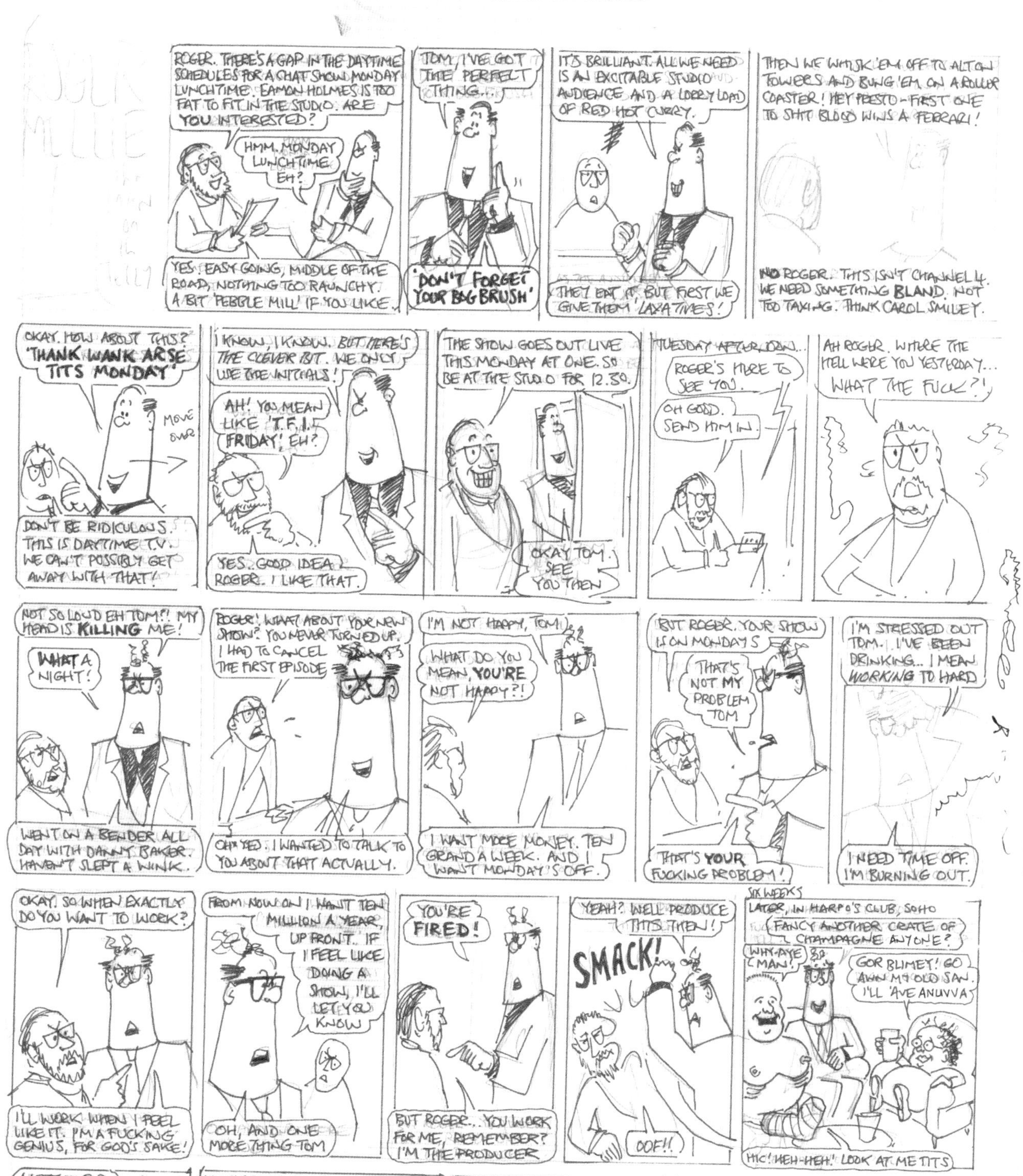

ROGER. THERE'S A GAP IN THE DAYTIME SCHEDULES FOR A CHAT SHOW MONDAY LUNCHTIME. EAMON HOLMES IS TOO FAT TO FIT IN THE STUDIO. ARE **YOU** INTERESTED?
HMM. MONDAY LUNCHTIME EH?
YES. EASY GOING, MIDDLE OF THE ROAD, NOTHING TOO RAUNCHY. A BIT 'PEBBLE MILL' IF YOU LIKE.

TOM, I'VE GOT THE PERFECT THING...
'DON'T FORGET YOUR BOG BRUSH'

IT'S BRILLIANT. ALL WE NEED IS AN EXCITABLE STUDIO AUDIENCE AND A LORRY LOAD OF RED HOT CURRY.
THEY EAT IT. BUT FIRST WE GIVE THEM 'LAXATIVES'!

THEN WE WHISK 'EM OFF TO ALTON TOWERS AND BUNG 'EM ON A ROLLER COASTER! HEY PRESTO - FIRST ONE TO SHIT BLOOD WINS A FERRARI!
NO ROGER. THIS ISN'T CHANNEL 4. WE NEED SOMETHING **BLAND**. NOT TOO TAXING. THINK CAROL SMILLEY.

OKAY. HOW ABOUT THIS? **'THANK WANK ARSE TITS MONDAY'**
MOVE OVER
DON'T BE RIDICULOUS. THIS IS DAYTIME T.V. WE CAN'T POSSIBLY GET AWAY WITH THAT!

I KNOW, I KNOW. *BUT HERE'S THE CLEVER BIT*. WE ONLY USE THE INITIALS!
AH! YOU MEAN LIKE 'T.F.I. FRIDAY' EH?
YES. GOOD IDEA ROGER. I LIKE THAT.

THE SHOW GOES OUT LIVE THIS MONDAY AT ONE. SO BE AT THE STUDIO FOR 12.30.
OKAY TOM. SEE YOU THEN

TUESDAY AFTERNOON...
ROGER'S HERE TO SEE YOU.
OH GOD. SEND HIM IN.

AH ROGER. WHERE THE HELL WERE YOU YESTERDAY...
WHAT THE FUCK?!

NOT SO LOUD EH TOM?! MY HEAD IS **KILLING** ME!
WHAT A NIGHT!
WENT ON A BENDER ALL DAY WITH DANNY BAKER. HAVEN'T SLEPT A WINK.

ROGER! WHAT ABOUT YOUR NEW SHOW? YOU NEVER TURNED UP. I HAD TO CANCEL THE FIRST EPISODE
OH YES. I WANTED TO TALK TO YOU ABOUT THAT ACTUALLY.

I'M NOT HAPPY, TOM.
WHAT DO YOU MEAN, **YOU'RE** NOT HAPPY?!
I WANT MORE MONEY. TEN GRAND A WEEK. AND I WANT MONDAY'S OFF.

BUT ROGER. YOUR SHOW IS ON MONDAYS
THAT'S NOT **MY** PROBLEM TOM
THAT'S **YOUR** FUCKING PROBLEM!

I'M STRESSED OUT TOM. I'VE BEEN DRINKING... I MEAN *WORKING* TO HARD
I NEED TIME OFF. I'M BURNING OUT.

OKAY. SO WHEN EXACTLY DO YOU WANT TO WORK?
I'LL WORK WHEN I FEEL LIKE IT. I'M A FUCKING GENIUS, FOR GOD'S SAKE!

FROM NOW ON I WANT TEN MILLION A YEAR, UP FRONT. IF I FEEL LIKE DOING A SHOW, I'LL LET YOU KNOW
OH, AND ONE MORE THING TOM

YOU'RE **FIRED!**
BUT ROGER... YOU WORK FOR ME, REMEMBER? I'M THE PRODUCER

YEAH? WELL PRODUCE THIS THEN!
SMACK!
OOF!!

SIX WEEKS LATER, IN HARPO'S CLUB, SOHO
FANCY ANOTHER CRATE OF CHAMPAGNE ANYONE?
WHY-AYE MAN!
GOR BLIMEY! GO AWN MY OLD SAN. I'LL 'AVE ANUVVA
HIC! HEH-HEH! LOOK AT ME TITS

A LETTER FOR YOU MR MELLIE
OH GOOD.
IT'S PROBABLY A PAY CHEQUE.

I DON'T BELIEVE IT. THEY'VE FREED ME FROM MY CONTRACT. I'VE BEEN SACKED
HEH-HEH! LOOK AT ME TITS!
THEY CAN'T TREAT YOU LIKE THAT! IT'S A FACKING DISGRACE!
WHY AYE MAN.
THEY WANT A BLEEDIN' SLAP, THEY DO.

TWO YEARS LATER...
ANYONE FOR MORE CHAMPAGNE?
WHY AYE MAN, ETC
GO ON MY SAN!
OH SHIT! THAT WAS THE LAST OF THE MONEY

SHORTLY...
HAVE YOU MET OUR NEW NEIGHBOUR YET? SIMON DEE
HI
CHAMPION. I LOVE A BIG FIRE, ME.
ANYONE FOR MORE METHS?

Label artwork and a discarded design for Top Tipple, Viz's brief foray into the world of brewing.

alc. 4.5% vol.
500ml e
BEST BEFORE DATE ON REAR
NICE VIZ BEER
TOP TIPPLE
TOP TIPPLE
Bar Code stripped in here
500ml of BEER ABV 4.5% BEST BEFORE END

NICE VIZ BEER
TOP TIPPLE

BAR CODE

Production stages from the cover of issue 114 (below left). Opposite: Preliminary pencil sketch. Left: Mock up. Below right: Finished artwork in pen, ink and acrylic.

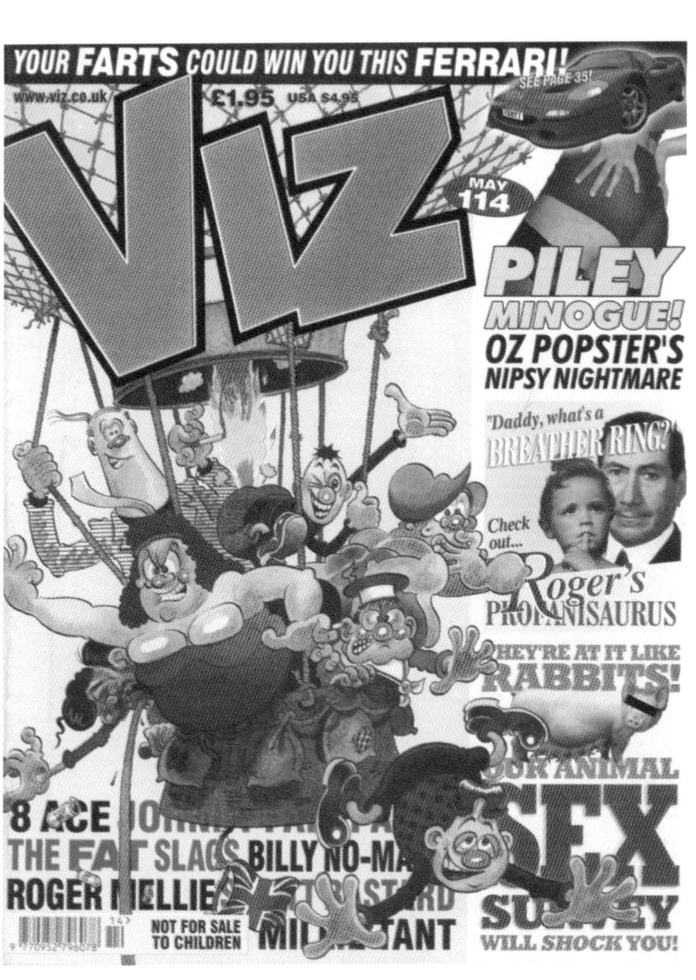

Production stages from the cover of issue 119 (above right). Opposite: Preliminary pencil sketches. Above left: Mock up. Left: Detail of finished painted artwork.

Preliminary sketches, finished ink drawings and computer-coloured artwork of the Fat Slags for 'The Viz Style Guide'. Overleaf: Full colour artwork from a Fat Slags double page spread before the addition of title frame and speech balloons.

RECEPTION

RECEPTION

RECEPTION

ACE

THE KING'S
HEAD
VIRGIN
BAR
L

VIRGIN

SPORT

VIRGIN

H
FULCHESTER
COCK
HOSPITAL

Various stages in the production of Les Dennis the Menace.

LES DENNIS THE MENACE
LES, CAN YOU GO OUT AND FETCH MY PAPER PLEASE?
OKAY DAD!
AND NO MINDING YOUR OWN BUSINESS! AND CRYING AS USUAL
COR LOOK! THERE'S AMANDA HOLDEN!
I DON'T REALLY KNOW! I DON'T REALLY KNOW! I DON'T REALLY KNOW!
EH? WHAT'S GOING ON? I DON'T REALLY KNOW?!
CHORTLE! NOW FOR A FEAST?!
OH! WAIL! OH, THE WOE! THE ANGUISH!!
MATERNITY HOME
WHAAA!
WHAAA!
WHAAAA!
WHAAA!!
GULP!! OUR SURVEY SAYS.... KICK ME UP THE ARSE?
BOOT
BOO HOO! MY POOR BACKSIDE BROKEN HEART! SOB SOB SOB
THERE THERE NOW. STOP CRYING.
HERE YOUR PAPER DAD!
CHEERS LES
HEADL
STUFF
SLAM
SLAM
SLAM
LIKE LES IS GETTIN SLAMMED BY THE PAPER AGAIN, EH?
Readers voice

Finished ink drawings and computer-coloured artwork of Gilbert Ratchet for 'The Viz Style Guide'.

RAT MAT
HOO YE - FUCK OFF!
THIS IS MY FUCKIN' TELLY
THIS - I TWOCKED IT MESELF

Preliminary sketches for the Viz computer Rat Mat, a gift for subscribers.

VIZ
RAT MAT
www.viz.co.uk

Various stages in the production of Ruby Murray and her Arse of Fire.
Overleaf: Cover roughs for issues 124 and 127.

RUBY MURRAY and her ARSE of FIRE

LISTS FOOD SHES ATE.

MR LATIFS ADVERT

SLIPPED AWAY WHILE HE PROMOTES RESTAURANT.

ERK! ARSE TEMPRAMENTAL

YAAH BOO!

HOT CHESTNUTS GONE OUT.

HMM....

HOORAY FOR RUBY AND HER ARSE OF FIRE!

URGHH! THERE ARE CHESTNUTS THEY'RE TAGNUTS!

GONE BLIND SO CAN'T GIVE CHASE.

TOXICARA

SHORTLY...

OHO! WHAT HAVE WE HERE!

CAR WON'T START

PLUG HAS

A HA!

OUR SPARK FROZEN, WE NEED A MAKESHIFT SPARK TO START THE ENGINE

JUST STICK YOUR ARSE IN THE PETROL TANK...

BADANG!

HA! WE NICKED THAT CAR AND WE'RE TRYING TO BURN IT OUT! THANKS FOR HELPING US!

HURTS ME MORE THAN IT HURTS YOU.

IS YOUR OFFICE READY FOR THE TERRORISTS?

…IC LUXURY CRAPPER!

…-TASTIC LUXURY CRAPPER!

VIZ

9-11 TO 5!

IS YOUR OFFICE READY FOR THE TERRORISTS?

124 APRIL

GOES TO …AR!

PLUS LES DENNIS THE MENACE

HEY! I'M AS THICK AS F[RUDDY]NG PIG[PLOPS]T, ME!

NOT FOR SALE TO CHILDREN

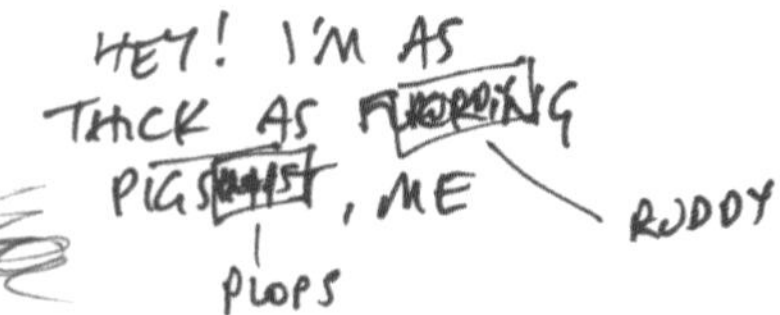

IT'S A ROYAL KNOCKOUT

ROD SAVE THE QUEEN

ANYTHING FOR THE WEEKEND?

SID the SEXIST

ROYALS at RISK! * SID the SEXIST * RAFFLES

VIZ

ANYTHING for the WEEKEND?

FREE HAIRCUT & A PACKET OF JOHNNIES for EVERY* READER

& a Packet

OI SAN. HOW MANY TIMES HAVE I TOLD YOU ABOUT TAKING THESE SCISSORS HOME TO TRIM YOUR

127

OH CORDY! IT'S THE FAT SLAGS!

PROFANISAURUS

Letterbocks

Top Tips

ROGER MELLIE * Morrissey's still a Tw

NOT FOR SALE TO CHILDREN

ROGER MELLIE

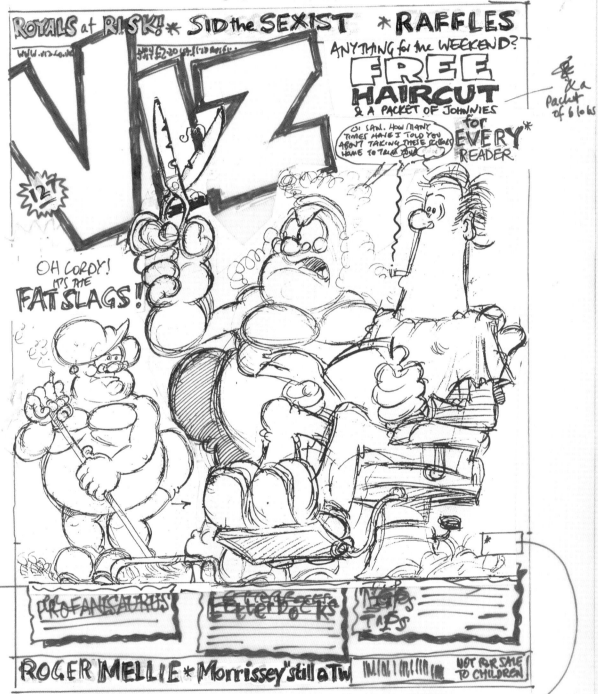

HARRY POTTER WAS MY IDEA – Says DRUNK.

POTTER RIP-OFF

* – who gets to the Barbers before the cash runs out.

ONE LUCKY READER MUST WIN
YOUR CHANCE TO WIN
VIZ
THIS £300000 DREAM COTTAGE!
129
DON'T GO IN THE WATER!
PATHETIC SHARKS
IT AIN'T HALF HOT MUM!
HELL!
PLUS
CILLA BLACKBEARD
RAT BOY

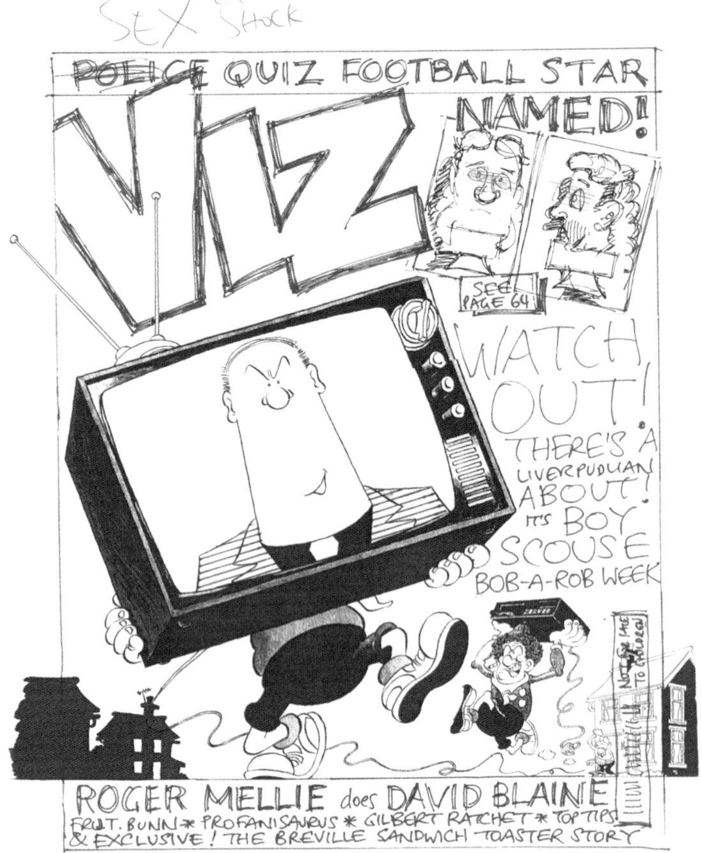

SEX SHOCK
POLICE QUIZ FOOTBALL STAR NAMED!
VIZ
SEE PAGE 64
WATCH OUT!
THERE'S A LIVERPUDLIAN ABOUT! IT'S BOY SCOUSE BOB-A-ROB WEEK
ROGER MELLIE does DAVID BLAINE
FRUT. BUNN * PROFANISAURUS * GILBERT RATCHET * TOP TIPS
& EXCLUSIVE! THE BREVILLE SANDWICH TOASTER STORY

Opposite: Original script, artwork and colour overlay for Billy Bottom. Overleaf: Camera-ready artwork for Viz postcards, 1987.

This page: Roughs and finished covers for issues 129 and 130.

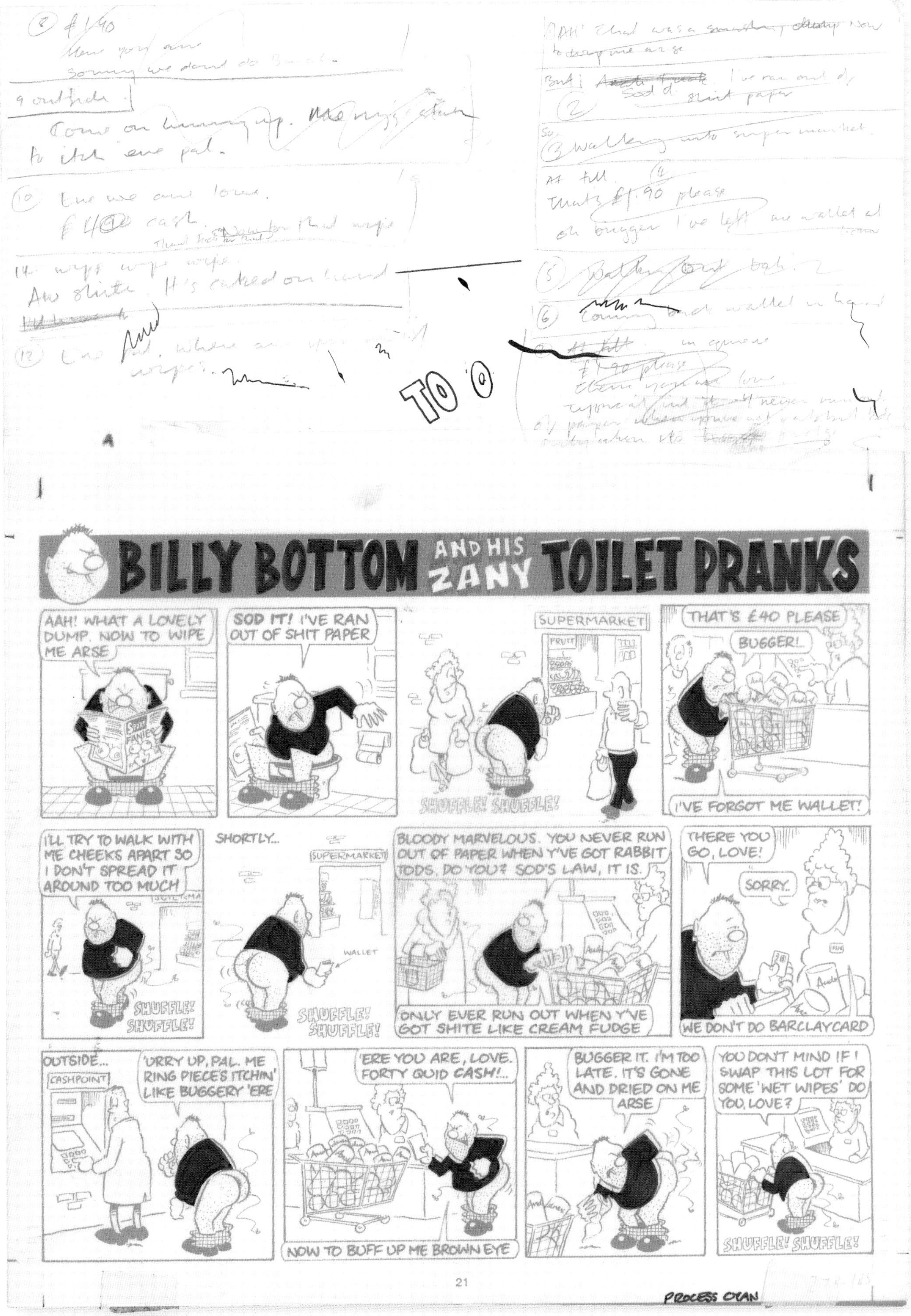

BILLY BOTTOM AND HIS ZANY TOILET PRANKS

21

PROCESS CYAN

TOO YOUNG TO LOVE
Their parents called it 'Puppy Love', but despite her tender years Camilla Johnson knew her love for Brian would last forever. And she intended to prove it...
I'LL SEE YOU TONIGHT DARLING. AND REMEMBER, I LOVE YOU, BRIAN

BILLY the FISH
ANOTHER BRILLIANT SAVE FROM THE 'FISH LIKE' KEEPER!
IT'S AMAZING! THIS FISH LAD CAN ALMOST SWIM THROUGH THE AIR!
DESPITE BEING BORN HALF MAN, HALF FISH, YOUNG BILLY THOMSON

I LOVE THIS HOT WEATHER. I CAN MAKE A FORTUNE SELLING ICE CREAM OUT OF MY UNDERPANTS
ONE PLEASE, FELIX
ME NEXT!
CD

AH, BUT LITTLE DOES DAD KNOW, THIS LONG, SL
PUMP WILL FORM A PROTECTIVE CUSHION ARO
MY BUTTOCKS AND SAVE ME FROM A WHACKING.

LATER...
FURTHER INQUIRIES HAVE PROVED FRUITFUL. I FIND 'PUNK ROCK' TO BE A FORM OF MUSIC; THE ART OF EXPRESSING OR STIRRING EMOTION BY A HARMONIOUS COMBINATION OF SOUNDS - SOUNDS SO COMBINED - RECORD OR SCORE OF THESE FOR REPRODUCTION. THE LATTER BEING THE ITEM WHICH I SUBSEQUENTLY PURCHASED.
EMI
NaZi

PREPARE FOR BOTTZKRIEG : ALL OUT BOTTOM INSPECTION!!
BOTTOM INSPECTOR
YES BOTTOMDANT LEYBURN, HEH! HEH!
HO! HO! HO!
HA! HA!

SECONDS FROM NOW I SHALL OWN THE WORLD'S FIRST SEX POWERED TELEVISION! NOT ONLY WILL I HALF MY ELECTRICITY BILL, BUT I WILL ALSO OWN THE MOST POWERFUL TELEVISION ON EARTH! USING 5000 STROKES OF SEX ENERGY PER SECOND!
SEX
THE EQUIVALENT OF 90 RHINOCEROS ORGASMS A MINUTE!!!
CD

AGGH! MY BOTTOM
THAT SHOULD PUT A STOP TO YOUR BANANA PRANKS, EH TOMMY? HO HO HO!
CD

DOCTOR. I'VE GOT AN UPSET STOMACH
BOO! SOB! I HATE YOU, I HATE YOU, I HATE YOU!!

TRANSFORMATION HAS TAKEN PLACE...
IT'S... THE BROWN BOTTLE!!
CH-CH-CH-CHEERS PAL, YA F- YA F- YAH FUKKAH!
TELEPHON

I PICKED UP THIS OLD REVOLVER FOR A FIVER... IDEAL FOR TOPPING MYSELF! HERE GOES...
BAM!
BAH! MISSED

E BEEN SAVING WHALES R ABOUT 4 YEARS NOW. YOU CAN SEE, THIS ONE AS GONE QUITE SMELLY.

WOMAN!! IT SHAT ON MY PARK!!!
WHAT'S GOING ON?!
BOOT!
YIP!

SAVE £££'s
RONCO 'THREE IN ONE' BANANAMATIC
IDEAL FOR ●HOLDING ●PICKING UP AND ●PUTTING DOWN BANANAS
PERFECT GIFT
PUTS AN END TO BANANA MISERY
FULLY ADJUSTABLE
BANANA ADHESION AT THE FLICK OF A SWITCH
ONLY £6-99
BUY SIX, GET ONE FREE!
Available now from all good chemists, most crap ones and major branches of WHSmiths

ENEMY PLANE AT 1-O-CLOCK
THAT'S GOOD. WE'VE GOT ½ AN HOUR TO SPARE, THEN

I'M OFF OUT DAD, T'CLOBBA SOMEONE IN THE MUSH
GIVE THE BASTARD ONE FROM ME, KIDDA
TITS!

Left and below left: Final version and camera-ready artwork of the Ronco Bottomatic advert. Below: Final version of a Viz advert. Opposite: Original artwork.

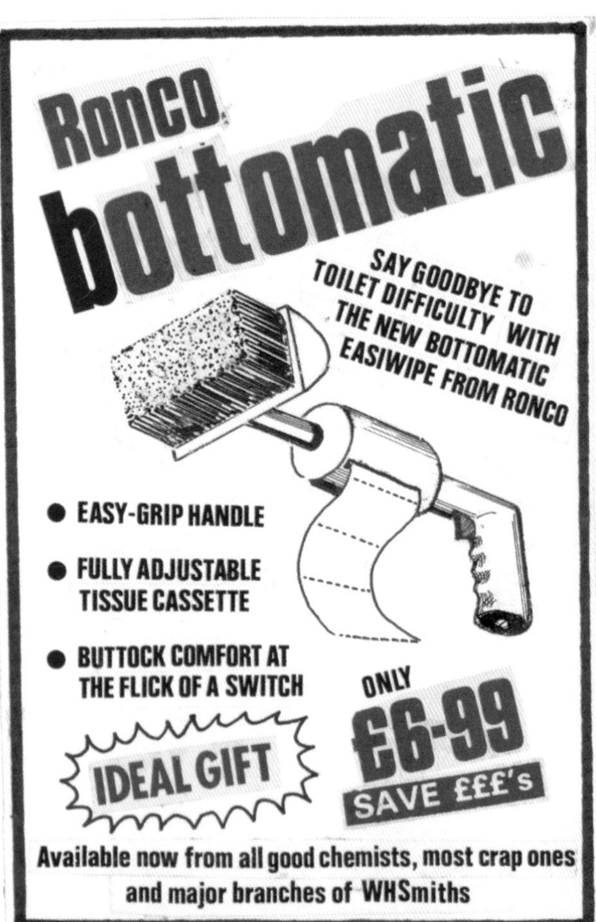

VIZ

Original ink drawings for spoof motorbike piano advert. Overleaf: Maps of 'the Shittish Isles' and 'Cuntinental Europe' given away with the comic.

MAP OF THE
SHITTISH ISLES

www.viz.co.uk

CONTINENTAL
EUROPE
Viz
MIR
www.viz.co.uk

MACHYNLLETH
MILFORD HAVEN BEAUTY SPOT

Detail from the original artwork of 'The Shittish Isles'.

Detail from the original artwork of 'Cuntinental Europe'.

SWITZERLAND
A VENDRE
£6M
CHI HA MANGIATO TUTTE LE TORTE
MONTE CARLO
NO OVER-TAKING
MARSEILLE
MONACO
ANDORRA
CORSICA
MAJORCA
SARDINIA

This page: A selection of Crap Joke camera ready artwork.

OUCH!
RIGHT MATE! YOU'RE NICKED!

DOCTOR. I'VE GOT SENSITIVE TEETH.
OOH! BOO! SOB! IT'S SO SAD.
SNIFF.
IT WAS THE BIT WHERE ALI McGRAW DIED THAT GOT ME.
DON'T START ME OFF.
ST.3.90.

Pop singer at record company joke
AXE the TAX
MAGGIE THATCHER MILK SNATCHER!
UP THE WORKERS!
IT'S NOT FAIR!
RECORD PRODUCER
ST-4-89
I'VE BROUGHT A DEMO WITH ME.

↑
QUALITY GAG.

Following pages:
Viz comic covers
from issue 1 to 137.

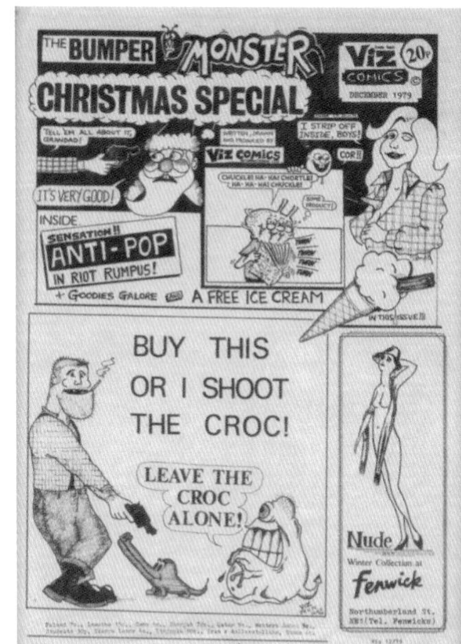

Issue 1 - December 1979

Issue 2 - March 1980

Issue 3 - July 1980

Issue 4 - October 1980

Issue 5 - March 1981

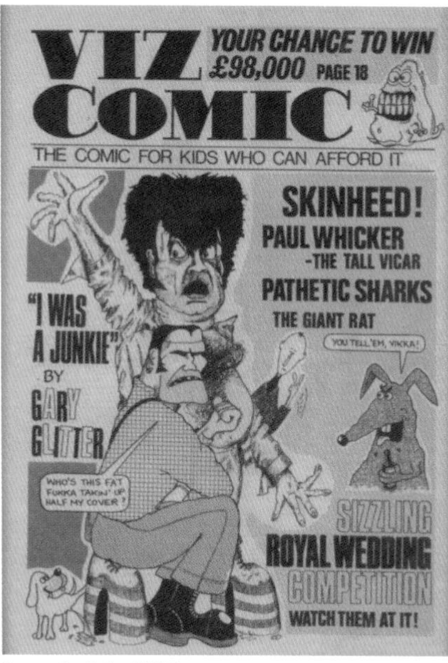

Issue 6 - July 1981

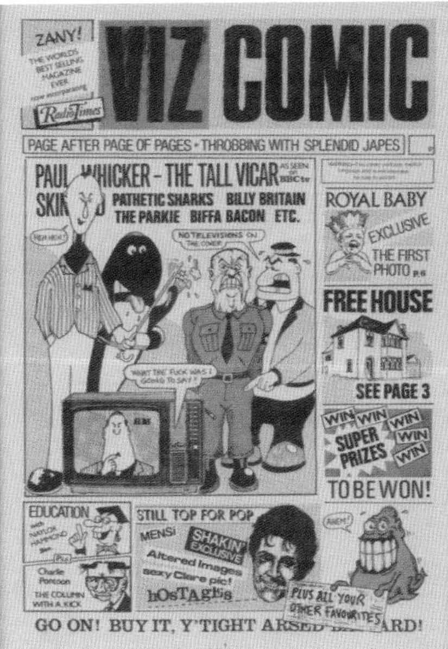

Issue 7 - December 1981

Issue 8 - May 1982

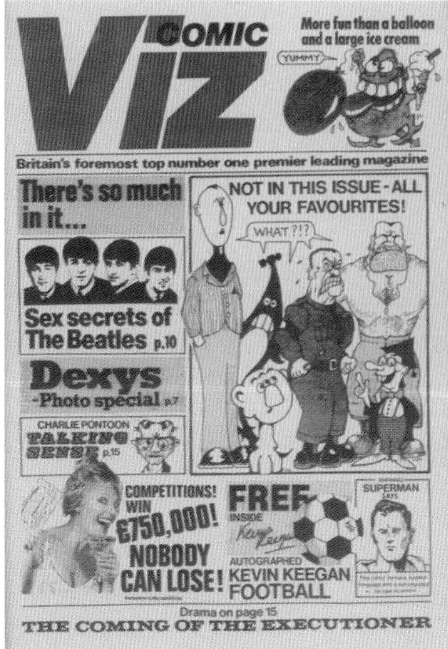

Issue 9 - November 1982

Issue 10 - May 1983

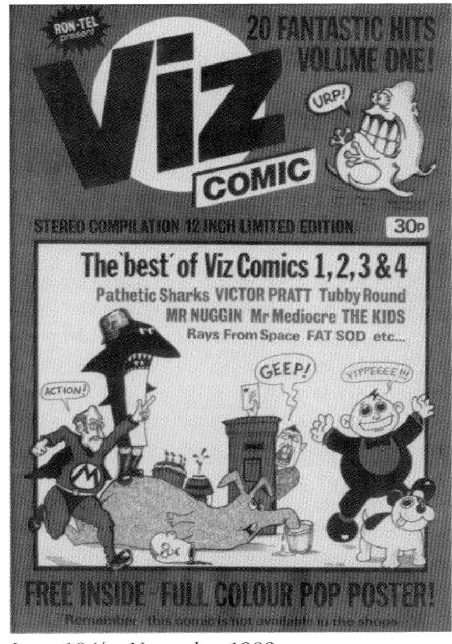

Issue 10 ½ - November 1983

Issue 11 - May 1984

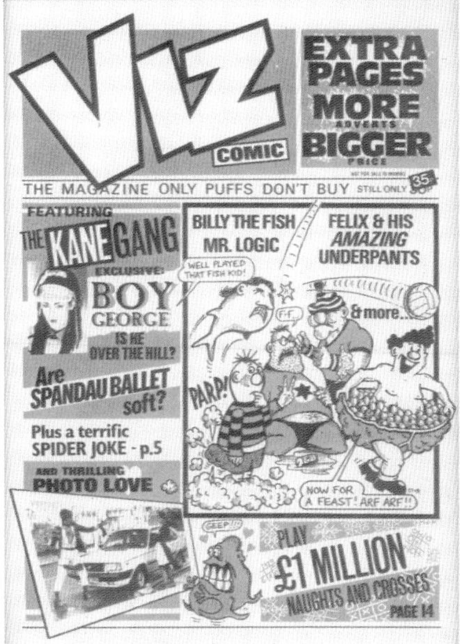

Issue 12 - November 1984

Issue 13 - August/September 1985

Issue 14 - October/November 1985

Issue 15 - December/January 1986

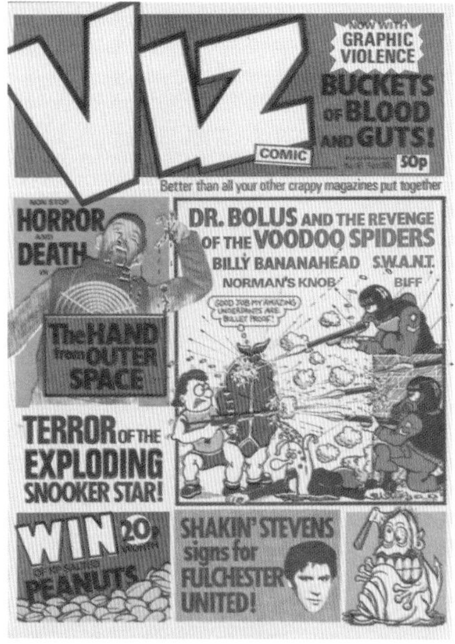

Issue 16 - February/March 1986

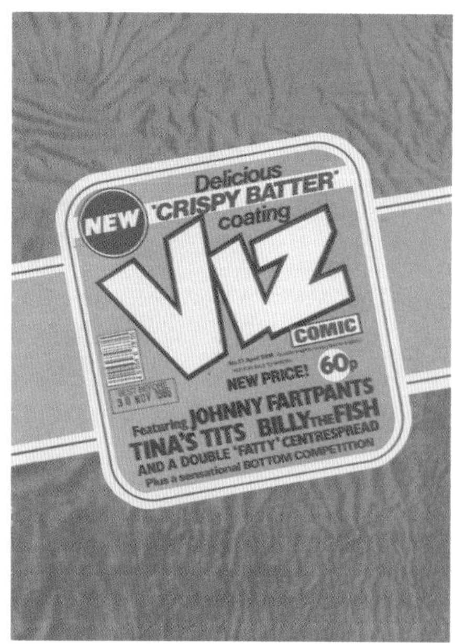

Issue 17 - April/May 1986

Issue 18 - June/July 1986

Issue 19 - August/September 1986

Issue 20 - October/November 1986

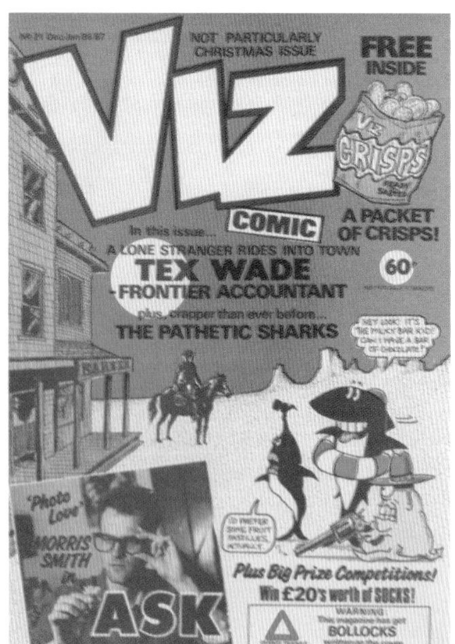

Issue 21 - December/January 1987

Issue 22 - February/March 1987

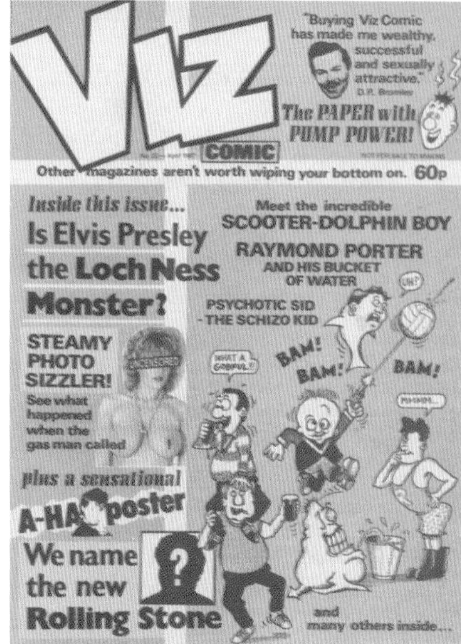

Issue 23 - April/May 1987

Issue 24 - June/July 1987

Issue 25 - August/September 1987

Issue 26 - October/November 1987

Issue 27 - December/January 1988

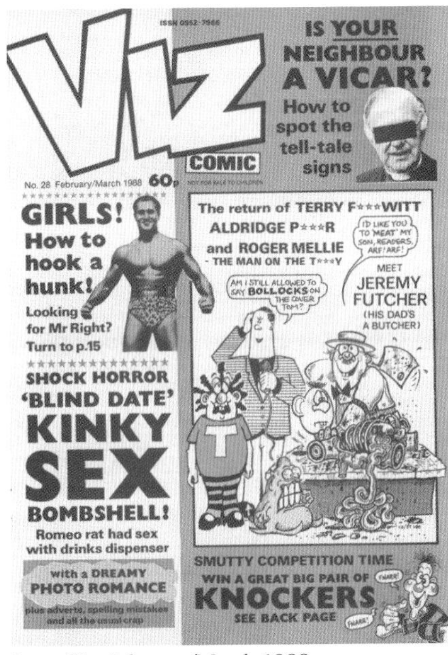

Issue 28 - February/March 1988

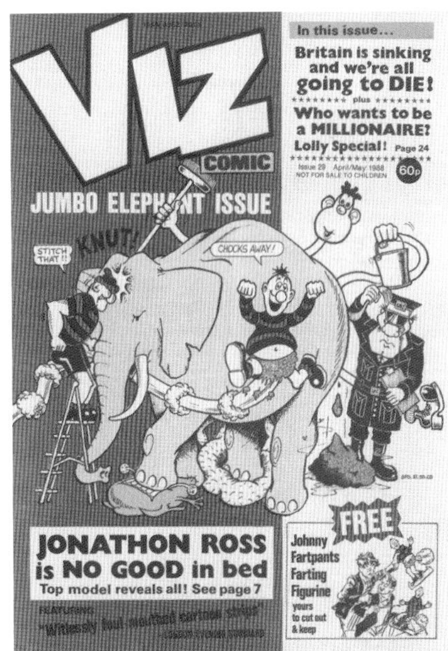

Issue 29 - April/May 1988

Issue 30 - June/July 1988

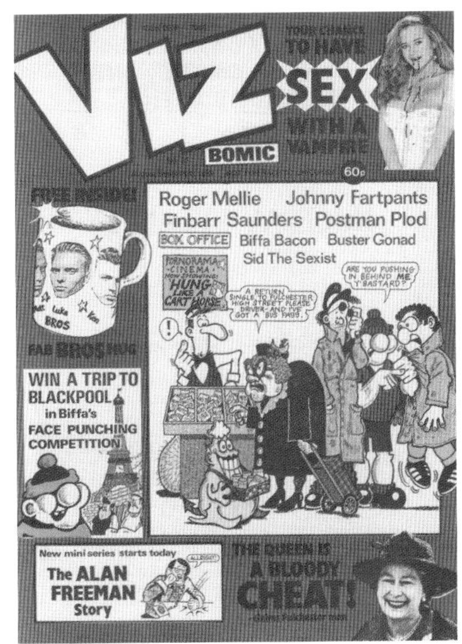

Issue 31 - August/September 1988

Issue 32 - October/November 1988

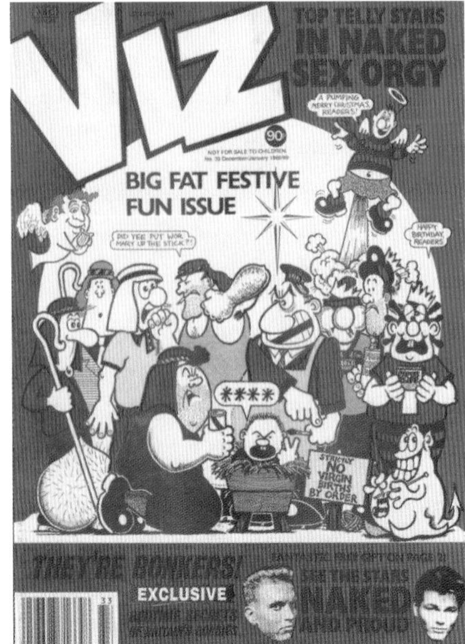

Issue 33 - December/January 1989

Issue 34 - February/March 1989

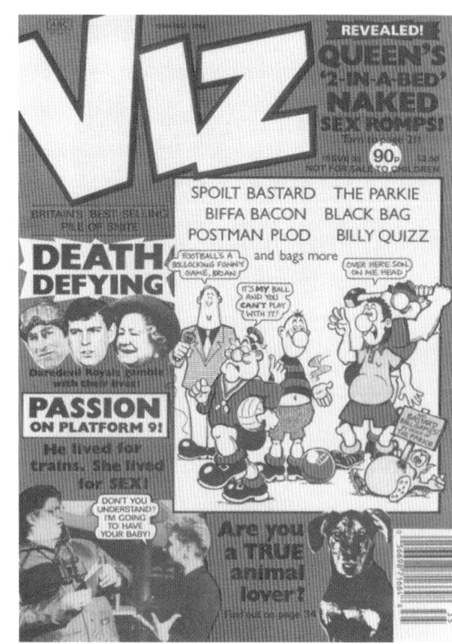

Issue 35 - April/May 1989

Issue 36 - June/July 1989

Issue 37 - August/September 1989

Issue 38 - October/November 1989

Issue 39 - December/January 1990

Issue 40 - February/March 1990

Issue 41 - April/May 1990

Issue 42 - June/July 1990

Issue 43 - August/September 1990

Issue 44 - October/November 1990

Issue 45 - December/January 1991

Issue 46 - February/March 1991

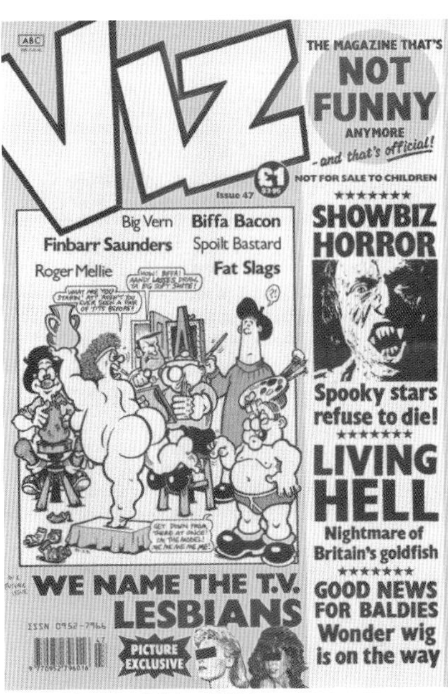

Issue 47 - April/May 1991

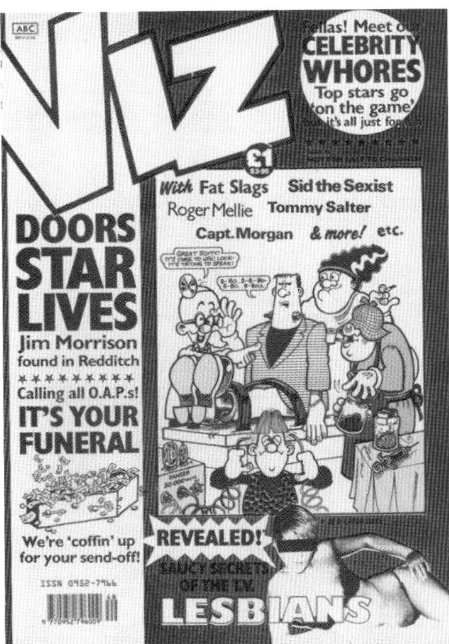

Issue 48 - June/July 1991

Issue 49 - August/September 1991

Issue 50 - October/November 1991

Issue 51 - December/January 1992

Issue 52 - February/March 1992

Issue 53 - April/May 1992

Issue 54 - June/July 1992

Issue 55 - August/September 1992

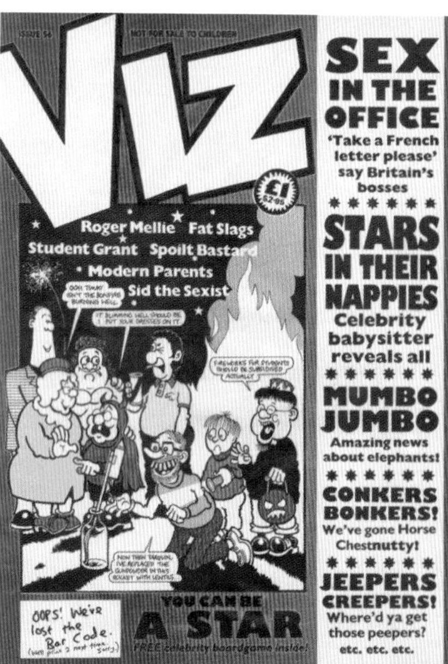

Issue 56 - October/November 1992

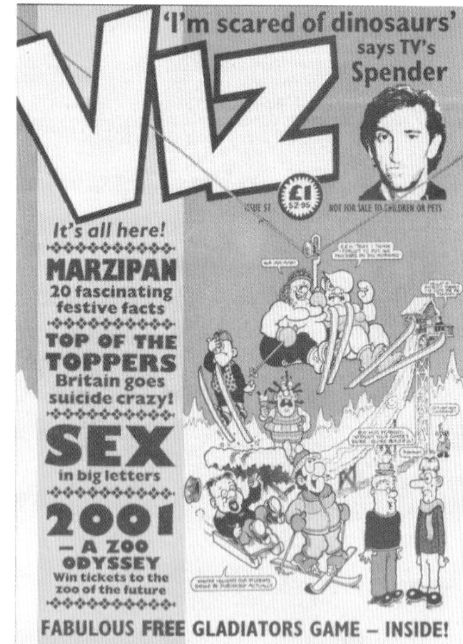

Issue 57 - December/January 1993

Issue 58 - February/March 1993

Issue 59 - April/May 1993

Issue 60 - June/July 1993

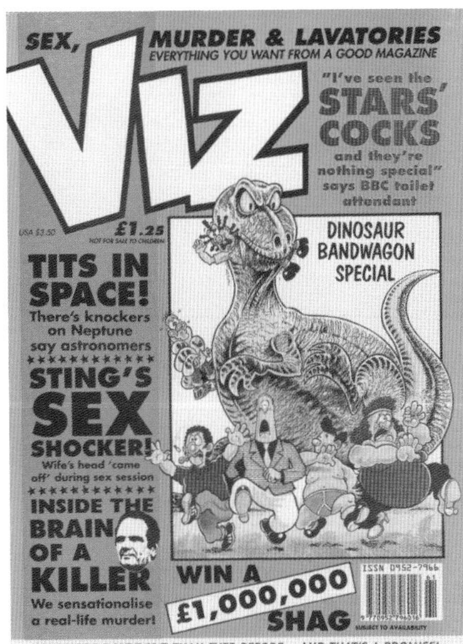

Issue 61 - August/September 1993

Issue 62 - October/November 1993

Issue 63 - December/January 1994

Issue 64 - February/March 1994

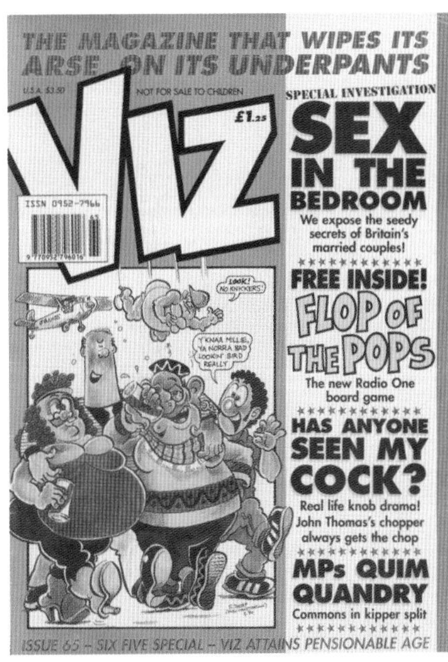

Issue 65 - April/May 1994

Issue 66 - June/July 1994

Issue 67 - August/September 1994

Issue 68 - October/November 1994

Issue 69 - December/January 1995

Issue 70 - February/March 1995

Issue 71 - April/May 1995

Issue 72 - June/July 1995

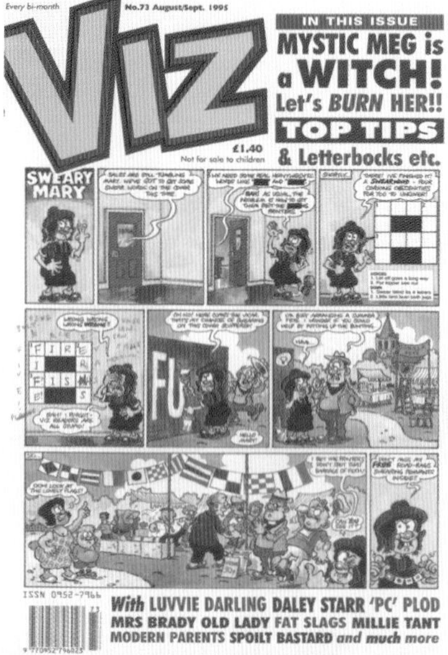

Issue 73 - August/September 1995

Issue 74 - October/November 1995

Issue 75 - December/January 1996

Issue 76 - February/March 1996

Issue 77 - April/May 1996

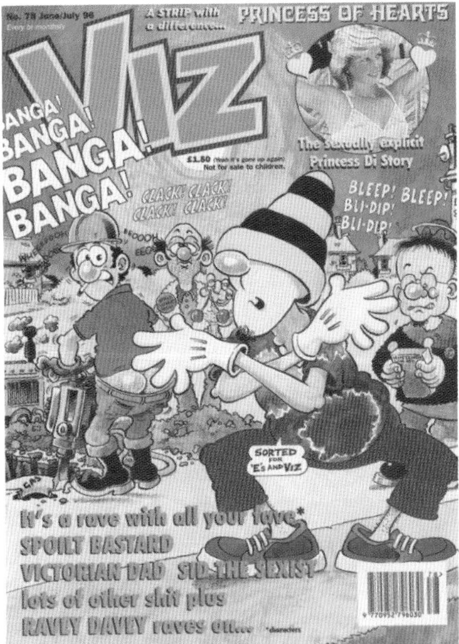

Issue 78 - June/July 1996

Issue 79 - August/September 1996

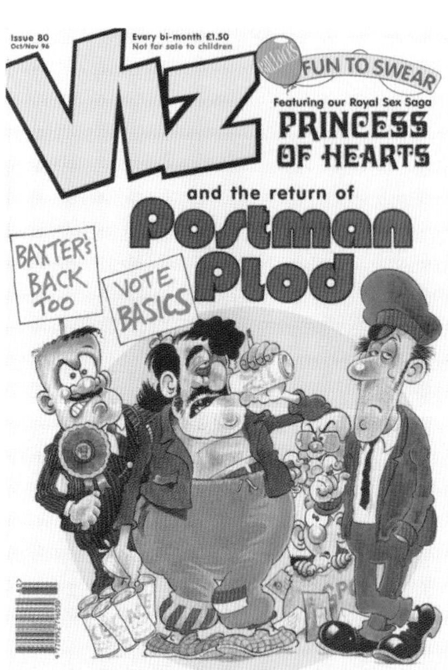

Issue 80 - October/November 1996

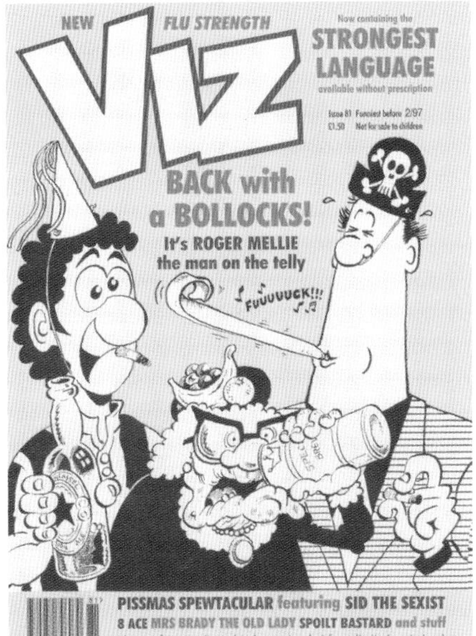

Issue 81 - December/January 1997

Issue 82 - February/March 1997

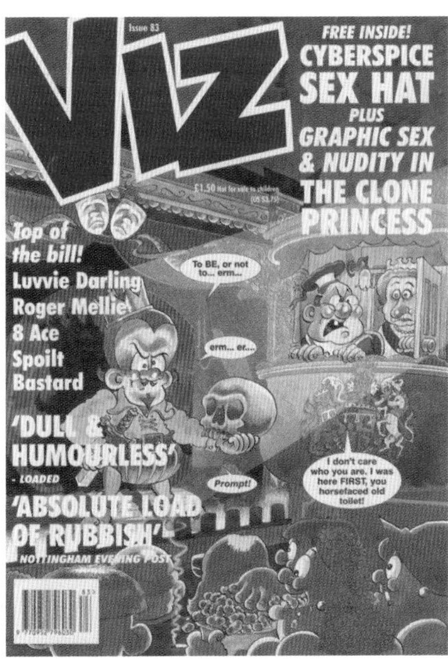

Issue 83 - April/May 1997

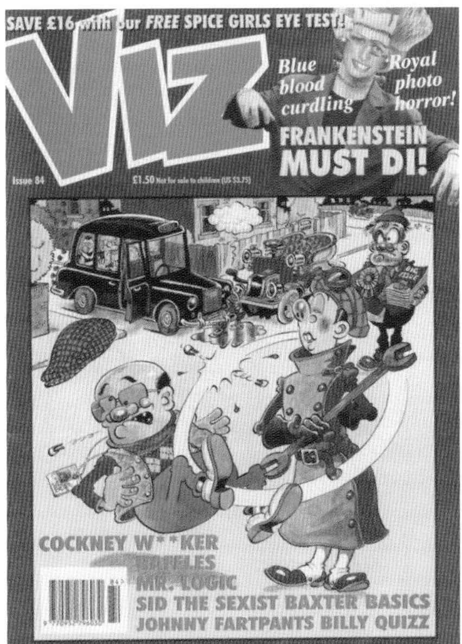

Issue 84 - June/July 1997

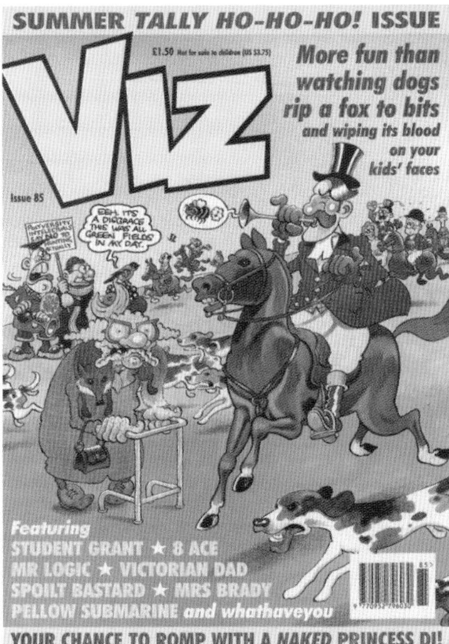

Issue 85 - August/September 1997

Issue 86 - October/November 1997

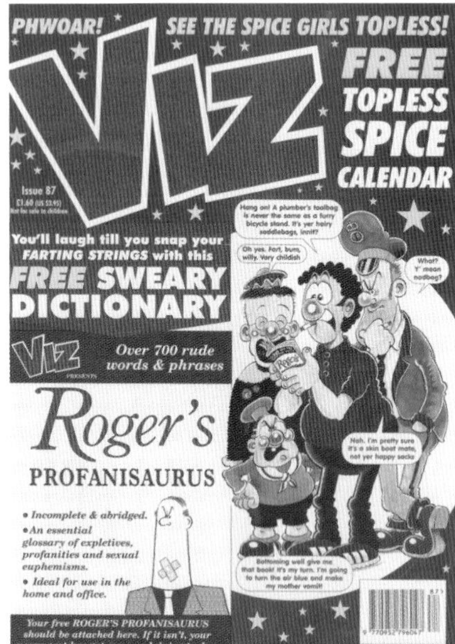

Issue 87 - December/January 1998

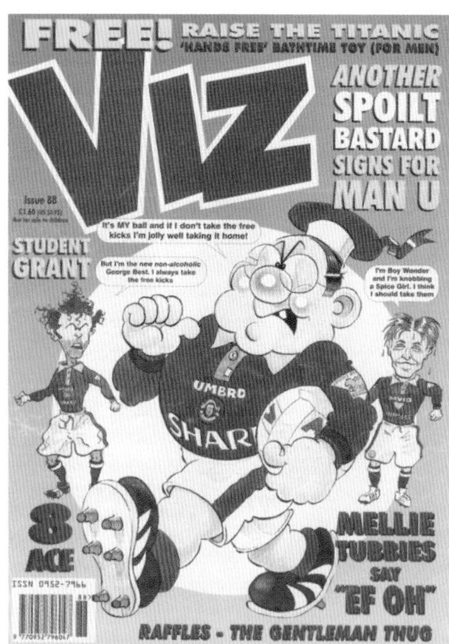

Issue 88 - February/March 1998

Issue 89 - April/May 1998

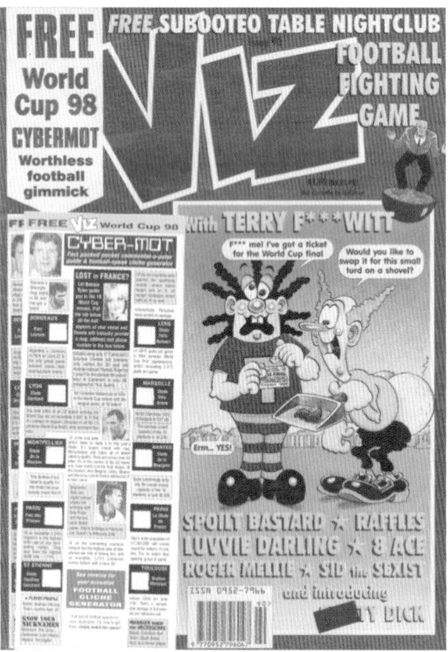

Issue 90 - June/July 1998

Issue 91 - August/September 1998

Issue 92 - October/November 1998

Issue 93 - December/January 1999

Issue 94 - February/March 1999

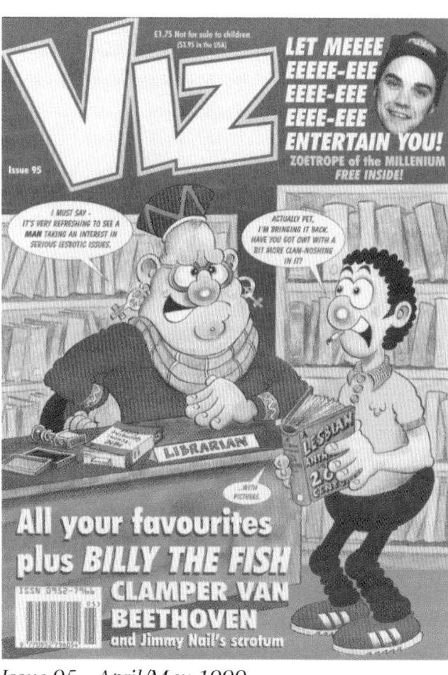

Issue 95 - April/May 1999

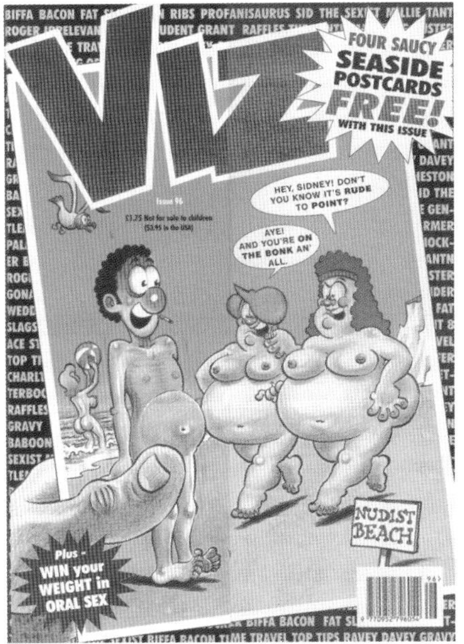

Issue 96 - June/July 1999

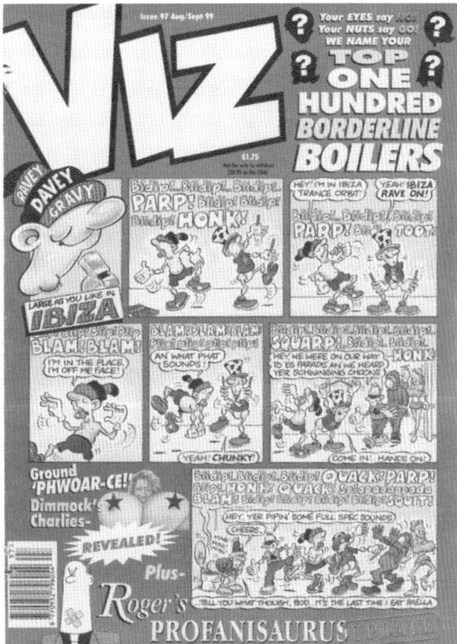

Issue 97 - August/September 1999

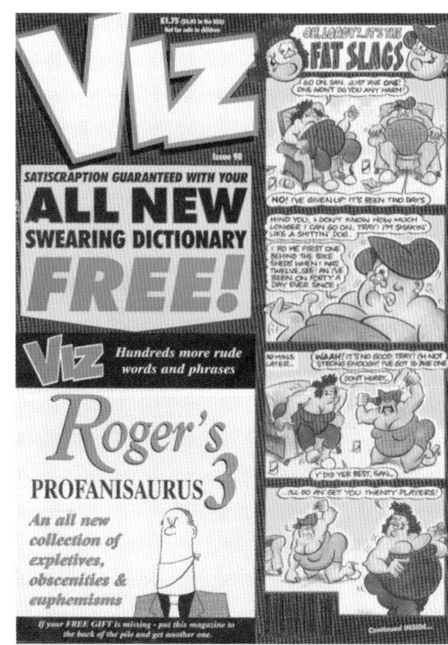

Issue 98 - October/November 1999

Issue 99 - December/January 2000

Issue 100 - February/March 2000

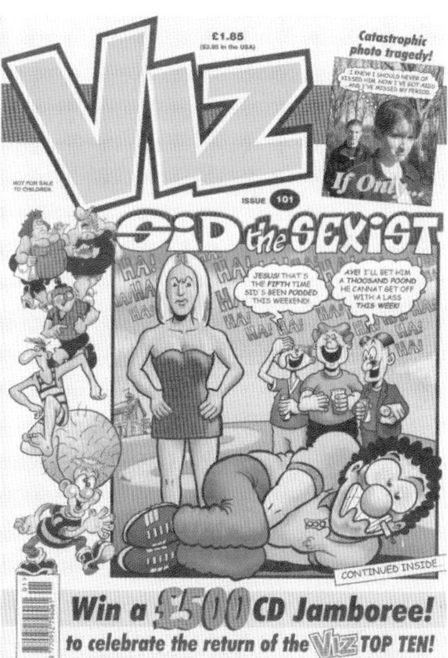

Issue 101 - April/May 2000

Issue 102 - June/July 2000

Issue 103 - August/September 2000

Issue 104 - October/November 2000

Issue 105 - December/January 2001

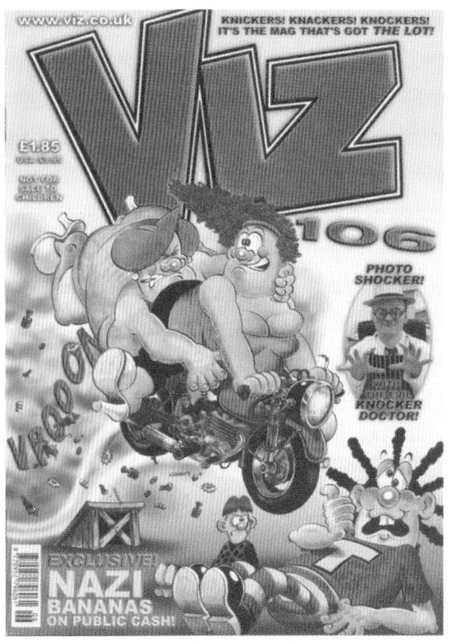

Issue 106 - February/March 2001

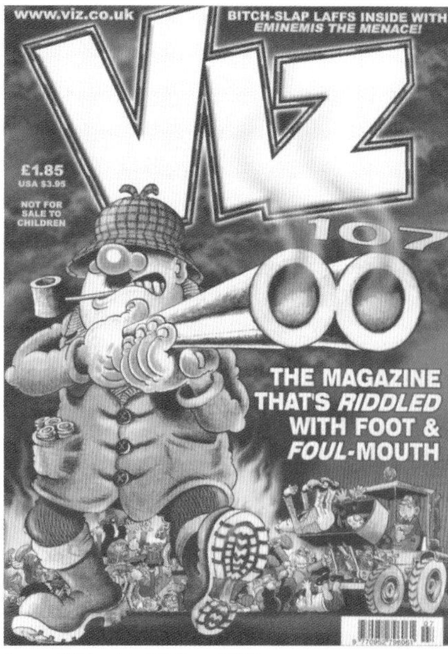

Issue 107 - April/May 2001

Issue 108 - June/July 2001

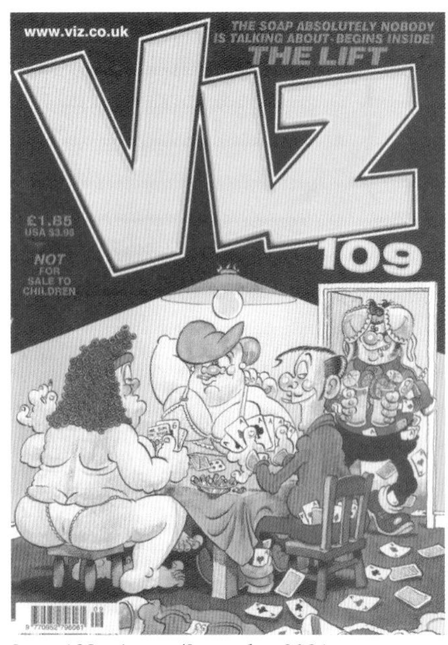

Issue 109 - August/September 2001

Issue 110 - October/November 2001

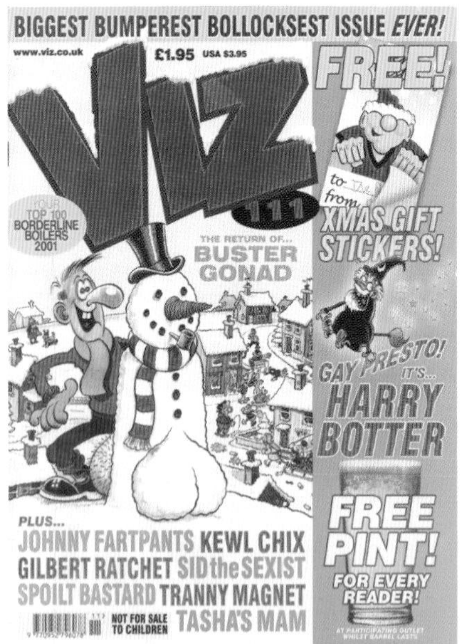

Issue 111 - December/January 2002

Issue 112 - February 2002

Issue 113 - March 2002

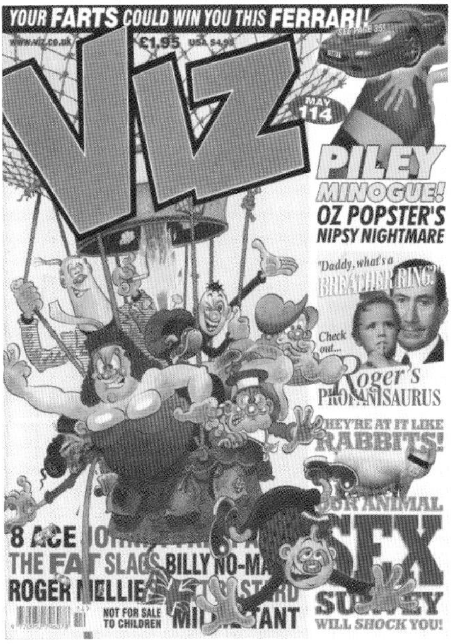

Issue 114 - May 2002

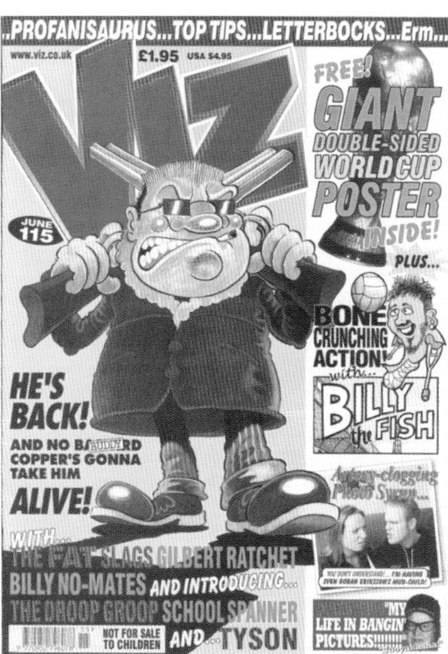

Issue 115 - June 2002

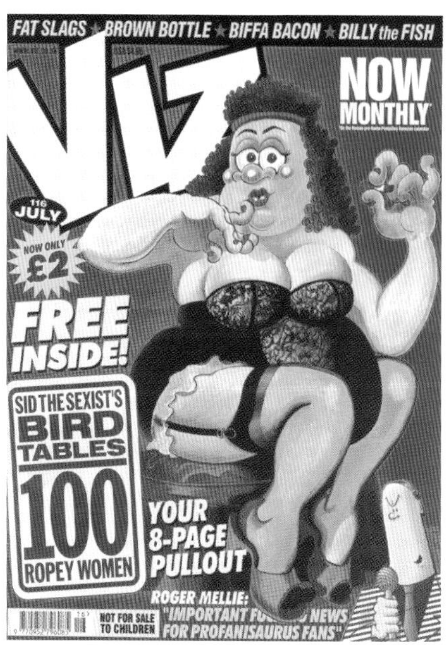

Issue 116 - July 2002

Issue 117 - August 2002

Issue 118 - September 2002

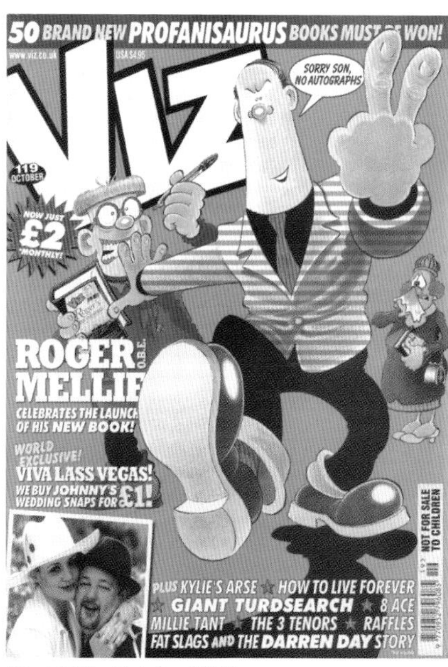

Issue 119 - October 2002

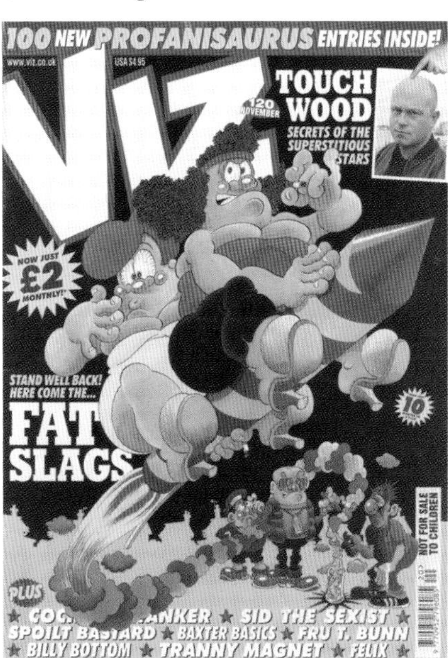

Issue 120 - November 2002

Issue 121 - December 2002

Issue 122 - February 2002

Issue 123 - March 2003

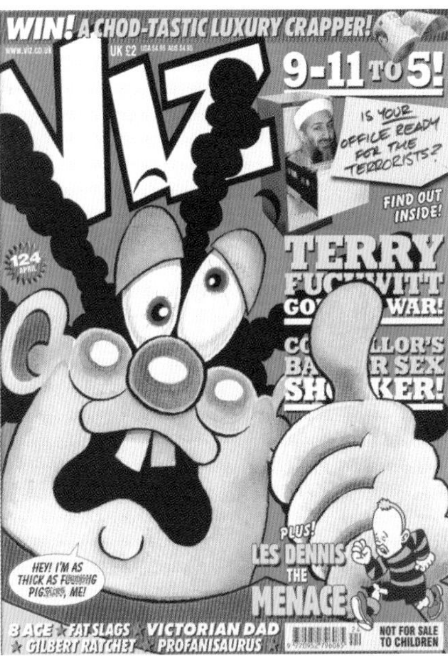

Issue 124 - April 2003

Issue 125 - May 2003

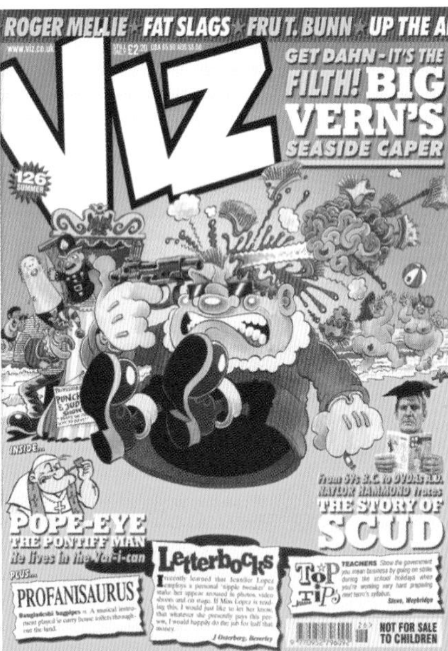

Issue 126 - June/July 2003

Issue 127 - August 2003

Issue 128 - September 2003

Issue 129 - October 2003

Issue 130 - November 2003

Issue 131 - December 2003

Issue 132 - February 2004

Issue 133 - March 2004

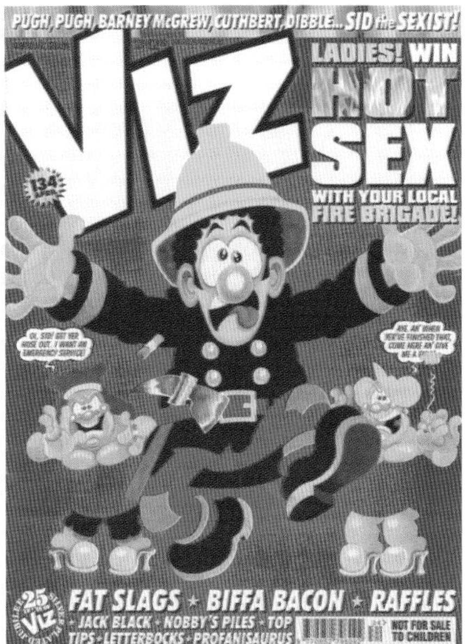

Issue 134 - April 2004

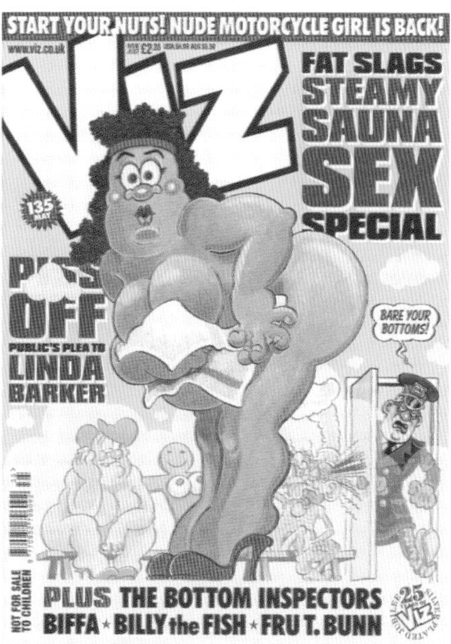

Issue 135 - May 2004

Issue 136 - June/July 2004

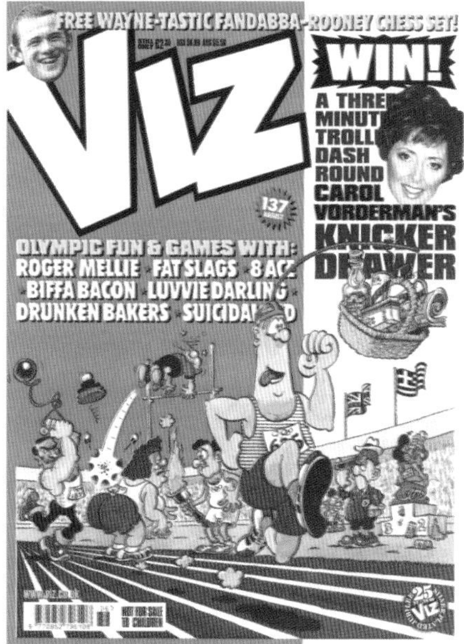

Issue 137 - August 2004

NOTES

1. *Observer*, 14 November 1999.
2. Sparks, BBC2, 1983.
3. *Comedy Review*, June 1996.
4. *Comedy Review*, June 1996.
5. *Independent*, 19 October 1999.
6. I, 19 October 1999.
7. Ibid.
8. *Loaded*, May 1994.
9. Ibid.
10. *Comedy Review*, June 1996.
11. Ibid.
12. *Independent*, 19 October 1999.
13. *Comedy Review*, June 1996.
14. Ibid.
15. Ibid.
16. Ibid.
17, *Daily Telegraph*, 5 March 1991.
18. *Viz* – The Documentary, Channel 4, 1990.
19. Ibid.
20. *Loaded*, May 1994.
21. *Guardian*, 7 November, 1989.
22. *Daily Mail*, 30 January 1997.
23. *Comedy Review*, June 1996.
24. Ibid.
25. *Daily Telegraph*, 25 June 1997.
26. *Guardian*, 29 November 1988.
27. *Sun*, 19 October 1999.
28. *Independent*, 20 December 1990.
29. *Daily Telegraph*, 25 June 1999.
30. *Independent*, 19 October 1999.
31. *Independent on Sunday*, 24 October 1993.
32. *Independent*, 26 May 2001.
33. *Guardian*, 12 July 1991.
34. *The Times*, 1 February 2001.
35. *Daily Telegraph*, 5 March 1991.
36. *Viz* – The Documentary, Channel 4, 1990.
37. *Guardian*, 27 November, 1989.
38. *Daily Telegraph*, 25 June 1999.
39. *Liverpool Echo*, 6 October 2001
40. Ibid.
41. Ibid.
42. *Guardian*, 28 August 1997.
43. *Guardian*, 30 August 1997.
44. Ibid.
45. *Guardian*, 29 November 1988.
46. *Guardian*, 5 December 1992.

ACKNOWLEDGEMENTS

Grateful thanks to the following, without whom this book would have been entirely cobbled together from old newspaper cuttings: Phil Branston, John Brown, Jim Brownlow, Tommy Caulker, Alex Collier, Colin Davison, Chris Donald, Dolores Donald, Simon Donald, Steve Donald, Graham Dury, John Fardell, Wayne Gamble, Stevie Glover, Marshall Hall, Andy Inman, Davey Jones, Abdul Latif, Lord of Harpole, Chris Moir, Brian Sandells, Anvil Springstien, Andrew Tait, Julie Thorp and Simon Thorp. Special thanks to Jake and Harry Wilson. And finally, thanks to Julian Alexander, Jacqui Butler, Ingrid Connell and Will Watt for all the grown-up stuff behind the scenes. Without their help, this book still would have been written – but almost certainly by someone else.

Fulchester Industries would like to thank: Maddie Fletcher, Anne Gates, Susan Patterson, Sheila Thompson, Deborah Graham, Claire Charlton and everybody who has ever contributed. Sorry, no refunds.

THE AUTHOR

William Cook is the author of *Ha Bloody Ha: Comedians Talking* (Fourth Estate, 1994) and *The Comedy Store: The Club That Changed British Comedy* (Little, Brown, 2001). He is the editor of *Tragically I Was An Only Twin: The Complete Peter Cook* (Century, 2002) and *Goodbye Again: The Complete Peter Cook & Dudley Moore* (Century, 2004). He has worked for the BBC, and written for *The Guardian*, the *Mail on Sunday* and the *New Statesman.*

VILLAGE LAMI...
AGAINST SETTING OF
IN PICTURESQUE COTSWOLDS
5'10" UGLY LESBIAN
PLANIC COUNCIL OFFICE

Britain's Cash-strapped
Mental Hospitals
running out of
Napoleon costumes.

* Steven Tin-fin

BLACK
Laboratory

Duffy the Vampire Slayer

SENSIBLE
PRECAUTIONS
OF PROTECTING
Y'SELF FROM
VAMPIRES

KEITH DUFFY the Vampire

BLACK BAG
FOOT 'n' MOUTH.

The A-Z of not getting
mollied off a vampire
JOHN STALKER

A - ALWAYS DON'T

ROOSTER
ER NO
3728.

I.O. Stevie £2000
at least.

#105
BILLY BOTTOM
PAY-TO-GET-IN
TOILET

Xmas
Buffa

WE'VE GOT
BACK

PAGE 31